T0007856

ALSO BY NEIL GROSS

Richard Rorty:
The Making of an American Philosopher

Why Are Professors Liberal and
Why Do Conservatives Care?

WALK
THE
WALK

WALK THE WALK

How Three Police Chiefs Defied the Odds and Changed Cop Culture

NEIL GROSS

METROPOLITAN BOOKS
Henry Holt and Company
New York

Metropolitan Books
Henry Holt and Company
Publishers since 1866
120 Broadway
New York, New York 10271
www.henryholt.com

Metropolitan Books® and m® are registered trademarks of
Macmillan Publishing Group, LLC.

Distributed in Canada by Raincoast Book Distribution Limited

Library of Congress Cataloging-in-Publication data is available.

ISBN: 9781250777522

Our books may be purchased in bulk for promotional, educational, or business use. Please contact your local bookseller or the Macmillan Corporate and Premium Sales Department at (800) 221-7945, extension 5442, or by email at MacmillanSpecialMarkets@macmillan.com.

First Edition 2023

Designed by Kelly S. Too

Printed in the United States of America

1 3 5 7 9 10 8 6 4 2

CONTENTS

THE OFFICERS

Stockton Police Department, California

Chief Eric Jones

Officer Drake Wiest

Officer Jesse Smith

Longmont Police Department, Colorado

Chief Mike Butler

Officer Vijay Kailasam

Detective Edna Munoz

Detective Sandie Campanella

LaGrange Police Department, Georgia

Chief Lou Dekmar

Corporal Robbie Hall

WALK
THE
WALK

INTRODUCTION

On a mild late spring night in 1993, a police officer in Berkeley, California, stopped a black-and-yellow two-door Chevy for a traffic violation. The officer was twenty-one years old, white. He was working a midnight shift in a lower-income neighborhood adjacent to North Oakland that had seen more than its share of violence, much of it linked to the trade in crack cocaine. The year before, 12 people were murdered in Berkeley, then a city of 103,000. Nearly 900 were robbed—someone coming up to them to demand cash, or jewelry, or their Walkman—and more than 700 were victims of aggravated assault, putting Berkeley's violent crime rate at twice the national average.

At 1:30 a.m., the officer was driving north on a mixed commercial and residential street, Sacramento. A block ahead, the Chevy was stopped at a red light in the left turn lane. Not waiting for the light to turn green, the driver of the car lurched forward, veering out of the lane to continue straight. This was hardly a serious offense. The streets were empty, no oncoming traffic. Still, it was illegal. The officer hit his overhead lights. "Adam 13, 11-95," he called on the radio. Car stop. One of a dozen he'd probably make that night.

Except the driver accelerated. The officer couldn't tell whether he was trying to get away or hadn't noticed the police car.

As the officer slowed to clear the intersection, the driver opened more distance between them. The policeman gunned his accelerator to catch up, the engine on his cruiser roaring to life. At the next street, the Chevy went left. The officer followed but the car had vanished. The only place it could have gone was Stanton, a small street that branched off, and as the officer drove past, he caught sight of the car's brake lights. He slammed on his own brakes, backed up, and barreled down Stanton until he reached the Chevy, which had parked in the driveway of a stucco house.

Like most small- to midsize police agencies, the Berkeley police department, with 180 cops in the early 1990s, didn't have its own police academy. When the officer joined as a recruit, he was sent to the academy run by the city of Sacramento, held on the grounds where the California Highway Patrol trained. There tall reeds billowed as future men and women of law enforcement took their morning runs; the recruits all idealistic in their own way, projecting impenetrability, driven to scratch some inner itch by pinning on a badge. Trainers taught them that car stops can be dangerous, even for minor infractions. Usually drivers and passengers are cooperative. But you never know—you might pull over someone with a felony warrant who'll do anything to keep from getting arrested, or a dealer with a stash and a gun hidden under the front seat, or a guy with anger issues looking for a fight.

Posters hung in the gymnasium, where the recruits practiced defensive tactics. One showed the CHP Survival Creed: "The will to live, to survive the attack, must be uppermost in every officer's mind. Fight back against all odds. . . . Don't let them kill you on some dirty freeway." CHP officers were trained to be on high alert when stopping cars. So were Sacramento police academy recruits. The cardinal rules were that you had to keep everyone contained, and hands had to be visible at all times.

There was no containment happening on Stanton Street. As the officer pulled up, a young man about his age, Black with cornrows, stepped from the passenger side of the car. He was shirtless, with pale blue shorts and blue Nikes. The driver had stayed at the wheel. The officer got out of his vehicle and yelled to the passenger, "Get back in the car and close the door!"

The man said flatly, “Why?”

“I’m stopping this car. Get back in and close the door.”

The man ignored him. He began walking toward the porch of the house, only a few paces away. The officer, trying to keep his eye on the driver, ran to the passenger and put his hand on his shoulder. The man flung it off. “If you touch me again, I’m going to kick your ass,” he said.

The two were face-to-face. The man had threatened a cop; he was going to jail.

“Get on the ground, you’re under arrest,” the officer ordered. He wanted the man seated or prostrate so it would be harder for him to make good on his threat. The officer, a recent graduate of UC Berkeley, had followed every twist of the Rodney King case, which had sparked protests and riots when the cops who’d beaten the Black motorist were found not guilty. But he wasn’t thinking about the symbolism of a white police officer ordering a Black man to the ground. He was thinking: if this guy’s willing to fight rather than sit in a car while I write his buddy a ticket, there must be something he doesn’t want me to know or find. His other thought was, don’t let them kill you on some dirty freeway.

He called for cover.

The driver, also Black and in his twenties, was out of the car now, too. The passenger again made a move toward the porch. This time, the officer grabbed him, pushing him against the hood of the Chevy, intending to apply handcuffs. The man pulled loose and swung at the officer, clocking him on his cheek. The officer stumbled a couple of steps and drew his baton. Few police had access to Tasers back then (the LAPD officers who assaulted Rodney King were an exception), so batons were the best nonlethal option.

As the passenger and driver squared off against the officer, on the radio he upped his request to “Code 3” cover—for an emergency. Sirens kicked on in the distance along with the intermittent beeping on police frequencies that signals trouble.

“Get on the ground! You’re under arrest!” the officer kept repeating, thwacking the passenger in his leg while the man stood ready to box. He grabbed the baton, but the officer wrested it back and hit him again in the leg, then once in the abdomen, a jab he'd been taught in defensive tactics.

His partner from the next beat over came running to cuff the driver. As the two of them fought, her baton tumbled from her hands. The driver went to snatch it off the ground and she tackled him. Meanwhile, an older couple had emerged from the house—the passenger's parents, it would later turn out—and were trying to restrain their son. The officer saw why: he was holding a sizable rock over his head and was about to throw it. Rocks are serious business.

A third cop arrived and rushed to help arrest the driver. The first officer unholstered his handgun, a stainless steel .40 caliber Smith & Wesson, and pointed it at the rock-wielding passenger, lining him up in his sights so he'd have a clean shot. "Put the rock down!" he screamed.

After a tense moment, the man did as he was ordered. The officer wasn't faced with the choice of shooting him in front of his parents or taking a rock to the head.

That Berkeley officer was me.

WE NEVER FIGURED OUT WHY the passenger had fought. He had an arrest record but wasn't on probation or parole. He had no warrants and no contraband on him. He'd been drinking but wasn't drunk. Taken into custody, all he would say was, "I'll be out, Gross. I'll find you."

* * *

THE STOP THAT NIGHT ON Stanton Street should never have escalated as it did; the outcome could have been horrific. The passenger wasn't blameless. He should have gotten back in the car when I asked. He shouldn't have threatened me or punched me in the face or tried to throw a rock. But I wasn't blameless either. Nor was the police institution that molded me into the cop I was.

As a rookie, I checked all the right boxes. I was born and raised in the Berkeley area and would be policing my hometown. I was educated. I was young but not completely inexperienced: I'd worked part-time for several police agencies while in college, including as a dispatcher. I had a clean record. I'd gone into policing with the best of intentions, to help people and make the community safer. And yet there I was, gun in hand, fighting with a young Black man over what? Over nothing, really.

What went wrong? I served as a Berkeley police officer for eleven months before quitting and going to graduate school to get a PhD in sociology, looking for answers to questions just like that. I've been a social scientist for more than two decades now, and I've thought often about the Stanton Street fight, with a mixture of guilt, sadness, and dismay.

At Colby College in Maine, where I teach courses about the police, I sometimes assess proposals for police reform by asking whether they would have prevented the kind of escalation that occurred. Could the whole incident have been avoided if my training had been different? If the department had different policies in place? If the police academy hadn't taught me to be paranoid about car stops, perhaps I wouldn't have perceived a passenger walking away as such a threat. If California had mandated meaningful de-escalation training for officers, maybe I would have thought to use a calmer tone or to say something less hostile than "get on the ground." Maybe I would have retreated after the man threatened me and waited for the arrival of more officers so that we could have arrested him safely through sheer strength of numbers. If department policy had established that lethal force could be used only when there was absolutely no alternative, maybe I would have ducked for cover when it looked like rocks were about to fly instead of drawing my weapon.

Maybe. But probably not. You can train and rewrite policy all day long, but done in isolation, that won't get you very far. If you've got a department full of cops who think of themselves as aggressive crime fighters locked in a life-or-death struggle against the forces of evil—which is how many officers saw themselves, even in liberal, educated Berkeley—then alienation and resentment are bound to spread in heavily policed neighborhoods. In the heat of the moment, you won't see police backing down.

Policy change is crucially important. But to fix policing, we need to change cop culture: the values, beliefs, and assumptions, the worldview of those in law enforcement. Right now, not enough people are talking about how to do that.

* * *

IN THE WAKE OF THE murder of George Floyd by former Minneapolis police officer Derek Chauvin and the massive Black Lives Matter protests that followed, the public has been exposed to near daily news reports about the deep-seated problems with American policing. The facts are well-known, even if the interpretations are in dispute. About a thousand people are killed annually by the police in the United States, a much higher rate of police killing per capita than in other wealthy democracies. Research by criminal justice scholar Frank Edwards and his colleagues shows that being killed by the police is the sixth leading cause of death for men of all racial groups between the ages of twenty-five and twenty-nine, behind accidents, suicide, homicide, heart disease, and cancer. Black people—young Black men specifically—are at the greatest risk of dying. Young Black men die in police shootings at an annual rate of about 3.5 per 100,000, compared with 1.8 for young Latino men and 1.2 for young white men. Cumulatively, 1 out of every 1,000 Black men in America will perish at the hands of a police officer, a lifetime mortality risk two and a half times that of white men.[1]

Fatal citizen encounters draw the most attention, but racial and ethnic disparities are evident in much of what the police do. A study published in 2020 found that Black drivers are substantially more likely to be stopped by law enforcement than white drivers, a gap that can't be accounted for by racial differences in driving behavior.[2] Black and Latino Americans are also stopped more frequently as pedestrians and patted down for weapons, an experience that can be frightening, humiliating, and enraging. Arrest rates for Black people and Latinos are higher, too, even for criminal offenses that are committed equally across racial and ethnic groups, like drug possession. Homicide cases with Black victims are less likely to be solved.

Other troubles with the police go beyond race: dealings with the mentally ill that end tragically, botched search warrants, illegal arrests, coerced confessions, violent policing of peaceful protest. There are police unions that dig in their heels and resist demands for accountability, departments using military equipment and tactics that petrify citizens, and police officers who are far-right sympathizers. The list goes on.

With nearly three-quarters of a million police officers in America scattered across more than eighteen thousand law enforcement agencies, there are legitimate questions to ask about the scope of these problems. Are they pervasive or concentrated among particular groups of officers, in particular locations? Are they problems of policing per se or symptomatic of broader societal issues like persistent inequality or the ubiquity of guns? Cops point out that journalists often report on police abuse but write almost nothing about the times police handle situations peacefully, respectfully, exactly as they should, fostering the impression that the entire occupation is corrupt. It's not always clear how well media narratives reflect complex truths on the ground.

Be that as it may, there is a public consensus that the time for police reform has come. On the eve of the Derek Chauvin verdict, a Vox/Data for Progress poll found that large majorities of likely voters supported such police reform ideas as mandatory use of body cameras, collecting better data on use of force, and banning choke holds.[3] Likewise, a CNN poll found that a mere 14 percent of American adults believed that "policing works pretty well as it is," and 53 percent favored major changes to the institution, with the remaining 32 percent preferring smaller-scale reforms.[4]

Politicians at the federal, state, and local levels (primarily on the Democratic side of the aisle) have tried to address this demand for change. The US Department of Justice, led by President Joe Biden's attorney general Merrick Garland, resumed investigating police agencies suspected of systematic patterns of abuse—an oversight mechanism used heavily during President Barack Obama's administration but sharply curtailed under the presidency of Donald Trump. Federal legislation (ultimately stalled in the Senate) sought to forbid choke holds and "no-knock" warrants, reduce liability protections for police officers, require implicit bias training, and much more. States, for their part, upped de-escalation training, instructed officers to intervene if they see their peers engage in misconduct, and changed laws governing the use of lethal force. Cities increased citizen oversight of police operations, pulled police out of schools, and even prohibited police officers from doing low-level traffic enforcement.

Some of these plans have shown promise. Federal investigations of problem departments, for instance, and the "consent decrees" they may lead to—where the Department of Justice and a police agency reach a court-approved agreement about necessary reforms—can improve policing, at least in the short term.[5] But other ideas, like training to counter implicit bias, are unlikely to make policing better. Despite the millions of dollars already spent on implicit bias training, little evidence exists that it has altered police behavior.[6]

Whether well-conceived or not, however, each of these plans for reform will quickly run up against a limit: the aggressive culture of policing that characterizes many American departments. That culture prioritizes above all tactical safety, putting bad guys behind bars, loyalty to other cops, and not taking flak from anyone on the street. Policy changes perceived to be at odds with those values—basically, anything that constrains the options cops have in dealing with what they see as dangerous people and situations—will be resisted and undermined at every turn.

We've been here before. After the 2014 death of Michael Brown in Ferguson, Missouri, and the subsequent protests and unrest, President Obama assembled a task force charged with developing a vision for policing in the twenty-first century. The task force issued policy recommendations, but its central insight was that policy change alone isn't enough to ensure good policing. "There's an old saying," the task force noted: "'Organizational culture eats policy for lunch.'" "Any law enforcement organization can make great rules and policies," the report continued, "but if policies conflict with the existing culture, they will not be institutionalized and behavior will not change." The reason for this is simple: in policing "the vast majority of an officer's work is done independently outside the immediate oversight of a supervisor."

Thus "consistent enforcement of rules that conflict with . . . culture . . . is nearly impossible."[7]

Despite the report's emphasis, proposals for reform typically aim at regulating or limiting the power of the police, not changing police culture. Politicians and pundits talk occasionally about the need for law enforcement officers to view themselves as "guardians" rather than "warriors," but it's difficult to know what that distinction entails, let alone how agencies could move in such a direction. It's as though policy makers can't imagine what ethical, effective, democratic policing might look like.

In some quarters, pessimism about the prospects for successful reform, tied to a critique of policing as inherently racist, has prompted calls for abolition, or a significant scaling back of police forces and their functions. Different versions of this argument command different levels of public support. Some activists have demanded that police departments be eliminated, proposing that community groups and social service organizations take responsibility for ensuring the peace. An Ipsos/USA Today poll conducted in March 2021 found that 11 percent of Americans endorse this position.[8]

Others call not for abolishing police departments altogether but for shifting municipal budget dollars toward social services, mental health, and education. The thought is that it's better to aid, treat, and empower those who might come to the attention of the police than to unleash a racist and punitive force upon them. Whether or not they favor abolition, 43 percent of Americans—as indicated by the same poll—support "tak[ing] a portion of the budget for police . . . and redirect[ing] those funds to social services."

The fate of these political efforts is uncertain. Cities such as Minneapolis or Seattle that sought to implement some version of abolition or defunding after George Floyd's murder found themselves backpedaling amid rising crime rates; citizens and business groups insisted that police staffing and service levels be restored. On the other hand, national interest grew in getting police out of the business of responding to certain types of calls—mental health calls, for example—which abolition advocates claim as a victory for their cause. Support for abolition or defunding is also highest among young adults, suggesting that these positions may gain further traction in the years to come.

While opinions differ on solutions, most people see value in improving policing now. And in that regard, not all hope is lost. The culture of policing *can* be transformed. I know this to be true because I've spent the last four years studying three unusual police departments dedicated to replacing the aggressive crime fighter with something different and better: with healthier, more socially responsible models of what it means to be a good cop. Many police forces promise change; these three are walking the walk.

One department is a work in progress. The other two have made it remarkably far down the road of transforming their cultures. In my observations, I have tried to identify the secrets to their success—while noting roadblocks to further reform—so that we can better understand how to change police culture nationwide.[9]

This book tells the stories of those three departments, and of the chiefs, officers, and detectives who are their lifeblood.

Stockton, California, with 320,000 residents—described by *US News & World Report* as "the most racially diverse city in the United States"—is in the Central Valley.[10] Chief Eric Jones, who graduated from the police academy one year after I did, hasn't turned Stockton PD into a policing nirvana. Stockton is a rough-and-tumble city plagued by gang violence, and many of the officers in the 428-person department there are old school, as hard charging as they come. But an increasing number are new school. Jones's achievement in introducing a palpably better approach warrants exploration.

In Longmont, Colorado, a high-plains town of 100,000 northeast of Boulder, Chief Mike Butler spent decades building one of the most progressive police departments in the nation, one already doing many of the things reform activists are calling for. The results are impressive: crime rates have fallen without resort to heavy-handed tactics, and the police are seen by locals as contributing to the social good.

Finally, LaGrange, Georgia, population 31,000, a pencil dot on the map not far from the Alabama state line. Improbably, perhaps, LaGrange police chief Lou Dekmar, a Republican and reluctant supporter of Donald Trump, has refashioned a once manifestly racist police department into one focused on racial reconciliation, equality before the law, and the preservation of life. How this was accomplished is instructive for any community looking to move forward from a blighted policing past.

My accounts of these departments are leavened by insights from social science. I draw on the latest research but also on classic studies in the sociology of policing. I teach my students about these classic studies. They deserve a place in today's national conversation about law enforcement.

While every community in the country faces its own challenges with police reform (including ones of scale for big cities like New York or Los Angeles), learning about Stockton, Longmont, and LaGrange opens a window onto what policing could be if we took seriously the charge of creating a more just America.

NOTE

Almost all the dialogue in these pages is verbatim (although slightly edited and condensed for clarity), recorded either by me during reporting trips or on bodycam, dashcam, or other video footage. In the rare cases where it felt important to include snippets of dialogue that weren't recorded, I relied on the recollection of people I interviewed, police reports, or court records.

In every scene involving interactions between police officers and civilians, I've used pseudonyms to protect the civilians' privacy, unless I was given permission to use the real name or the person had been identified in news stories. Where necessary, I obscured identifying characteristics.

The police are a notoriously closed group, suspicious of outsiders. That I was once a cop may have helped the chiefs, officers, and detectives who appear here feel comfortable enough to be forthcoming about their lives and jobs. I've tried to repay their trust by offering more personal portraits so that readers might go a mile in the officers' boots, gaining an intimate understanding of the most controversial job in America, and of what may be done to set it right.

PART I

STOCKTON

1

MUDVILLE

Chief Eric Jones commanded his officers from an expansive office on the top floor of the Stewart-Eberhardt Building, a four-story office block in dilapidated downtown Stockton. Through a picture window a view of the city presented itself. The view was better—maybe only slightly—than it was for Billy Tully, the protagonist of Leonard Gardner's gritty 1969 Stockton boxing novel, *Fat City*. Tully looked out his flophouse window to see a "stunted skyline" of "business buildings, church spires, chimneys, water towers, gas tanks and the low roofs of residences rising among leafless trees between absolutely flat streets."[1] Eric saw some of the same dreariness. But when he'd allow himself the occasional contemplative moment in the late afternoon, after his meetings and calls for the day were done, he saw something else out the window. Hope.

Stockton—Mudville, as it was called back in the day—is an eighty-mile drive east of San Francisco. From the Bay Area there are two main ways to get there. One is to take Highway 580, with its harried commuters and Amazon tractor trailers, up and over the Altamont Pass. That drops you into the fertile San Joaquin Valley, the midsection of the Central Valley. Soon 580 connects to 5, California's monotonous, utilitarian north-south thoroughfare, which runs through Stockton like a crooked pipe cleaner. The second route, this one more northerly, is Highway 4, traversing the levees and sloughs that define the capillary topography of Northern California's Delta region. No matter the route, when you arrive in Stockton, you know you've left the glittering Bay Area bubble far behind.

Stockton was established during the gold rush as a way station for miners and materials, a halfway point between San Francisco and the foothills. Charles Weber, the city's founder, was an enigmatic German who'd come to California in the early 1840s seeking his fortune. He headed to San Jose, where he and his business partner, Guillermo Gulnac, started one successful enterprise after another: flour mill, shoe factory, saltworks, hotel. California was then part of Mexico, and Weber acquired a large Mexican land grant covering an area in the San Joaquin Valley where the Yokuts and Miwok peoples had lived and French-Canadian fur trappers were acquiring pelts.[2]

When California fell to the United States in 1846 and the Mexicans retreated, General José Castro took Weber prisoner, finally releasing him into the desert, horseless, two hundred miles east of the small ranching city of Los Angeles. Somehow surviving the trek to the coast, Weber was given refuge by Commodore Robert Field Stockton of the US Navy. In gratitude, Weber named the town he started after him.

Did Weber know that Stockton, a leading figure in the movement to send freed American slaves back to Africa, was also a swaggering racist who would declare, before the Civil War, that if "our religion and our free institutions should be checked in their progress, or every n—— should be massacred, I'd massacre the n——?"[3] Unclear. In any case, when gold was discovered in 1848, and thousands of people made their way into the foothills, the trading post Weber had set up was perfectly situated to receive them. A rambunctious, vice-filled Wild West city arose overnight, with boats under sail and later steamers arriving daily on the San Joaquin River.

Because Stockton was in the Delta, floods would sometimes wash through its unpaved streets, earning the town its nickname. Ernest Thayer, who wrote "Casey at the Bat," the famous 1888 baseball poem—"there is no joy in Mudville—mighty Casey has struck out"—lived in

San Francisco. He could have been writing about Stockton, which fielded a championship team. Or he could have been writing about Holliston, Massachusetts, another Mudville, near where he was raised. Stocktonians prefer the former interpretation.[4]

By the early twentieth century, Stockton had matured. Agriculture was flourishing in the valley, and the town became a different sort of hub, a place for warehousing, transportation, canning, and milling, as well as banking and commerce. Mexicans and Filipinos took up residence in large numbers. Industry was robust, too, thanks to the Holt Bros. Company, which invented caterpillar treads for tractors in time for them to be used on American and British military equipment during World War I. Shipbuilding during World War II drew Black Americans.[5] In the 1970s, Cambodian, Vietnamese, and other Southeast Asian refugees came.

Stockton today remains a diverse working-class city, one to which coastal California pays little mind. "I could pass that bitch like Stockton (it ain't nothin')," the rapper Jack Harlow declares.[6] But with much of its heavy manufacturing lost (victim to the same deindustrialization that hollowed out cities in the Northeast and Upper Midwest), Stockton struggles.[7] Because of its proximity to the Bay Area, its location off I-5, and its deepwater port on the river suitable for cargo ships, nearly 30 percent of the Stockton-area workforce is employed in "trade, transportation, or utilities," the single biggest employment category in the local economy. Many of these jobs are unionized; they pay well. So do the smattering of professional positions. Other jobs don't. The workforce is poorly educated—only 19 percent of Stocktonians have finished college, while just under a quarter never graduated high school—and low-end service sector gigs are as commonplace as the 49ers decals on bumpers and rear windows. The city's median annual household income is about $20,000 less than the California average. The official poverty rate, 17 percent, is damagingly high and is even higher in Stockton's Latino and Black communities.

Sprawling homeless encampments filled with trash and bicycle parts—an alternative currency for the city's dispossessed—line the sloughs. In some neighborhoods, gunfire and wailing sirens regularly disturb the night. Yet Stockton is beautiful in its way, in the sweet dampness of the air at dusk, in its determination and lack of varnish; for its resolute urbanness jutting from the fields of the Central Valley, what the writer Gerald Haslam has called "the other California," where pickup trucks are the preferred mode of transportation and idealism a luxury few can afford.[8]

• • •

DRAKE WIEST DIDN'T THINK MUCH of idealism. As he keyed in the code to walk through an unmarked door leading to the police department, the only thing on his mind was food. An officer in Stockton PD's gang unit, Drake, twenty-eight, was starving. It was five o'clock in the afternoon in the early winter of 2020, and he'd been at work for eleven hours, coming in before sunrise to help execute a search warrant on a Cambodian gang member. The man had been terrorizing his neighbors doing target practice with a handgun every morning in the front yard of his north Stockton triplex. With the search completed, along with several hours of more routine law enforcement, the door to the department was the only thing standing between Drake and an ahi tuna poke bowl he'd picked up for dinner.

Pink-faced, the sides of his head shaved, the short dirty blond hair on top combed back and shellacked, Drake was the butt of just about every joke told in the twenty-officer unit, which worked closely with specialized gang detectives to police the fifteen hundred or so known members of Stockton's estimated seventy-three active street gangs. In 2019 Drake was named Officer of the Year, partly for how well he and his old partner Yanell Ysais had handled a domestic violence case when he was still assigned to the patrol division. An associate of La eMe, the Mexican Mafia prison gang, had been holding his girlfriend hostage in a motel for several days, telling her he was going to break her neck. She escaped and called the police, but the boyfriend fled. When he returned hours later, Drake and Yanell were able to arrest him, probably saving the woman's life.

Drake's gang unit colleagues were proud of him for winning the award but couldn't pass up the opportunity for some ribbing. With a wink at his fame, they taped three large publicity photos of Drake on the wall above the team's cubicles. They dismantled a clock and put a cutout of Drake's face at the center so that time revolved around him. They made a label for his bodycam that said "Manatee," a reference to Drake's ample frame. When he ate pizza for lunch, dipping the slices into copious amounts of ranch dressing that inevitably fell onto his radio microphone, they laughed until their sides hurt and warned him of the dangers of joining the 300 club.

They could make these jokes because the truth was obvious. At six feet three and 290 pounds in his uniform gear (a little more since his daughter's birth that past summer), Drake and his size were assets. He towered over most of the young men he stopped. He was an incongruously fast runner, and he'd always have your back in a fight. Great instincts, too. Each year he'd take twenty, twenty-five guns off the street.

Besides, when the others dished it out, Drake would dish it right back. The team spent their downtime cracking each other up. That was how they blew off steam. Drake loved it as much as the rest of them.

The other officers in the unit were already in the breakroom; they always ate together. Today the talk was about coffee. That, and how Stockton's city manager didn't appreciate them. (Stockton has a mayor, but because of the way the municipal charter is written, the city manager, a professional administrator appointed by the city council, has more power.)

Rob Barrington was the only cop not in uniform. He was sporting a sweatshirt and jeans and working an undercover car, which required, among other things, timing your liquid intake right. If a surveillance ran long, you might have to pee into a wide-brimmed plastic Costco juice bottle.

Rob was sipping water from a hydro flask with a coffee company sticker on it. Drake gestured at the sticker.

"Is Black Rifle Coffee really that good?" Drake asked.

"The first bag of coffee I got from them I didn't like. But I was like, fuck it, I'm still going to drink it based on what they stand for." (The company is veteran owned and reportedly promotes a "pro-military, pro–law enforcement" message.[9]) "The entire month of November, for every bag they sold, they matched it one for one and sent a bag overseas to a deployed unit. That's a lot of coffee."

Drake seemed unimpressed. He turned to Conner Nelson and asked if he used Keurig pods or ground coffee. "I just switched to the ground," Drake said. "So much better."

"Do you get whole beans and grind it yourself?" Rob asked.

"Should I do that?" Drake replied. "Do you use a French press, too?"

"I used to," Rob said. "Terrible investment. I used it four times, and then I was like this is too much. It's been sitting in the back of my cupboard ever since."

Discussion drifted to contract negotiations between the Stockton Police Officers' Association and the city. Relative to other California police agencies, Stockton doesn't pay its officers particularly well. The city has pressing needs: failing schools, the homelessness crisis, infrastructure begging for upgrades. But being underpaid for risky work felt like a slap in the face. The sentiment in the breakroom was that if the city didn't come back to the table with a raise in the 20 to 30 percent range, there'd be an exodus of Stockton cops to better-funded Bay Area departments.

For Drake, this wasn't idle speculation. He had an hour's commute to Stockton. At his wife's urging, he'd applied a few months earlier to a department much closer to home, Fairfield PD, and had made it past the oral boards. He expected an offer soon, once his background investigation was done. The top step salary in Fairfield was almost forty thousand more than in Stockton, which would come in handy now that he had a kid.

Rob's phone buzzed. It was a Stockton officer assigned to a federal fugitive task force. He and his partner had gotten a lead on a man wanted for attempted murder, and they now had eyes on him. The man was with some friends in the Kings Card Club, a cardroom in the Valley Oak neighborhood. As well as gang policing, Drake's team often assisted with high-risk arrests.

The cops rushed out of the Stewart-Eberhardt Building, known as the SEB, and got into their cars, black-and-white SUVs with silver Stockton PD badges painted on the sides. They headed to a staging area a few blocks from the cardroom—a residential intersection—while Rob drove his undercover unit discreetly into the club's parking lot.

It was dark now and cold outside, at least for California. The uniformed officers milled about on the sidewalk, waiting.

"Is this our attempt homicide?" Drake asked Sergeant Alex Guerrero, one of the team's supervisors.

"I don't know. It's a US Marshals case. A love triangle. Somebody got stabbed a bunch of times." As the team's task was simply to help nab the suspect, the details of the crime hadn't been made clear.

Another officer assisting with surveillance, Apolonio Garcia-Rangel, popped onto the gang unit's radio channel. "He's wearing a black jacket and a brown 49ers baseball hat," he said in a low voice. The team had gotten a text with the suspect's photo and a description of the car he was driving, a gray Chevy Impala.

"Stand by. We're going to try to take him down before he gets to his car to avoid pursuit. If he gets to the car, to the driver's seat, come in and just block them."

Drake looked concerned. "Sarge," he said to Alex, "I think we're too far away. It's going to be hard to get across Swain and pin him in."

Alex thought for a second. "Right across the street, the real estate office, the gate's usually open. On Tam O'Shanter."

The team moved, mustering their SUVs in the real estate office parking lot, which was a thirty-second drive from the club but not too visible from it. The arrest would happen soon, so the cops stayed in their cars. Drake cranked the heat and started playing *Call of Duty* on his phone.

Over the radio, Rob said, "Hey, Garcia, is that him in front of the car right there?"

"It looks like, yeah."

Drake tucked his phone in his pocket and zipped from the lot. His tires screeched as he took turns through the cardroom's parking area. He pulled up behind the Impala at the same time the fugitive task force officers did, in their gleaming unmarked pickups with tinted windows. The pulse of red and blue lights from the police cars combined with the neon signage of the cardroom to produce a weird purple glow.

The fugitive guys had their guns trained on the car. Drake leaped out and drew his weapon. His gang unit colleagues parked behind him and took positions around Drake's vehicle. As the fugitive task force officers instructed the suspect—a middle-aged Black man with a beard and a resigned expression—to step slowly from the Impala and walk backward toward them with his hands in the air, Drake focused on the passenger in the back seat, who'd thrust his hands out the window. Drake's instructions were clear and calm, and he handcuffed the passenger without a problem.

High-stress situations like this didn't faze Drake all that much. He tried to be in good spirits not only with his team but with everyone he dealt with. That didn't always work out, but Drake found that he got more cooperation by being relaxed and pleasant and a bit of a goofball than by coming off as intimidating—as a cop who might shoot first and ask questions later. It was a lesson he'd learned the hard way.

Drake's policing style appealed to his former partner Yanell, with whom he'd spent six months on the midnight patrol shift. They'd both been partnered with other cops before that and would occasionally wind up on the same calls. When the opportunity arose, they decided to work together. They figured that a huge white guy and a Latina would be a winning combination. Sometimes people didn't want to talk to a hulking white cop, so Yanell would take charge. Sometimes they *only* wanted to speak to a man, so Drake would do the honors.

Not to put too fine a point on it, but some cops are assholes. They're assholes to civilians and assholes to other cops. Drake, by contrast, was a genuinely friendly person. He'd strike up a conversation with anyone. Someone stopped for a traffic violation, a witness to a crime, a store clerk. Someone waiting around for a tow. To break the ice, Drake might make a joke or ask the person about something they were wearing or the car they were driving. Or he'd unintentionally come out with some malapropism, his mouth running faster than his brain, and then laugh at himself. One time he stopped a car as winter was approaching and instead of saying, "It's really cooling down and getting darker earlier," he said, "Well, it's really cooling up and getting darker lighter!" Friendly conversations and banter usually led to frictionless encounters. That's how Yanell tried to police, too, by putting folks at ease and talking to them, human to human. It's what Eric Jones wanted of every Stockton officer.

All the same, Drake could go hands-on when he needed to. Most people he and Yanell encountered were cooperative, but some were not. They'd get in their face, try to run, resist, or even attack them. The moment things got physical, Drake was on it, using his size to subdue the person and get the situation under control. Yanell knew that Drake would do anything to protect her, and she'd do the same for him. They'd take a bullet for each other. In the world of policing, that meant everything.

Yanell also admired Drake's drive. He found gangs fascinating and had been clear from the beginning that his goal was to become a gang cop. Not in an obnoxious way, like, "I'm destined to work gangs, fuck you and fuck patrol." More like, "I'm a patrol officer now. I'm devoted to my job, but if I work hard and prove myself, then maybe someday I'll get this cool specialized assignment." So Drake took any opportunity to learn about Stockton's gangs. When he'd chat with people wearing red or blue, he'd ask them what set they were claiming and get them to talk about their neighborhood. He'd hop on social media to see what the Stockton crews were doing. He paid attention to graffiti. He memorized the names and faces and affiliations of different gang members, something Yanell wasn't good at. When Drake was asked to join the gang team, Yanell was happy for him and for Stockton. She knew he'd serve the city well.

Back at the Kings Card Club, the attempted homicide arrest was a wrap. Once the car was searched and the passenger—who had no connection to the crime—released, the fugitive task force guys were all smiles. They'd gotten their man. Drake was satisfied as well. It was a good arrest to cap off a long, productive day. But something was nagging at him. He knew that moving to Fairfield PD, a smaller, quieter agency where he'd have to go back to working patrol, made logical sense. It was the responsible thing to do for his family. But could he really give up the thrill of being a gang cop, whose every gun or violent crime arrest made Stockton a little safer? Could he give up this team, these guys? This department?

• • •

Some police chiefs favor civilian attire, but Eric, forty-nine, with a cleft chin, rectangular face, and short reddish hair, always wore his navy blue uniform at work, the sleeves crisply pressed, the four gold stars signifying his rank pinned neatly along each collar. A black T-shirt peeked out between the buttons, the urban officer's camouflage. Eric was an executive, but he wanted his people to remember that on the inside, where it mattered, he was a cop, not some out-of-touch suit.

He was born in Chico, California. From there his parents moved to Modesto and then, when Eric was a kindergartener, to Ripon, a tiny farming community south of Stockton. His mother was a community college English professor, his father an equipment engineer who designed conveyor belts for food products. Eric and his older brother were raised on five acres, where they were expected, in their spare time, to tend an olive and almond orchard. The family had been in the San Joaquin Valley for generations. Eric's grandparents ran a cattle ranch, and his parents wanted to make sure that their kids knew how to work the land, that its feel and smell would be with them forever.

But Eric didn't want to be a farmer or a rancher, or an English professor or an engineer. He wanted to be a cop. As a child, he was crazy for detective stories. When he was ten, his grandparents got ripped off, after someone forged a signature on a check. Eric was on the case. On a family trip to Washington, DC, he visited FBI Headquarters. He was taken with the grandeur of the building, the fingerprint and forensic technology, the investigative techniques he learned about on the tour. In high school, Eric studied Tae Kwon Do, thinking he might one day need to defend himself.

At Cal State Sacramento, his interest in policing lapsed. He'd also been into computers as a kid, a passion cultivated on an old Commodore 64, and for a while he considered majoring in computer science and going into tech. But he wasn't sure. He told a sociology professor that he was still pondering law enforcement. The professor told him to forget it; he was way too smart to be a cop. Rodney King was the talk of the nation, and the man warned Eric that joining the police force meant signing up with a racially oppressive institution.

Eric got angry. The sociology class covered the problems of urban America: poverty, violence, racism in the criminal justice system. If the goal was to tackle those problems, he thought, smart people who want to make the world better are *exactly* who should be going into policing.

He was hired by Stockton PD in 1993 and sent to a five-month training program in Santa Rosa. He was thrilled. Stockton was the big city for him, and now he'd be in the thick of it.

Long a haven for gangs, Stockton had been hard-hit by the national epidemic of street violence that crested around the time Eric was in high school. In the late 1980s and early 1990s, it maintained the dubious distinction of ranking twenty-fifth in the nation for most dangerous large city based on homicide rates; it was the third most dangerous in California, behind Oakland and Los Angeles.

Starting as a beat cop on patrol, Eric ascended the ranks: sergeant, lieutenant, captain, deputy chief, assistant chief, as if his rise were preordained.

• • •

By 2005, when Eric had been on the force a dozen years, it seemed like Stockton might be turning a corner. Housing costs in the Bay Area were off the charts. Thousands of workers were compelled to move their families to the San Joaquin Valley and make the commute. Demand for new builds soared. Houses and condos went up in subdivisions on the outskirts of town, in neighborhoods like Weston Ranch on the west side of I-5, fetching prices no one would have dreamed possible a few years earlier. With tax revenue flowing in, the city felt the time was right to invest in a major redevelopment of the waterfront, building a sports and concert arena, and to renegotiate pension contracts with city workers. Stockton appeared poised on the brink of a kind of prosperity.

Then the housing bubble burst at the end of 2007, and Stockton home prices plummeted. Building ground to a halt, and construction jobs vanished. Unemployment spiked to an unheard of 17 percent while interest rates rose. Many Stockton home buyers had gotten subprime mortgages. Now they couldn't make the payments. Stockton ended up with the highest foreclosure rate of any city in the country, with almost one out of every ten homes underwater in 2008.

The tax base was dealt a blow, and Stockton, locked into spending agreements, faced a budget emergency, a shortfall of $26 million. According to Michael Fitzgerald, a retired columnist at Stockton's *Record*, the situation was exacerbated by fiscal mismanagement, including flagrant overtime spending in the fire department. The result was that every city agency had to make cuts. Stockton PD laid off or forced into early retirement one hundred officers—nearly a quarter of its force—and slashed pay for those who remained. The police union started a billboard campaign: "Dear Stocktonians, due to cuts in the budget we can no longer guarantee your safety." In 2012, the city declared bankruptcy.

Laying off cops in a financial crisis is a risky proposition. When jobs evaporate, the underground economy grows, often in tandem with violence. To the surprise of criminologists, crime did not increase nationwide during the Great Recession.[10] But it did in a place like Stockton. Researchers have found a connection between the number of police officers employed by a city and the homicide rate, with every additional ten officers preventing about one homicide annually.[11] Fully staffed departments could keep a lid on recession-related crime; Stockton wasn't in a position to do that. The murder rate climbed each year from 2008 to 2011. In 2012 there were seventy-one homicides in the city, including nine killings in a two-day period. That's when Eric was called to lead, replacing an interim chief who was the latest in a run of short-tenured, ineffective appointees.

After taking over the department in March 2012, Eric delivered an impassioned speech, promising a crackdown. Standing behind a wooden podium and in front of pleated purple curtains, he said that his motto going forward would be "two simple words: 'combat crime.'" He pledged to focus the department's attention squarely on gangs and guns. Almost all the city's homicides and nonfatal shootings had been gang related: one group of young men beefing with another over territory or a drug deal gone bad or a challenge laid down to someone's honor. An ambush and a squeeze of the trigger on a stolen Glock or Beretta was all it took to produce sudden vindication and an endless cycle of retaliation and grief.

No more, said Eric. From there on out, he and his staff would be taking a "flexible, real-time approach." The ranks of the department might be thinned, but Stockton PD would compensate by giving watch commanders the ability to immediately redeploy officers to hot spots where danger was brewing instead of sticking with fixed deployment patterns. The department would also add officers to its gang unit to more effectively monitor Stockton's gang members and go after their guns. "In the pursuit of the criminal element, we're going to be very aggressive," Eric vowed.

In those early days, Eric's main concern was stopping the bloodshed. But another goal burned in him—an ember, not yet a flame: to remake the police department, with its core of committed officers but also a well-deserved reputation for brutality, into something Stocktonians could take pride in.

2

I DON'T GANGBANG NO MORE

Among progressives, it's an article of faith that poverty is the root cause of street crime. Improve socioeconomic conditions in impoverished neighborhoods—by creating good paying jobs, strengthening the social safety net, or fixing schools so that more kids go on to college—and you'll naturally bring down the rate of burglaries, robberies, and shootings. Such a view is broadly consistent with findings from social science research, though the relationship between poverty and crime is governed by many other factors, from social bonds among neighborhood residents (which can buffer poverty's effects) to differential exposure to environmental toxins (which can compromise impulse control).[1] But studies also make clear that cities can take steps to reduce crime even when they're unable in the short term to change the economic fortunes of high-crime areas.

When it comes to gun violence, a rough consensus has emerged among experts as to what those steps should be. In most cities, a small number of individuals are at the highest risk of becoming either shooters or shooting victims. These are often young men deep into gang life, whether they belong to large-scale criminal organizations or smaller, more informal cliques. If the police can identify the likely shooters before they shoot, deprive them of access to weapons, be present on the block to deter them from acting on their worst instincts, encourage them to settle grievances without resorting to violence, and maybe peel a few of them away from gangs, they stand a reasonable chance of making the streets safer.

This ambitious approach, which requires more of cops than aggression, is the brainchild of David M. Kennedy, a professor of criminal justice. In the 1980s, as a writer and researcher at Harvard, Kennedy was assigned to projects involving close contact with the Boston Police Department. He came to know the BPD well and the struggles it faced to contain the city's then rampant violence problem.

While studying homicide in Boston, Kennedy learned something interesting. Gang cops and city outreach workers told him that nearly everyone shot in the city was already on their radar, and that they'd know right away who did it because, as frontliners with their ears to the ground, they knew who was beefing with whom.

Shouldn't there be some way, Kennedy thought, to reach the warring parties ahead of time and act to stave off the violence? The cops and outreach workers were doing some of this, but Kennedy envisioned a large-scale violence-prevention effort.[2]

Together with his Harvard colleagues, local and federal law enforcement, and social service providers, Kennedy developed a program that came to be called Operation Ceasefire. The group first surveyed Boston's gangs, mapping out patterns of conflict and alliance. One or two representatives from each gang who were on probation or parole (a lot) were next instructed by their probation or parole officers to come to a "forum," where they'd sit with police, outreach workers, and community representatives, including ministers.

In addition to stressing that violence wasn't the answer, the team had a message for the gang representatives. "We're changing the way we operate. We'll help anybody who wants help." Job training, getting a GED, making a better life for their families? All was possible. But the team bundled these carrots with a stick: "After you leave here today, we're going to be watching for the first body to drop. Whichever group is responsible, we're going to organize police, probation, prosecutors, the feds, everybody to look at every law you're breaking, every open case, every unpaid fine, every outstanding warrant, everything, for everybody in that group.

We're telling you ahead of time because we don't want to do it." If moral suasion and opportunities weren't enough to keep a gang member from shooting a rival, maybe the fear of having the police breathing down the neck of everyone in his crew would do the trick. (The team thus deployed a strategy of "focused deterrence," where the consequences for illegal behavior are communicated directly to the potential criminal, increasing the chances that they'll heed the warning.)[3]

Ceasefire worked. Coupled with other crime-reduction strategies and a more cooperative relationship between law enforcement and the community, it brought about a "63 percent reduction in youth homicide and a 50 percent reduction" in gun violence, according to one study.[4]

Stewart Wakeling, also a criminal justice researcher at Harvard, assisted with a replication of the project in Lowell, Massachusetts, but was eager to return to his home state, California. In 1997, Wakeling persuaded Stockton's city manager and police chief to try a version of Ceasefire; a wave of drive-by shootings had the city on edge. In the years that followed, violence began trending downward, as it had in Boston. But Stockton's commitment to the Ceasefire model faltered. With neighborhoods more peaceful, the city manager decided that the money would be better spent on other things.

Faced with a skyrocketing murder rate in 2012, Eric Jones decided to bring Ceasefire back; he called on Wakeling, who had since formed an organization called the California Partnership for Safe Communities, to consult. Drake Wiest's gang unit, the Community Response Team, was conceived as Ceasefire's main operational arm. Along with gang detectives, CRT would gather intel on players in the gang scene. They'd discuss Ceasefire in community meetings. They'd participate in "call-ins" (Stockton's term for Boston's forums) with higher-ups in the department. They'd stop gang members and tell them about the program. And they'd bring the heat to those who refused to cooperate.[5]

• • •

DRAKE FLIPPED ON HIS LIGHTS and whooped his siren. The driver of a white Ford sedan pulled into the parking lot of the Red Sea Market, a neighborhood grocery with a faded 1970s-era Pepsi sign and bold red-and-blue lettering painted on a whitewashed exterior announcing "Beer * Wine * Liquors / Productos Mexicanos * Groceries."

The driver, a large Latino man in his thirties wearing a black T-shirt, hadn't come to a complete stop at a stop sign. But the real reason Drake lit him up was because his face was covered with gang tattoos. Stopping gang members and searching them for guns was a big part of the CRT mandate.

Community Response Team. The officers thought it was a dumb name, Orwellian even, a politically correct title for what they really were: gang cops. But CRT was such a plum assignment, an adrenaline rush every day, that no one was going to raise a stink.

Drake usually recognized the people he was stopping before he pulled them over. It was as though he'd downloaded a database of Stockton gangbangers directly into his brain. "There goes two guys from Vickeystown," he'd say. Or, "This gentleman here is Flyboys." If the individuals he'd spotted were on probation or parole, he didn't need probable cause to make the stop; a condition of their release was that they could be stopped wherever, whenever. In situations like this one, where Drake didn't recognize the guy but could tell from a glance that he was a gang member, he needed some sort of violation to make the stop legit.

"Can you roll down the back windows, too?" Drake said as he approached the car. The Ford's other occupant was a very small boy, perhaps four or five years old, who sat wide-eyed in a car seat in the back.

"How's it going?" Drake asked the driver.

"It's OK, I just got this one a haircut," the driver said, motioning toward the back seat.

With a boy in the car, this was going to be a chill stop. The driver wasn't looking for trouble, and the last thing Drake wanted to do, as a new father himself, was jack someone up in front of their kid. He stood casually next to the driver's door, his left arm outstretched, resting on the frame. The man didn't bother to ask why he'd been stopped.

"When did you get those tattoos?" Drake asked. Drake's own tattoo of St. Michael, the patron saint of law enforcement, was visible beneath the left sleeve of his uniform shirt, the words "St. Michael Protect Me" in curly script.

"A long time ago," said the driver.

The man had vertical lines running up his neck, markings all across his forehead, and a red kiss mark tattooed on one cheek. On the other cheek, the number 3600. (Gang sets sometimes identify themselves by the numbers of the street blocks they claim as their own.)

He had a bowl haircut with a tail, a gold earring, and bags under his eyes.

"How long? 'Cause the 3600 looks pretty fresh, bro."

"Nah, it's a different ink," the driver responded.

Drake asked the man if he was on probation or parole. He was on parole, had only recently been released from prison, and had gotten the 3600 tattoo inside.

He was done with gangs, he told Drake. He was getting too old for them.

Drake's backup, Sergeant Wesley Grinder, arrived. Drake asked the driver to step out of the car and then handcuffed him out of sight of his child, placing him in the back of the police SUV. Before they started looking through the Ford, Drake and Wesley gingerly released the kid from the car seat.

"Cool haircut," Wesley said to the boy, who began playing a game in the parking lot. "Would you like a sticker?"

Wesley wasn't Drake's main supervisor. That responsibility fell jointly on Alex Guerrero and another sergeant, Jason Underwood, whose cubicle in the SEB was adorned with a sign christening him "Sgt. Underpants." There was some tension between Drake and Jason. At the very least, Drake preferred Alex's leadership style. A Stockton native, Alex stood ramrod straight and could hold his own as the guys swapped war stories over a meal at Susy's, an all-day Mexican restaurant and diner. When Alex would ask the team to huddle, pointing out habits and ruts they seemed to be falling into that were limiting their productivity in getting guns off the street, Drake ate it up like it was machaca and eggs.

The Ford contained nothing illegal. Drake walked back to his SUV and continued where he'd left off on the tattoos, cracking the door so he and the man could talk.

"That 3600 looks super fresh, but you're saying you dropped out. All your other face tattoos are faded like crazy, and that one's not," Drake told him. "I'm just being truthful. Like, how long have you had that kiss on your face?"

"Listen, I don't gangbang no more. Why you keep asking?" said the man.

"So here's the thing. I'm not fucking with you just to fuck with you. We're the gang cops. You're a gang member. So I'm gonna talk to you. Are you still claiming, or what's going on?"

"No, I work," the man replied, shaking his head.

"Where do you work at?" Drake asked.

The man gave the name of a grocery store chain.

Wesley asked the boy, who was still playing, "Do you want to sit back in the car? Do you want me to zip up your jacket?"

The man called out, "He's got a lollipop, he got it after his haircut."

"A little incentive!" Drake said jovially. More quietly he asked the man, "You ever been arrested in Stockton?"

"Yeah."

"You weren't with any set?"

"I used to be with the North, but I don't run around with anybody no more."

The North—Norteños—are the dominant Latino gang family in Northern California. Gang members displaying "XIV" tattoos (for "N," the fourteenth letter of the alphabet) and red clothing (because it's the opposite of the blue worn by their archrivals, the Southern California–based Sureños) can be found in every major city.

"Is this your girl's car?" Drake asked the man, having looked up the registration.

"Yeah. We got twins on the way. Girls."

"Twins on the way? Congratulations, man! That's crazy," said Drake. "Girls are cool. I got a girl. My buddy put it pretty good. Your daughter is the first girl you'll fall in love with right away."

Drake ran the man's name through the system. No warrants. He asked where he lived. Lodi, to the north.

"The southside Lodi guys don't trip off you?" Drake asked, as he pulled the man out of the SUV and released the handcuffs.

"You know what? They do. . . . Nah, they don't, 'cause I don't see none of them. I'm thirty-two."

"Yeah, I mean shit's different from when you were gangbanging," Drake said.

"Yeah, it is," said the man.

"Now if you piss someone off on social media, they go around and shoot up your house," Drake said. "There's no more fisticuffs or anything like that. It's just everyone shoots each other. Over stupid shit, too."

The man said: "See, my thing is, I work graveyards, so I go to work at ten o'clock. I get off, you know what I'm saying. I wake up about three o'clock in the afternoon, my day is gone."

Drake told the guy that he could hook him up with someone who could remove the face tattoos, if he wanted. He took out his business card. Wesley cajoled a high five out of the little boy, who hadn't said a word the whole time.

• • •

What type of officer are you going to encounter when one pulls you over with your kid in the back seat, or hails you on the sidewalk with a "Hey, you," or shows up at your doorstep in response to a call? What attitude will he or she bring? Will your rights be protected or trampled? Will the cause of justice be helped or hindered?

Americans have been asking questions like these since police departments were founded in this country in the mid-nineteenth century. Boston was the first to be set up, in 1838, then New York in 1844 (both modeled on London's newly created Metropolitan Police), then a host of others in quick succession. In northern cities, the departments replaced the informal "constable-watch" system that had come before, in which citizens were pressed into service to make arrests and respond to cries for help. In the South, in places like New Orleans, Savannah, and Charleston, the police evolved out of military-style "city guard" units concerned first and foremost with capturing runaway slaves and quelling slave rebellions. In the West, on the frontier, uniformed police officers took the place of town marshals, who worked with county sheriffs to enforce the law. That was the story in Stockton, which elected a police chief for the first time in 1862.[6]

Some people, especially those with money and power, welcomed the advent of police forces. Crime and disorder, including political violence, were characteristic of fast-growing cities, and the police promised a solution.[7] Elites also backed the police in the hope that they'd keep the "dangerous classes"—the poor, immigrants, striking factory workers, Black people—in line.[8]

By the early 1900s, support had ebbed. Reformers drew attention to the corruption that was endemic in big-city departments. Cops had grade school educations, received no formal training, supplemented their meager salaries with bribes, and were treated by politicians as hired thugs. Barely showing up for work, they had a minimal effect on crime. During Prohibition-era inquiries into corruption, civil libertarians highlighted the brutality officers used to extract confessions. One writer on the subject of the "third degree," Ernest Jerome Hopkins, wrote that if the term was understood to encompass "cruel and inhuman forms of torture," "blows, slaps, kicks, floggings," and "the use of sleeplessness, hunger, cold or heat, threats, lies, trickery," then "there are but a few exceptional American cities where the third degree is not practiced in most felony arrests."[9]

In the late 1930s and early 1940s, the NAACP and other civil rights organizations exposed the vicious racism of the police, particularly in the South, where police departments enforced the terms of Jim Crow, and where their connections with the Ku Klux Klan were tight.[10] Things weren't much better in the rest of the country. In the racial unrest that broke out during World War II, in Detroit, Harlem, Los Angeles, and elsewhere, the police—almost exclusively white—could be counted on to side with white rioters. Scores of Black and Latino Americans were killed in these clashes.

It was around this time that social scientists first got into the business of studying the police. They came less to criticize (or celebrate) than to understand. Two studies in particular laid the foundation for what would become a dynamic field of research. Both put police culture at their center.

"Violence and the Police" appeared in 1953, written by William Westley, an American sociologist teaching at McGill University in Montreal.[11] In graduate school at the University of Chicago, Westley had met Joseph Lohman, a man with one foot in academia, the other in criminal justice administration.[12] Chicago sociologists were known for using a distinctive method to explain human behavior: they tried to grasp how social environments shaped the way people thought about the world, and how those perspectives influenced their motivations and choices. Westley wanted to use this method to study policing, so Lohman helped him gain access to the department in nearby Gary, Indiana.

The main question Westley took up in his research was why cops so often utilized violence, even when they weren't defending themselves against attack. Westley had no way to measure the amount of gratuitous police violence in Gary, but in response to the question "When do you think a policeman is justified in roughing a man up?" seventy-three officers ticked off a range of circumstances in which they thought he was. Forty percent of Gary cops said that "disrespecting the police" was justification for a beating, while 20 percent approved of violence to get an uncooperative suspect to hand over information. One officer told Westley, "Most of the police use punishment if the fellow gives them any trouble. . . . If there is any slight resistance, you can go all out on him. You shouldn't do it in the street, though. Wait until you are in the squad car."[13]

Westley's explanation for this behavior focused on what policing is like as an occupation. "The policeman," Westley wrote, "finds his most pressing problems in his relationships to the public. His is a service occupation but . . . he must discipline those whom he serves. He is regarded as corrupt and inefficient by, and meets with hostility and criticism from, the public. He regards the public as his enemy, feels his occupation to be in conflict with the community, and regards himself to be a pariah. The experience and the feeling give rise to a collective emphasis on secrecy, an attempt to coerce respect from the public, and a belief that almost any means are legitimate in completing an important arrest." Westley concluded, "These are . . . basic occupational values."[14]

Westley's study is still relevant. Contemporary research reveals that perceived challenges to police authority, which trigger the occupational insecurities Westley identified, can indeed increase the risk of police brutality. When sociologists Geoffrey Raymond and Nikki Jones analyzed videos of police stops in 2021, they found that the interactions became more tense and veered toward violence when police interpreted people's actions or responses as resistance, even if the people didn't intend them that way.[15]

In the second key study, Jerome Skolnick, a professor at UC Berkeley, investigated the police department in a midsize city he called Westville (which we now know to have been Oakland). He interviewed patrol officers but mostly considered the detectives in Westville's vice squad who dealt with prostitution and narcotics. Later, he conducted a smaller-scale study of an East Coast police department—"Eastville"—in order to have a basis for comparison.

The book Skolnick wrote from this research, *Justice without Trial* (1966), explored how policing practices in the two departments affected the pursuit of justice.[16] Would residents of Westville or Eastville have been better served if different practices were in place? If vice detectives didn't rely so heavily on shady informants, for example? Or if the police didn't see constitutional protections afforded to suspects as technicalities they could freely sidestep? Skolnick's answer to these questions was an unqualified yes.

The practices reflected police culture, which Skolnick believed was a major factor explaining why the administration of justice came up short. He described this culture, equally present in Westville and Eastville, as "the police officer's working personality." It had two major components: an abiding concern with danger and social isolation. Skolnick noted that the "*raison d'être* of the police officer and the criminal law . . . arises ultimately . . . from the threat of violence and the possibility of danger to the community."[17] Because of this, cops are always attuned to danger and on the lookout for individuals who might prove to be a threat. But the things officers consider to be signs of danger may not be. They might signal prejudices the officers hold, leading them to be suspicious and potentially violent toward people who've done nothing to deserve such treatment.

As for social isolation, the officers Skolnick interviewed—much like the cops in Gary—felt they had little public support and that people they met in their off-duty lives didn't like them because of their job. Even generally law-abiding citizens break the rules sometimes. They speed, drink too much, get into fights. They're not going to feel friendly toward officers of the law who might arrest them.

Thus police tend to socialize principally with other cops. And that, Skolnick argued, has profound effects. They come to believe that lawmen are the only people they can trust and that the most important thing is to protect their brothers in blue, even if it means lying to cover for wrongdoing. Officers who are cut off socially from the communities they serve are also much more likely to trade in crude stereotypes, racial ones included.

From the standpoint of democratic law enforcement in a diverse society, Skolnick noted, both elements of police culture—the singular concern with danger and the us-versus-them mentality—are bad. Since they emerge from the nature of the occupation, what hope is there for change?

For a time, the belief among social scientists was that change is impossible. That wherever you looked, the culture of the police would be pretty much the same, and awful.[18]

There was a problem with that theory. It wasn't necessarily true.

• • •

In 2012, Eric and his command staff put their all into getting Ceasefire off the ground. There were late nights, seven-day workweeks, kids' soccer games and dance recitals missed, marriages strained. Beyond the logistical challenges of Ceasefire, morale in the department was at an all-time low. The cuts had forced out so many officers. Everyone who remained was feeling the effects of the slashed pay, even as the agency was overwhelmed with calls. Eric made the rounds. He met with his troops, told them he knew how tough things were. He implored them not to leave Stockton for other agencies, not to lose their commitment to the job. He listened to what they had to say and reassured them that he was right there with them. "The community needs you now more than ever," he said. His officers saw him as a beacon of calm and strength.

Six months in, the crime situation stabilized. Shootings went down, and the murder rate returned to something approaching Stockton's historical average—atrociously high but not Cartagena-level.

The decrease probably had more to do with Stockton PD finding its bearings again under Eric's leadership, or the changes he'd made to officer deployment patterns, or random fluctuations, than with Ceasefire. According to Scott Meadors, the captain in charge of the department's field operations division, a problem with the violence-prevention program became apparent. The cops would arrange call-ins with gang members and instruct them to come to the station or some neutral location. Many never showed up. Those who came didn't trust what the officers had to say. How could they be sure Ceasefire wasn't a trap to trick them into confessing to some crime? They were used to Stockton PD being all stick, no carrot. The police faced skepticism from the men's families, too.

No one could say the skepticism was baseless: the department was notorious for overzealous policing and violence. Wilisha Beatty-Cherry, an outreach worker at a Stockton elementary school, knew that as well as anyone. One night back in 2002, when she was twenty years old and sound asleep, she got a frantic phone call from her stepmother, Erica. "When the sun comes up, Wilisha, I know they're going to kill him," she cried. "You need to get here."

Wilisha's father, Bobby Carl Washington Sr., with eight kids and a love of fishing, was having a breakdown. His mother had died the year before—it was the anniversary of her death—and he'd been laid off from his construction job. That night, Bobby started talking about taking his own life and maybe killing his family. He might have been on PCP. His brother, who lived next door on a quiet cul-de-sac, called the cops. Soon the house was surrounded by the Stockton PD SWAT team.

Wilisha sped over. She got out of her car and approached the officers who were maintaining a perimeter. She told them she was Bobby's daughter. She was sure she could calm her father down. All she needed was a chance to speak with him. Her stepmother had told her that the police wanted her there as a mediator.

The cops on the scene peppered her with questions as if she were a suspect: her name, age, what she did for work, her father's age, how many children he had. "Just let me get to my dad!" she yelled. They said no. She started screaming and swearing. "I don't even know what's going on, let me get to my dad!" She became so agitated that the cops handcuffed her and placed her in the back of a police car. Hours later, she received word that the SWAT team had shot and killed her father.

The police said Bobby had pointed a gun at them, but Wilisha's uncle insisted he hadn't. The family is Black, and the Stockton chapter of the NAACP promised to launch an investigation. The San Joaquin County District Attorney's Office found the shooting justified. Legality aside, in the weeks and months after the shooting, no one from Stockton PD thought to contact the family, to offer condolences, to explain what had happened in those final minutes—or to apologize to Wilisha for putting her in handcuffs.

Bobby's death cut a hole in the Washingtons. Wilisha took in two of her younger siblings. Three more went into foster care. Her stepmother became homeless. Wilisha told a reporter for the *Record* that Erica had "lost hope. She lost everything. It's like standing on a little rug and somebody snatching it from under your feet—you get knocked over, and she just never got up. I think that is what the police took from her."[19]

Other tragedies unfolded in Stockton, other abuses. Some made headlines: a sixteen-year-old who carjacked a van and was chased by Stockton police officers and a sheriff's deputy. The cops rammed the vehicle, causing the kid to crash into a garage. Then they fired dozens of rounds, killing him, claiming he'd been about to back up and run them over.[20] There were less dramatic incidents: lawyers with the San Joaquin County Public Defender's Office who believed that cops had beaten their clients but were unable to prove it.

In 2010, the department made more than ten thousand arrests, which works out to one for every twenty-nine people living in Stockton, an appallingly large number. In the 1990s, when Eric was coming up as a cop, Stockton had bought into the zero-tolerance policing model of the time—stop everything that moves, make every arrest you can, hope the judge will throw away the key—and had carried it forward. Huge racial disparities were evident in these arrests, reflecting the color of poverty and social dislocation in Stockton—as well as, no doubt, bias on the part of the officers. The department held press conferences announcing gang sweeps, displaying arrestee posters filled with Black and brown and Asian faces. In some parts of the city, the police were seen as an occupying army, there to haul off young men of color.[21]

Michael Fitzgerald, the retired *Record* columnist, put these policing practices in the context of Stockton's history. As the city's economic fortunes waned in the decades following World War II, there was a rise not only in poverty but in deep poverty, families living below 50 percent of the poverty line, many who'd remain stuck there for generations. It was out of these families that Stockton's violent gang culture emerged. Stockton PD stood ready with a solution, Fitzgerald said: for years, it tried to control the crime problem by employing cowboy cops, often white and racist, who'd swarm high-crime districts and bloody heads. That tradition of violence remained alive in corners of the police force that Eric had inherited.

The cops kept killing people. In 2012, four men lost their lives at the hands of Stockton PD (one after shooting an officer in the stomach). Angry protests erupted outside the main police department building on East Market Street.

There's hard data to show that the most beleaguered Stockton residents had all but lost faith in the police. In 2015, three years after Eric was installed as chief, the Urban Institute conducted a study of attitudes toward the criminal justice system among residents of disadvantaged neighborhoods in six US cities, Stockton included.[22] The study found that only about a quarter of Stocktonians in those neighborhoods believed that the police made fair decisions, treated people with dignity and respect, or usually followed the law. Nearly 60 percent thought that the police acted on the basis of bias or prejudice. Trust was almost nil. Among Black people who responded, a mere 9 percent said they personally trusted the police.

It began to dawn on Eric that he couldn't serve the city well—that he couldn't bring about a substantial reduction in crime through programs like Ceasefire or get cooperation from citizens—if people had no reason to trust that the cops were acting in good faith. Changing that would require taking on Stockton's culture of policing.

3

PJ

As social science research on the police accumulated in the 1960s, scholars continued to work with William Westley and Jerome Skolnick's theory of police culture, which held that all police "see the world similarly."[1] Then a book by political scientist James Q. Wilson changed the conversation.

In the mid-1960s, Wilson had undertaken a study of police bureaucracy, examining twenty-five American departments, eight intensively. Like other researchers, Wilson recognized that discretion—the judgment calls police make about how to handle cases and situations—was an essential feature of the job. In *Varieties of Police Behavior* (1968), he pointed out that there are two components to the police role: enforcing the law and maintaining order.[2] Discretion comes into play in both because general legal and departmental rules have to be applied to real-world situations, requiring officer interpretation. Does it make sense to ticket someone driving two miles an hour over the limit? When is a blasting stereo too loud, such that a cop could reasonably ask its owner to lower the volume?

As Wilson saw it, police discretion and the risks and complexities of law enforcement are what give rise to a recognizable occupational culture among cops; the culture functions to guide officers in making discretionary choices. Criminal justice scholar Elizabeth Reuss-Ianni later called this "street cop culture" to differentiate it from the culture of police managers, and she identified several "maxims" that encapsulated it: "show balls," "be aggressive when you have to, but don't be too eager," "watch out for your partner first," and "protect your ass."[3]

Under the influence of this culture, the police were as concerned with controlling people's behavior through threats (and protecting their own careers) as they were with lawfulness. That made policing an unusual type of public bureaucracy, one where achieving supervision and accountability was particularly challenging.

But something else stood out to Wilson and his research team: police culture wasn't entirely the same in the different agencies they'd studied. You could walk into a squad room for roll call in Albany, New York, or Highland Park, Illinois, and though certain things would be similar, others wouldn't. Leaving aside superficial differences like regional variations in uniforms, Wilson determined that what varied from one department to another was the extent to which officers in each agency prioritized law enforcement versus maintaining order, and the degree to which officers felt bound by law and policy. In this respect, the agencies fell into three types, each one indicating a particular cultural style layered over the commonalities of street cop culture.

In Albany, Wilson observed a "watchman" style: the cops tended to ignore minor offenses, including vice-related ones; they didn't make many proactive stops; by and large they stayed out of minority neighborhoods unless they were called; and in place of arrests, they would issue warnings or mete out street justice, inflicting beatings on those they thought deserving of them. Watchman-style cops prioritized maintaining order and shrugged off legal constraints on their behavior.

Other departments, like Oakland PD, exhibited a "legalistic" style. The cops there focused more on enforcing the law across the board. They issued loads of traffic tickets. They responded to minor offenses. They could be found zealously patrolling crime-prone neighborhoods. They dealt with juvenile delinquents formally, by arresting them and bringing them down to the station. They accepted (if grudgingly) that police officers should abide by rules and laws, too.[4]

Finally, some departments had what Wilson called a "service" style. In these agencies—which he said were typical of "homogeneous, middle-class communities" such as Nassau County, Long Island—"the police intervene frequently but not formally."[5] The officers would be in your business in a second if they saw you doing something suspicious, but they were more apt to give you a talking to than bring you in or kick your ass. They were less bureaucratically inclined than their peers in legalistic agencies.

What accounted for these differences in culture? One factor loomed large: the political tenor of the city in question, which influenced who was appointed chief. Watchman-style departments often arose in cities with "caretaker" political cultures, where the goal of local politicians was to have city government offer "a minimum of public services at the lowest possible cost."[6] Laissez-faire chiefs installed in such cities set the tone for their officers. Legalistic departments were more common in racially or ethnically heterogeneous cities run by city managers, especially managers who'd been hired "with a mandate for change."[7] In trying to address problems, city managers selected chiefs who promised to professionalize the police, which usually meant making the departments more rule-bound. In well-off suburban communities, citizens wanted high-touch service from government but didn't want to be hemmed in by excessive law enforcement.

The period in which Wilson's book was published saw a great deal of urban strife involving clashes with the police. Historian Elizabeth Hinton documents 4 major incidents of racial unrest nationally in 1964, another 4 in 1965, rising exponentially to an astonishing 613 in 1969.[8] Although these incidents were described as "riots," as in the infamous 1965 Watts riots in Los Angeles, Hinton argues that they're better characterized as rebellions against the oppressive conditions faced by Black Americans. Grievances with police mistreatment were the main motivator; social and economic exclusion lay in the background. Unrest continued into the 1970s, with the police, and occasionally National Guard troops, responding with ferocious force. Between police mishandling of these events and their failure to deal appropriately with peaceful protest around the Vietnam War, as during the Democratic National Convention in 1968 when Chicago cops beat protesters, it seemed to many policy makers, scholars, and activists that policing had reached a crisis point. Commissions were launched, reports written, all with the goal of better understanding the crisis and finding some way forward.

Few readers of Wilson at that time saw him offering the definitive analysis of American policing. For one thing, his comments about street justice aside, his book said more about police behavior than misbehavior. Wilson's typology made no sense of the abuse regularly doled out by cops in Los Angeles, for example, or in Chicago's Grant Park, where many of the 1968 clashes took place. A second problem was that while Wilson hadn't meant for his styles to be mutually exclusive, he often discussed them as though they were. When a reviewer for the *Boston Globe* noted that Boston PD was a "confusing potpourri of various styles of police procedure," he was pointing out a flaw in the argument: Wilson gave little thought to how the styles might combine.[9]

Nor was it clear what policy lessons Wilson intended readers to draw. He registered advantages and disadvantages to the three styles of policing, meditating on a possible "trade-off between leniency and equity."[10] If you wanted to change police culture in your community but were powerless (as most people were) to upend local political culture—Wilson's key explanatory variable—what were you supposed to do?

Nonetheless, *Varieties of Police Behavior* established that the cultures of police departments aren't all alike, a point that hadn't been adequately acknowledged before. Evidently there was some flexibility, some give, in the fabric of the occupation.[11] So in principle, at least, police culture might be changed and improved. In the 1970s and 1980s, the book set off a scramble among researchers to identify better styles than the ones prevailing in leading departments and articulate the steps that would bring them about. The model of police reform Eric Jones would end up championing in Stockton was a legacy of these inquiries.

• • •

Procedural justice, the police philosophy Eric got behind, is rooted in the work of Max Weber, the German social scientist most famous for his essay "The Protestant Ethic and the Spirit of Capitalism."

Weber wrote extensively on the conditions under which people will agree to be governed by political authorities, whether kings or bureaucrats or party leaders. The threat of force can generate compliance, Weber observed. So can monetary incentives, when a corrupt politician stays in power because voters think he's good for their pocketbooks. A more efficient and stable form of authority, however, comes about when people believe those in power have the right to be there, when authority is seen as legitimate.[12]

The concept of legitimacy is at the core of *Why People Obey the Law*, a 1990 book by psychologist Tom Tyler.[13] Crunching data from a survey of Chicago residents, Tyler examined why some were more likely than others to avoid unlawful behaviors like littering, drunk driving, speeding, or stealing. Those people concerned with getting caught, losing the approval of peers, or violating their personal morality were less prone to lawbreaking. That much is common sense. But people's perception of the legitimacy of the authorities had an impact, too. If they thought well of the Chicago police or the court system—thought the cops were honest, deserving of respect, believed the courts were fair (thought, in other words, that the procedures they'd be subject to were just)—that increased the odds that they'd comply with the law's demands.

The implication was that if the police and court system could be refashioned to operate more fairly regardless of race or class, and if they could demonstrate that they were operating fairly, the population would become more law abiding. Law professor Tracey Meares, writing with Tyler nearly three decades later, argued that when it comes to the police, "the public wants to be listened to when policies are being created, as well as to have an opportunity to state their case when dealing with individual police officers. They also want explanations for police actions that allow them to determine that the police are acting in unbiased ways and in accordance with policies that connect to understandable and shared objectives." If these conditions are met, Meares and Tyler asserted, people will "trust" the police, "defer to their authority," and also "cooperate by reporting crimes and criminals, providing testimony, and otherwise helping to hold offenders accountable."[14]

Procedural justice, or PJ, as it's called in law enforcement circles, where everything has an acronym, became popular among police executives when Barack Obama was president. It was the focus of the report of the President's Task Force on 21st Century Policing—the one that claimed "organizational culture eats policy for lunch." The best way to improve policing, the report argued, would be to infuse the ideals of procedural justice into the culture and thinking of street cops everywhere.

Eric had first heard about procedural justice from Stewart Wakeling, the man who'd brought Ceasefire to Stockton. The more he read and learned, the more excited he became. The vision of the good cop that Eric had clung to in college, a trustworthy officer who'd arrest lawbreakers while doing right by the community, was a model of procedural justice. That was the ideal he'd set for Stockton PD. From Eric's perspective, some Stockton officers were already putting the philosophy into practice, whether they knew it or not. If he could shift the culture of the entire department in that direction, that would be something. It could help cultivate the trust of the community, which had been so sorely lacking, impeding the success of Ceasefire.

Halfway across the country, the Chicago police department, with the assistance of Meares and Tyler, had been experimenting with procedural justice. In the fall of 2013, Wakeling organized a trip for a group of Stockton officers to take the PJ course that Chicago had designed. The cops stayed downtown, enjoyed the crisp weather, ate some deep-dish pizza. They took what they learned back to Stockton, developing their own one-day training for supervisors and officers. The training explained the tenets of PJ, highlighting four principles officers should follow when interacting with citizens: be transparent about what you're doing and why, give citizens an opportunity to speak and be heard (on the street and in the community), prioritize fairness, and remain an impartial decision maker. Stockton PD labeled these trustworthiness, voice, respect, and neutrality. Trainers discussed the notion of implicit bias, explaining how procedural justice and reducing prejudice go hand in hand.

Talk about the four principles could get a little abstract, so trainers showed videos of real-life police-citizen encounters that illustrated procedural justice in action. After the videos played, trainers would lead discussions about how the principles had been applied. If the officer on a video explained patiently why he'd stopped someone, the trainers would ask how that demonstrated transparency and trustworthiness. If a videoed officer said, "What are you upset about tonight? Talk to me," the class was asked to reflect on how this represented giving citizens a voice. Trainers would point to specific words that exhibited respect, such as "sir" or "ma'am," and would ask questions of the cops to get them to explore neutrality in decision-making, like whether a police action seemed justified by the facts or may have revealed bias.

Critics of procedural justice have argued that integrating elementary ideas like trustworthiness, voice, respect, and neutrality into policing won't produce much of a concrete change in how, and against whom, the government's punitive capacity is deployed.[15] Proponents counter that there's a vast difference between a cop who treats everyone with dignity and respect—even if an arrest must be made or force used—and a cop who reserves such treatment only for those who are white and middle-class.

Stockton's course paired discussion of the four PJ principles with something else: an examination of the historical reasons communities of color often mistrust the police. The officers studied a timeline of police mistreatment of Black and brown citizens, from the early history of slave patrols to police brutality against civil rights protesters. For later versions of the course, Stockton PD asked Elizabeth Hinton, the historian, to comb the archives looking for instances of racial injustice in Stockton, such as police overreaction to unrest in the city's Sierra Vista housing project in 1968. Officers learned that they were policing against the backdrop of that history; if they weren't plainly fair in their dealings with people, there'd be no way to win trust.

Every officer on the force cycled through the course. Some cops told the trainers—fellow officers who'd been chosen for having both street cred and an intuitive understanding of the issues—that whatever the racial atrocities of the past, they weren't personally responsible for them. The trainers would agree. Even so, they'd add, when people look at you, at your uniform and badge, the history might be what they see. Initially the course lasted only a day, but in time it swelled to three days, the class sessions spaced weeks apart so the officers would have time to think about and absorb the insights.

Gary Benevides was one of the trainers. When he began teaching procedural justice in 2015, he was a recently promoted sergeant with experience as a K-9 and SWAT officer. A cop's cop. His very first class, he had a skeptic in the room. The man kept reading a newspaper, putting on a show of sighing loudly and shrugging as Benevides went over the goals for the day: setting expectations for how the department wanted new officers to police; providing an opportunity for veteran officers to reset or recalibrate their practice; and reinforcing what good officers in Stockton were already doing.

During break time, Benevides went up to the guy. It seemed as though he wanted to provoke a confrontation: he'd act oppositional, prodding Benevides to come down hard on him, and then the cop could tell his buddies that procedural justice was a stupid idea being rammed down everyone's throats. Benevides took a different tack. "Hey, you look miserable. That's the last thing we want. I have no problem with you going home for the day and skipping the training if you want."

This caught the skeptic off guard. Unsure how to respond, he fumbled. "No, it's fine," he said. "I'll stay." As Benevides tells the story, the simple act of acknowledging the officer's feelings seemed to mollify him, and he eventually proved among the more engaged students in the session. Benevides's response legitimized procedural justice because he had shown the same respect and care he was asking officers to show citizens.

Two other parts of the procedural justice program took shape. Soon after becoming chief, Eric had started a community advisory board. It met monthly, in different locations around the city, to give him input on policy and procedure. Board members reported on their community's fears about crime. They were also livid about police brutality.

Annette Sanchez, then vice president of El Concilio, a social service nonprofit, served on the board from its inception. Eric asked the board to "inform him of the good, the bad, the ugly of what was taking place with the citizens, and with his own staff." Board members would float ideas about what Stockton PD might do differently—Sanchez pushed for hiring more Latino officers—and Jones would ask their thoughts on policy changes under consideration. He didn't accept all the recommendations he heard, and some of the most strident critics of Stockton PD were never asked to join. But members like Sanchez welcomed the opportunity to converse with the chief of police.

Eric had been an advocate of community partnerships for some time, from before he learned about procedural justice. When he began reading about PJ's emphasis on voice—the idea that legitimacy is enhanced not only when cops let citizens speak, but when residents have a say in how criminal justice is administered—he recognized that this was what the board could offer. The board *was* procedural justice, and he doubled down on his commitment to it.

The other piece was a series of trust-building workshops. As the national conversation around procedural justice advanced, there was increasing talk about the need for reconciliation between the police and minority communities. Scholars and practitioners envisioned workshops where officers would sit at a table with citizens who'd felt the bite of police oppression. If the citizens could share stories while officers gave their perspective on the job, maybe that could spark a change, with the police becoming more compassionate and the community recognizing that not all cops are bastards.

This approach, emphasizing dialogue and mutual understanding, had been used in conflict resolution in places like Northern Ireland and South Africa, and Eric decided it was worth a try in Stockton. The department arranged a series of meetings.

Wilisha Beatty-Cherry attended one such event fourteen years after her father was killed by Stockton cops. She'd seen recent news coverage of Stockton PD shootings and her heart was heavy with grief for the dead and their families. It was her grief, too. She'd come at the invitation of a friend who worked at Fathers and Families of San Joaquin, the nonprofit where the workshop was being held. Twenty-five Stockton residents and five police were present to take part in what were billed as "courageous conversations." The attendees broke into groups. In Wilisha's, people began introducing themselves. When it was her turn, she said, "In 2002, Stockton PD robbed me of my father."

She noticed that the officer at her table, a white man in his forties, looked uncomfortable. Something about his body language. He asked Wilisha her father's name, and when she said, "Bobby Washington," he shifted in his chair. "I was there that night," he said. It was Captain Scott Meadors, one of the officers who'd traveled to Chicago to learn about procedural justice.

Wilisha broke down. In the years since her father's death, she'd never talked to any of the cops involved. When she regained her composure, she told the group how her family had been devastated by the shooting and how awful it felt that Stockton PD had never offered them support.

As the conversation drew to a close, Scott handed his card to everyone except Wilisha. Hmm, she thought. Was he trying to avoid her? But then Scott came over and apologized on behalf of the department for neglecting the family. He seemed truly contrite and empathetic. He wrote his cell phone number on a scrap of paper. "If you ever need anything, call me," he said.

Never in a million years did Wilisha think she would. But life works in mysterious ways. Two weeks later, her eight-year-old son, Khe-Len, started having nightmares. Their house had been burglarized, and Khe-Len was terrified that someone would break in while he slept. He was also scared of ghosts, and of police officers, who'd killed his grandfather. Wilisha and her husband bought a home security system. They told Khe-Len that ghosts don't exist. But they couldn't assure him that most police are there to help, not hurt. They couldn't believe that themselves.

Wilisha remembered that she had Scott's contact information. She hesitated, then dug it out of her purse.

"Is there anything you can think of to say that would make my son feel better?" she asked Scott.

"I want to meet him," Scott replied. "We can bring him to the station, take him on a tour, show him good officers," he suggested.

"I'll even talk to him about ghosts."

4

TAKE SOME GIRLS

The Metro Narcotics Task Force was a mixture of officers from Stockton PD, the San Joaquin County Sheriff's Office, Probation, the FBI, and other agencies. Its job was to go after major narcotics traffickers. Everyday gang policing wasn't its thing, so the guys on CRT didn't spend a ton of time hanging out at the Metro offices, located in a nondescript, low-rise industrial building near downtown.

But CRT had a unique role in the department. Besides stopping gang members and helping with high-risk arrests, the team was the go-to unit for vehicle pursuits with suspects thought to be armed and dangerous. CRT officers, some of whom did double duty on SWAT, were recruited in part because of their tactical skill, expected to excel at suspect takedowns, entry into residences for probation or parole searches, and especially performance driving. Once on CRT, they quickly gained outsized pursuit experience; it was the rare week when they didn't get into a chase with someone they were trying to pull over. That's why, every few months, CRT made the trek over to the Metro facility, parking their battered SUVs on the street out front. If Metro was planning a bust that might result in a vehicle pursuit, CRT would get called in.

The Metro briefing room had a long table with a whiteboard at one end. Twenty or so mismatched chairs were positioned around the table, with more along the walls. By the door, unflattering photos had been taped up of drug dealers (and some cops) exposing their beer bellies, looking stunned by the camera, or being otherwise caught in an embarrassing moment. On the right side of the whiteboard was a sketch of a bearded man's face. That was Jenkins. When Metro officers met in the room, you'd hear someone yell, "You can erase everything but Jenkins. He's been here for like fifteen years!" People would chuckle, even those who had never heard of Jenkins.[1]

One decorative item in the room wasn't funny. At least, Drake Wiest didn't find it funny when he took a seat next to it in 2019 for a briefing on a controlled buy involving twenty pounds of crystal meth (thousands of hits), a drug courier from Southern California, and a Mexican cartel. That item was a life-sized plastic skeleton draped in fabric and holding a scythe. Santa Muerte, the folk saint of death, is an icon rejected by the Catholic Church but worshipped in Mexico and Central America, where it's best known for its association with the criminal underworld. Many Mexican jail cells are said to contain altars to the "Bony Lady."[2] But Santa Muerte has also amassed a large following among non-prisoners, who feel that they can pray to her for protection and assistance if they aren't righteous enough to win God's ear. If they've done things they don't feel good about. She's popular on this side of the border as well. Drake would often see a Santa Muerte statuette or votive candle in the homes of Latino gang members when he and the team conducted a probation search or went to make an arrest. Did he believe in Santa Muerte? Did he pray to her for protection? No. But while the skeleton may have been a joke to other cops in the room, or an oddity, to Drake she had come to command a certain level of respect.

Drake grew up in Vacaville, a small city that lies between Oakland and Sacramento along I-80. With its tracts of farmland and historic downtown, Vacaville evokes old-timey California and is a good place to raise kids; it's a rare Bay Area locale where you can be blue-collar and not feel poor.

After Drake's parents split when he was young, his mother remarried, to a guard for the California Department of Corrections and Rehabilitation. The department operates two prisons in town and is its largest employer.

In high school, at Vacaville Christian, Drake didn't know what he wanted to do for a career. When he was younger, he aspired to be a mechanic like his dad; that interest faded. In Drake's senior year, his stepfather encouraged him to consider the highway patrol: good salary, good benefits. He couldn't see himself writing tickets all day, and he didn't like the idea of stopping cars on the freeway, where one step in the wrong direction could turn you into roadkill. But the suggestion got him thinking about law enforcement.

Sometimes Drake's stepfather would regale him with stories about the gang members he encountered as a prison guard. Drake would hang on his every word. Gangland was its own world, with distinct social structures, morality, languages, symbols. Drake didn't want to join that world. He wasn't totally straight edge and never applied himself in school, but he was basically a law-abiding kid. Still, he imagined himself getting close enough to gangs to know them well, crack their inner workings and secrets, and counter the threat they posed.

City policing, that's what he'd do. After two years at community college, he enrolled in the police academy. Stockton PD was the first department to offer him a job when he finished. "Are you sure?" asked his then girlfriend, now wife, Shelby, the brains of the family, a lab tech at a pharmaceutical company who went on to earn an online master's degree from Johns Hopkins. She knew—everyone knew—how bad things were in Stockton.

Drake's career got off to a fast start. Too fast, he felt, looking back. He spent much of the late spring and summer of 2014 in field training. Then on a July afternoon, twenty-two-year-old Drake was waiting for his shift to start when his field training officer—who happened to be Jason Underwood, Drake's supervisor five years later—told him to hurry up and get their car ready. Shit was going *down*.

Gilbert Renteria belonged to a particularly callous set of Norteños. He had a rap sheet with arrests for dealing drugs, guns, and sex trafficking his girlfriend. Alex Martinez had been arrested for selling meth to an undercover officer and had caught several gun cases of his own. On that July day, Renteria and Martinez teamed up with Jaime Ramos and Pablo Ruvalcaba to rob a Bank of the West branch on Thornton Road.[3] Renteria and Martinez had robbed the same bank at the end of January.

Around 2:10 p.m., Ruvalcaba dropped off the other three. Renteria, Martinez, and Ramos stormed the bank. They were wearing hoodies, sunglasses, fake beards, and gloves that were taped to their sleeves to make sure they left no trace of DNA. All three had handguns; Martinez was also carrying a semiautomatic AK-47-style rifle. Shouting "Don't be a hero!" and "Don't push the button!" they forced everyone except an old woman to lie on the floor. They restrained a security guard and several male customers using zip ties, and ordered the branch manager, Kelly Huber, to go into the back and unlock the vault. Huber did as she was told. She'd been there for the robbery in January; she knew the drill. While Renteria and Ramos stood guard, Martinez went with her. He scooped cash and put it in his backpack, angry because there was less than he expected.

Back in the lobby, the trio yelled, "Who has a car, we need a car!" Huber offered hers. It seemed like the responsible thing to do, trading her blue Ford Explorer for the safety of her staff and customers.

But instead of taking her keys, the men grabbed Huber, held a gun to her, and forced her outside. That's where they encountered the police. Monitoring the bank's cameras remotely, Bank of the West corporate security detected the robbery in progress and called in the cops. One witness who saw Renteria, Martinez, and Ramos enter the bank told an officer who was getting lunch. Stockton cops rushed to the scene, barely concealing their presence. That was a mistake. When the three robbers stepped out with Huber, they saw the officers, one of whom yelled for them to drop their weapons, and they promptly went back inside the bank.

Renteria, who seemed to be in charge, asked Huber if there was another exit. She said there wasn't. That's when he growled, "Grab them! Take some girls!" The men turned their guns on Stephanie Koussaya, a bank teller, and Misty Holt-Singh, a customer who'd stopped by the ATM on the way to get her hair done, leaving her twelve-year-old daughter in the car. Renteria, Martinez, and Ramos exited the bank again, this time with three hostages.

The same Stockton officer who'd ordered them to drop their weapons was now wielding a handgun and a rifle. He knew that if he opened fire, the hostages could be killed. The gang members certainly knew it. Renteria and his pals moved toward Huber's SUV, using the women—who were screaming for help—as shields. They forced them in and told Huber to start driving.

Inside the Ford Explorer, pandemonium. Huber drove, though she had no idea where she was supposed to be going. Renteria was next to her. Ramos was in the back seat with the other hostages. Martinez squeezed into the luggage compartment. As the SUV peeled out of the parking lot, Stockton police units were right on its tail. Two minutes later, bang! Huber saw blood pouring from her leg.

"Oh shit, I'm sorry!" said Ramos. He'd let a round go by accident. The pain was so intense Huber could no longer drive. Renteria pushed her out of the car and took the wheel.

As the police began to close in, the SUV's back window was shattered by bullets. It was Martinez shooting his AK-47 at the cops. The gun started chewing up police vehicles, even as officers swerved to avoid getting hit. Windshields were shot, tires blown. As cop cars were put out of commission, their place in the chase was taken by units behind them.

Renteria was driving like a Hollywood stuntman, headed toward Lodi at speeds approaching 120 miles an hour. At one point he veered off the freeway, racing recklessly down a side street. The police lost sight of the Explorer for a second, but then other officers spotted it, and the pursuit resumed, Renteria backtracking into the city.

The Stockton PD SWAT vehicle soon caught up with the chase. The vehicle, a dark gray BearCat made by the Lenco company, was a 17,000-pound modified Ford truck with armor plating and one-inch-thick bulletproof glass. It was expensive, but the Stockton SWAT team served so many risky warrants that the agency felt they couldn't do without it.

The officer driving the BearCat tried to ram the Explorer. But Martinez shot out one of the vehicle's tires, its Achilles' heel. (The BearCat had a "run flat" system, so it wasn't put completely out of commission.)

The chase continued like that for more than an hour, with the Explorer getting off and on the freeway, Martinez shooting round after round, and the cops mostly holding their fire for fear of killing a hostage.

After looping through the Stockton area several times, the Explorer made its way toward Thornton Road, not far from the bank. In the car, Stephanie Koussaya sensed that things were coming to an end. If she didn't get out now, she'd die in the cross fire. At the next opportunity, she hit the lock, flung open the door, and jumped. Misty Holt-Singh was the only hostage left.

Drake and Jason Underwood had followed the Explorer across the city. When the SUV took a U-turn, they moved up closer to the front of the line of pursuing vehicles. Drake got a clear view of Renteria with his hoodie and sunglasses, Martinez with his rifle. He and Jason were maybe ten cars behind. It was unreal. Drake called Shelby from the car. "I just want to call and tell you I love you," he said. "I'm in a shooting, and I'll call you as soon as I can." He hung up while she had a full-blown panic attack.

Then they saw Stephanie Koussaya bail out. Early in the pursuit, Drake had heard on the radio that there were three hostages, two adult females and a young girl, a mistaken reference to Misty Holt-Singh's daughter. Later, someone said the girl had been found safe. The officers knew that the first hostage had been tossed from the SUV, so when they saw Koussaya jump, they thought she was the last one. Only bad guys were left now, they believed. In Drake's mind, the time had come to end this before anyone else got hurt.

On Thornton Road, two cops took cover behind an electrical box. As the SUV raced by, they shot and punctured its tires. It came to a stop by the Stockton Ballroom, an event space across a wide street from some homes. Several police cars were hastily arranged about fifty feet behind the Explorer. More cars were put in positions around these. The gunman got off a few last shots. That's when the fusillade began. Thirty-two officers fired more than six hundred rounds, with some cops shooting not because they could see a specific target but because the officers next to them were firing. Drake emptied his magazine as did Jason and the cops around him. When the smoke cleared, Renteria and Martinez were dead. Ramos survived, apparently by positioning himself behind Misty Holt-Singh, who also died, killed by Stockton PD bullets.

The Bank of the West heist and chase was an incident so out of control, so unpredictable, and so poorly handled by the department—from the initial response to the failure to deploy basic equipment (like spike strips in the road, which might have stopped the Explorer) to the communications failure about the number of hostages and lack of planning for the endgame—that it remains an object lesson for cops in California in how not to respond to a bank robbery. Investigations, lawsuits, recriminations followed. Eric Jones, though proud of his officers' bravery under fire, faced searing questions from the community, and from his conscience. Had he placed enough emphasis on tactical training? On buying the right equipment? On managing the challenges of running an agency down one hundred senior officers and full of rookies? On countering the take-no-prisoners mentality his officers had displayed? The heist would prove to be a turning point for Stockton PD. Eric had set his sights on reform, and now it was imperative. No one could deny that.

It would take years for the lawsuits to conclude. Misty Holt-Singh's family settled its wrongful death suit against the city for $5.75 million (as part of the settlement, a Stockton softball complex was named after her), while Kelly Huber and Stephanie Koussaya failed in their efforts to hold the city liable for their injuries.

Ramos, the surviving robber, was sentenced to life in prison without the possibility of parole. Ruvalcaba, who'd driven the other three to the bank, got twenty-five to life.

As for Drake, he took solace in the fact that the cops had prevented anyone else from being shot—no drivers, no police officers, no bystanders, including the hundreds of people who'd flocked from their houses to watch the pursuit, alerted by live news coverage. They'd cheered as the Explorer drove past, although Drake didn't know whether they'd been cheering for the cops or the robbers. Maybe they'd been moved by the spirit of the Bony Lady. From that July day forward, death and the power to wield it would never be far from Drake's mind, his easygoing policing a liturgy to keep her at bay.

5

ENEMY NUMBER ONE

Wilson Way, an eastside Stockton commercial strip, was a hot spot for prostitution. So when Officer Jesse Smith spotted a young woman with white spandex pants and heels strolling down North Wilson, waving at passing cars, he had a pretty good idea what she was up to.

It was 4:30 p.m., nearing the end of what had been an unusually slow day shift. Jesse attributed the quiet radio to a murder that had happened the night before. If people on the street knew who was responsible, they'd be lying low.

The lack of calls meant that Jesse, assigned to a unit that dealt with nuisance behavior, was free to do some proactive policing. And if you asked those who lived in the houses off Wilson, on streets like North Sierra Nevada, what low-level crime bothered them the most, they'd say prostitution. While sex workers did much of their business out of cheap motels, sometimes johns preferred to stay in their cars, parking on side streets in plain view. When time permitted, Stockton PD went after prostitution—not only because the community demanded it but also because many of the women were being trafficked, held against their will or manipulated by pimps, some of them with gang connections.

Jesse drove slowly past the woman in spandex and made the block.

He was looking for her associates. When he came around again, he saw her walking out of Superior Thrift Store, holding a piece of paper and waving it like a pennant. It was weird, but weird doesn't justify a stop.

He pulled into the lot of a nearby McDonald's. A few minutes later, the woman—who looked to be in her early twenties, Black and Latino, Jesse thought, with bright eyes and freckles—marched up to the police car and signaled for Jesse to get out.

"Excuse me, officer, can I talk to you?"

He obliged. Black, with medium-length hair that sat high atop his forehead, Jesse was a former professional football player, in the arena league, and looked the muscle-bound part.

"Why were you watching me?" the woman asked. "I was getting a job application from my aunt in the thrift store." She presented the piece of paper for his inspection.

"Look," Jesse said, "when I see a young woman walking up and down Wilson Way, and you didn't see me, but you were waving, trying to get someone's attention, I automatically assumed one thing, and we both know what that is."

"I was waving at my cousin," said the woman, without missing a beat. "Did you see him stopping in a Hyundai?"

Jesse took in the scene. Traffic on Wilson was becoming brisk. Across the street, another woman, this one white and goth and probably homeless, was yelling incoherently.

"He saw me waving," the first woman continued. "Because I'm trying to get into the Whistle Stop"—a bar—"but I don't have my ID, and they told me that I can't go in there without my ID. And I told him that."

Jesse peered at her, trying to break through the flow of information. "But you understand what I'm saying, right?"

"Yeah, of course."

JESSE, THIRTY-SIX, WAS STOCKTON BORN and raised and no stranger to hardship. His mother had been in the clutches of a crack addiction for much of his childhood, his older brother a member of a Stockton set of the Hoover Crips. When he was fourteen, his home life became so bad that his churchgoing grandparents took him and his younger brother in full-time. His grandmother was there for him as he honed his athletic talents—football and track—at Bear Creek High.

Down at Fresno State, Jesse set a team record for the Bulldogs in the 100-meter dash. For a time after he graduated, it seemed as if arena football could be a stepping stone to the NFL. But then it wasn't. So Jesse allowed a new dream to jell: law enforcement. He'd ensure public safety while being the type of officer he wished had patrolled his neighborhood when he was a kid, an officer who would be fair and only use force judiciously, unlike the Stockton cops who'd harass his older brother and friends.

Jesse vowed to be a cop who'd care about the community, who might run into a young person living an unspeakably difficult life and offer a hand up. Jesse believed this drive came from God, who had a plan for him: he had suffered so that he could help others suffer less.

After quitting arena football, Jesse put himself through the police academy at Fresno City College. Through the six months of coursework, he kept hoping that some NFL team, maybe the Cleveland Browns, would belatedly recognize his talents. He signed on to Stockton PD in 2013, one year after Eric Jones took the helm.

Given Stockton's budget crunch, only a few officers were hired that year. But Jesse was everything Eric wanted in a recruit. There weren't many Black officers on the Stockton force, and Eric was learning through his PJ work how crucial it was that the department look more like the city it served. More important than Jesse's skin color, however, were the skills he brought. He knew the city's geography inside out. He knew the quickest way to drive from Ray's, a market and restaurant where he'd go for lunch, eating red snapper while *Predator 2* played on the TV, to the Spanos Park neighborhood in the north, where he'd attended high school. He was as familiar with Stockton's cultural geography: its racial and ethnic fault lines, how to get along with people from diverse groups. He was college-educated and could write a mean police report.

And as an athlete, Jesse could run after suspects. He knew how to tackle and was physically intimidating. Other cops would rib him about his size: "Hey, Jesse, stop shortening your shirtsleeves, you're making the rest of us look bad." To which Jesse lobbed back: "Nah, I grow my muscles the old-fashioned way." More than anything, Jesse had integrity; that was clear as day.

Jesse told the woman on Wilson Way what he was going to do. "I'll get your name," he said. "I'll let it be known that I spoke to you." He'd pass her information on to one of the vice detectives, who might connect the woman to a social service agency.

"Your aunt, too," Jesse said. "I'll let her know, if she has any questions about why you've been followed by the police." Jesse knew there was no aunt working in the store, a fact he confirmed afterward by going in there and talking to the employees. But he saw no benefit to calling the woman out.

"My thing is," he said, "I don't like to pass judgment. I have to do my duty. As long as everything checks out, you're free to walk up and down the street all day. But as a police officer, you start to put two and two together. You happen to see people waving at people, I have to check it out to make sure."

"Be safe walking around," he added. "If you're not doing nothing, that's fine. Even if you are, still be safe. There's nothing out here that's worth you getting hurt."

• • •

When Jesse first heard he'd be going through procedural justice training, he wasn't sure what to expect. He knew that the lack of trust between Stockton PD and the community was real. He had felt it acutely growing up, and as a cop, he saw it every day. He was well versed in Stockton's gangs—through his brother—so Jesse was assigned to the Community Response Team after field training, before rotating off to his current assignment. (Mostly because of burnout, CRT rotations generally lasted only a few years.) The team would arrest a gang member for a weapons charge or a parole violation. They'd tell the man about Ceasefire. Almost without exception, the guy wouldn't buy it, suspicious of a scam or a ruse. Jesse found that the only way to get past this distrust was to talk about where he came from and what he'd been through. When he did that, he'd add, "Look, I'm willing to go the whole length with you to make this work out." Then magic could happen; Jesse believed he'd persuaded more than one person to step away from violence.

When procedural justice training started, a year into his time on the force, Jesse quickly realized it was all about building trust. The instructors were making good points. They touched on fairness, race, using force only when necessary. Act right and trust will follow, was the message. Yes, thought Jesse. This is what policing should be. Procedurally just policing was what he'd been trying to do on CRT. It was what had been lacking in Stockton when he was younger. Now he had a name for it, a policing philosophy he could adopt for himself.

Procedural justice spoke to Jesse. The officers sitting to his left and right? Not so much. Jesse's classmates seemed checked out. They were scrolling on their phones, blank expressions on their faces. White, Latino, Asian—it didn't matter. Jesse had already reached the conclusion that many Stockton officers had a narrow perspective. They considered themselves good and viewed most of the people they dealt with on the job as dirtbags. There was no middle ground and therefore no need to build trust. For these officers, procedural justice training was just some administrative bullshit they had to endure. Jesse hoped that would change.

The officers' response is hardly unprecedented. Studies of police reform offer many examples of well-meaning efforts to modify the culture of policing that foundered on the shoals of cops thinking they were bullshit.

Two police departments, Schenectady and Syracuse, New York, turned to PJ not long before Stockton did. They didn't invest in the philosophy or promote it as much as Eric Jones did, but both departments had reform-minded chiefs who believed that citizen satisfaction was an important metric of success. Residents of Schenectady and Syracuse had thought favorably of their police forces before the cities embarked on reform. Yet trust in the police was higher among white than Black residents, while a series of scandals, particularly in Schenectady—

excessive force cases, officers arrested for DUI or domestic violence, public feuds between the departments and other city agencies—cast the cops in a bad light.

Political scientist Robert Worden and criminal justice scholar Sarah McLean studied what happened after these two departments embraced a "customer service" model of policing, based in procedural justice ideals.[1] Beginning in 2011, they tracked the implementation of the model and discovered that talk about a customer service approach by the chiefs (though sincere) was, in the end, only that—talk. The cops didn't change how they policed, and citizens didn't notice any difference.

To explain these findings, Worden and McLean invoked an idea developed in the 1990s by two other criminal justice scholars, John Crank and Robert Langworthy: the institutional environment of policing.[2] For an organization in any field to be successful, it has to do two things: perform its tasks well, and get along with other organizations (government bureaucracies that regulate it, suppliers, even competitors). Those other organizations make up the institutional environment.

The problem is that sometimes it's impossible to satisfy expectations from the institutional environment *and* perform a task well. For example, a hospital might be expected by insurance companies to keep costs down, though this would mean that doctors are discouraged from ordering expensive tests they believe are essential.

So organizations resort (often inadvertently) to "loose coupling." Internally, they continue to do whatever they think is required, while the parts of the organization that face outward make window-dressing changes consistent with the expectations of others.

Crank and Langworthy gave examples from the world of law enforcement. Periodically, police departments face crises—instances of brutality or corruption. The chief dutifully takes his or her licks, promising to implement reform. Often, chiefs glom on to fixes that are politically popular, without evidence that they will be effective. The important thing is that they're in line with community expectations. To satisfy those expectations, chiefs usually put on a big show when rolling out reforms, hoping that the media will cover how the cops are turning things around.

It might seem that the department has made a major change. But if sergeants and lieutenants with immediate control over frontline officers think the reform will interfere with their mission, they'll either ignore it or discourage cops from following through, hoping that no one will be the wiser. This is loose coupling.

That's what Worden and McLean believed happened in Schenectady and Syracuse. The chiefs had gotten behind procedural justice at least in part to satisfy outside groups. But many of the supervisors and officers viewed their job in light of traditional police culture and considered procedural justice "incompatible with police work."[3] Cops, they held, are supposed to be menacing toward lawbreakers and not so concerned with the appearance of bias that they fail to make stops when their instincts are telling them something's amiss. The officers ignored the new approach while their supervisors let them. This wasn't hard for them to do: the chiefs had no tools to assess whether individual officers were treating citizens in a procedurally just manner—no performance measures—so there was no accountability.

Worden and McLean concluded their study with a warning: "In an agency that publicly espouses" procedural justice, "there might well be wide divergence between public pronouncements" and "day-to-day performance on the street." These pronouncements "might add to the department's legitimacy," but standard practices "would continue unaffected."[4] They called their book *Mirage of Police Reform*.

Judging by the lack of interest displayed by Jesse's colleagues, that seemed the likely fate of procedural justice in Stockton, too. But that's not quite how things turned out.

• • •

STICKING WITH THE STATUS QUO in Mudville wasn't an option. After the Bank of the West debacle in 2014, the climax of a horrible period for the city, Eric and his staff began doing the work to turn his emerging vision for a better department into reality. Each subsequent year—straight through to 2019—saw improvement. As recovery from the financial crisis gained momentum, the city's budget became less constricted. Eric could now hire a steady stream of recruits fresh from the police academy, and Stockton PD wasn't shy about letting them know how much they were needed. At their first roll call, a sergeant might ask them to publicly pledge not to leave the agency for a better-paid position in the Bay Area. Some officers would go anyway after a year or two, having gained more experience in Stockton than they would in a decade anywhere else, increasing their appeal to South Bay departments—Silicon Valley—that paid ridiculously well. But others stayed, finding Stockton a good fit, a challenge, an adventure.

Over time, Eric replaced most of the one hundred officers lost to budget cuts, getting the agency close to full staffing. So when Stockton residents called the cops, they'd show up without too much of a delay, which matters for citizen satisfaction and—as some studies have found—for solving crimes.[5] Stockton's homicide rate remained level while it ticked up in other cities like Baltimore, Chicago, Houston, and Milwaukee.

The department could buy equipment again, although Stockton's still lean budget meant that expensive items needed alternative funding. City funds helped to upgrade the force's Tasers, purchase less-lethal beanbag shotguns, acquire ballistic shields, and get more of those spike strips that would have been useful in the Bank of the West chase. To launch Stockton's body-worn camera program, purchase aerial drones, or buy new rifles, the department had to set up a nonprofit—the Support Stockton Police Foundation—to accept private donations. Many police departments supplement their budgets with assistance from foundations of this sort. Critics point out that rich people, local businesses, and corporations with a stake in the city are the biggest contributors, and they question whether that gives them undue influence with law enforcement.[6] Chiefs respond that good policing is expensive. If municipal budgets are inadequate, what other choice is there?

Hiring and equipment were essential, but no less important was that during this time, Eric worked out a strategy for more thoroughly integrating procedural justice into the department. Effective police leaders need an instinctive feel for dynamics in their agency. Eric knew that if he simply went through the motions with procedural justice, it would fail. Stockton had an entrenched traditional culture of policing, and although standout cops like Jesse took to PJ right away, others were reluctant. Yet Eric also sensed that if he introduced PJ and then turned the screws, monitoring his officers' every move and disciplining them whenever they did something at odds with the philosophy, he'd wind up with a bunch of disgruntled cops who'd grouse that they'd lost their autonomy. They'd leave the department or start dragging their feet at work, which could affect public safety.

Faced with this dilemma, and a redoubled commitment to transforming Stockton PD after Misty Holt-Singh's death, he chose to take a slow, incremental approach, resolving to stay one step ahead of his officers, not three steps. Combating cynicism and putting in place modest measures of procedural justice performance were the cornerstones of his strategy.

• • •

One way of thinking about procedural justice is that it's an antidote to what criminologists call legal cynicism. A conventional explanation for the prevalence of crime and violence in some communities is that the culture of those places tolerates bad behavior. But in 1998, sociologists Robert Sampson and Dawn Bartusch discovered that this explanation wasn't true.[7] Looking at data from a survey of nearly nine thousand Chicago residents, Sampson and Bartusch found that people who lived in high-crime areas were every bit as angry and upset about crime as anyone else. What differed was that those residents had grown cynical about the criminal justice system and its ability to provide safety and security. That cynicism contributed to a withdrawal from collective neighborhood life, which in turn allowed crime to flourish. While providing legitimacy, PJ might also make residents less cynical about the police.[8]

Yet there's another form of cynicism that's equally pernicious: cynicism among agents of the justice system. The wellspring for studies of police cynicism is a 1967 book by sociologist Arthur Niederhoffer.[9]

Niederhoffer, a former cop, noted how common cynicism was on the force, came up with a way to measure it, and traced the evolution of cynical attitudes over officers' careers.

The best update of his work comes from sociologist Peter Moskos. As a graduate student at Harvard, Moskos set out to conduct an in-depth study of urban policing. He came to realize that the only way to get the access he wanted was by joining a force and viewing things from the inside. He got hired by the Baltimore police department, went through the academy, then spent a little over a year as an officer before quitting to write his PhD dissertation and first book, *Cop in the Hood: My Year Policing Baltimore's Eastern District*.[10]

Moskos described the shift in worldview that many cops undergo early in their careers. Most of the men and women who joined Baltimore PD were idealistic: they wanted to help people, make the community safer, be guardians and heroes. After a short time stationed in high-crime districts, however, that idealism faded, replaced by a sense that nothing the police did mattered; that liberal judges let criminals go with a slap on the wrist, so there was no point in officers putting themselves in danger; and that the police department was a bloated bureaucracy run by political hacks. As one officer told Moskos, "Sure, you start off wanting to do good, help. . . . But then you see how things are. All the junkies. Everybody lies. Victims won't tell you anything because they're criminals themselves. Then you start to ask, 'Why am I here?'"[11] Cops who developed this attitude became prone to laziness, corruption, and violence.

If a department is trying to shift officer conduct toward the practice of procedural justice, officer cynicism will be enemy number one. Cops won't buy into some new philosophy based on respect if they think that nothing that they do matters, the people they police don't deserve respect, and the department they work for is a sham. In Stockton, cynicism would be the most likely source of resistance to PJ and any loose coupling attached to it. Cynical officers would be the first to declare PJ bullshit.

Officer cynicism had been on Eric's mind since his first promotion, to sergeant, in 1999. The root of the problem, as he saw it now, was that

Stockton officers—like their peers around the country—had grown used to thinking of themselves as call responders, nothing more. A 911 call would come in, they'd do whatever they had to, and then leave and move on to the next call. The same pattern would repeat shift after shift, month after month, year after year. (Stockton was such a busy agency that officers frequently spent their entire shifts responding to calls.) The cops might do important work on those assignments, but it was never enough to effect change in a neighborhood. Being reactive meant that the police were Band-Aids on a wound that would never stop bleeding.

So PJ trainers in Stockton designed a strategy to combat cynicism, which in their opinion peaked after about five years on the job. The crucial part was figuring out when cynicism had first taken root and why. Was it because of specific encounters? Or because many of the officers didn't live in Stockton and came across only the city's most lawless residents? Had they worked with cranky cops and learned that the best way to fit in was to strike the same jaded stance? Or had they had a negative experience with the department itself—with a sergeant, say—that had marred their outlook?

Trainers asked officers to reflect on these questions. Then they were asked to recall why they became cops in the first place. The trainers would remind them that most of the reasons people go into law enforcement are good and noble and that they shouldn't lose sight of them when dealing with the reality of enduring social problems.

Hardened cynics weren't won over by this. If the exercise was effective for officers on the verge of bitterness, it's because it resonated with other efforts in the department to help cops hold on to some of their youthful idealism. The pep talks Eric gave his officers served this purpose, as did informal meetings his staff organized between cops and citizens at gyms, coffee shops, and community centers. While the police sometimes faced criticism in these meetings, they also heard from people who valued them and their contribution to the city. That kind of thanks goes a long way. Police cynicism is a knotted thread. Pick at it from different angles, and maybe a cop would become receptive to suggestions for change.

Eric's attempts to combat cynicism internally benefited from the friendly relationship he forged with the union. In Minneapolis, another city where the police attempted procedural justice reform, the union head, an outspoken Trump supporter named Bob Kroll, was derisive. "Ask them, love them," he said of the public, "give them their space and give them their voice. This is what they're training new officers." He went on, "Our cops went through that and they're going, 'Oh my God.' Yeah, procedural justice. And the theory behind it being that . . . white men have oppressed everyone else for 200 years."[12] Kroll had his critics among the rank and file, but the union's dismissive attitude probably made Minneapolis cops more resistant to procedural justice, accounting in part for the failure of the philosophy to take hold in that department.[13]

Things with the union were different in Stockton. Historically, the association was very conservative. With all the post-bankruptcy turnover in the ranks, however, a somewhat younger, more open-minded guard of union leaders rose to power. They saw value in procedural justice. Sergeant Chuck Harris, a burly white cop who was elected union president in 2016 after a decade and a half on the force, enjoyed working for an agency that was committed to continuous improvement. Harris had participated in some of the trust-building workshops Eric organized and went through mandatory procedural justice training like every other Stockton officer. He found both experiences "eye-opening." He'd been moved by his conversations with community members, who described the indignity of being stopped by the police for what they perceived to be no reason. And it was important, he thought, for officers to be reminded of the bleak history of police-community relations in Stockton and the nation—of the origins of the city's mistrust, and the repair work that respectful policing could accomplish.

It helped that Harris appreciated Eric and that the two had developed a reservoir of goodwill. They disagreed on occasion, yet Harris thought Eric was a smart and capable leader. He'd been around Stockton PD forever and had proved his mettle. He'd respond right away when Harris texted him about needs that weren't being met. And he was fair-minded about officer discipline. If you were a cop trying to do your job well, Harris thought, Eric would have your back. Eric was a true believer in procedural justice, and since Harris had confidence in him, he became a believer in procedural justice, too.

It's relevant that Eric came to PJ because of the problems he'd encountered with Operation Ceasefire. Once he learned about the philosophy, he was all in, but he'd discovered it while trying to bring down gun violence, a traditional law enforcement goal if there ever was one. If, by contrast, the department had embraced PJ because activist groups or politicians were demanding it, or to go along with the latest fad in police administration, the effort would have been tainted—at least in the eyes of the union. As it was, union leaders were encouraged to see procedural justice as a pressing attempt to solve an authentic police problem, which justified its necessity and led them to give it the benefit of the doubt.

• • •

To avoid loose coupling, it was also critical to establish employee performance measures. Eric and his team took a multipronged approach: They built procedural justice into officer evaluations by making clear that fair, courteous treatment of citizens was the department's expectation. Field training officers evaluating rookies were supposed to consider how well they delivered procedural justice in interactions with citizens. Sergeants kept a lookout for experienced officers whose policing seemed disrespectful or biased. Those cops would be brought in for more training. Any officer seeking promotion needed a solid understanding of procedural justice to score well on exams or interviews.

The department also monitored adherence by investigating citizen complaints. With a formal complaint in hand, or on the basis of a tip received at a community meeting, or in any major use of force incident, the department would pull bodycam footage.

Stockton PD could have designed much more stringent performance measures, like random spot checks of bodycam footage not connected to complaints, perhaps aided by artificial intelligence algorithms designed to detect procedurally unjust policing.[14] In the short term, such measures might have ensured greater compliance with PJ principles. But Eric worried that they would have come at a heavy cost and would have been in tension with his strategy of not leaping three steps ahead of his officers.

Sociologist Sarah Brayne studied the fallout from the LAPD's introduction of big data technologies to help cops predict where and when crimes were likely to occur and to assist with investigations.[15] The officers had mixed feelings about the tech, but one thing many of them agreed on—cops not being immune to double standards—was that while big data might be OK for monitoring civilians, it shouldn't be used to monitor police. Workers want some independence and privacy on the job. Several LAPD officers explained to Brayne that a nice thing about police work is that you don't have your boss in your face every second, watching you and telling you what to do. Fully trained officers are supposed to be trusted by their departments to figure out most situations on their own.

In Stockton, Eric worried that random checks of bodycam footage and other monitoring technologies would suggest that the department didn't trust its officers. That would have sapped their morale, undercut their confidence in Eric's leadership, and sunk union support for reform. In time, Eric feared, he would have wound up with bigger problems on his hands than inconsistent adherence to procedural justice; he could have faced a department in revolt in a city whose policing needs were especially pressing.

Eric struck a bargain: he and his team would make a case for procedural justice at every opportunity, hoping to pull officers in and secure some gains for police culture. Officers would always be required to follow department policy, but they wouldn't be forced, on pain of unpaid days off or termination, to conduct themselves at every moment as PJ trainers would have them do. They'd be strongly encouraged, but not compelled, to fit within the department's new ideological mold.

• • •

Just because the union got behind procedural justice, and trainers had strategies to combat cynicism, and the cops were held to performance measures—none of these things ensured that every officer would take PJ principles seriously. And many didn't. A Stockton cop might finish a PJ class, give it a nice evaluation, and go right back to policing the same way he had before, yelling obscenities at some young man he'd stopped or humiliating a kid before hauling him off to juvie. Despite PJ training, he might offer to let someone go after a traffic stop if the guy would agree to bite a raw fish he had in the car only to withdraw the offer at the last second after the psychological damage had been done (not a hypothetical allegation, unfortunately). Those cops, in the privacy of patrol cars on the midnight shift or in the parking lot of a gas station on Country Club Boulevard or standing around shooting the breeze, would make merciless fun of PJ. By no means was it out of bounds for Drake and the jokesters on CRT, though the truth (which Drake knew full well) was that the principles of PJ had informed his policing style.

While more serious transgressions weren't tolerated, the department didn't worry too much about the bad-mouthing. Cops grumble and complain and wisecrack about everything—a coping mechanism for dealing with trauma and stress. If officers were making fun of PJ, then they knew what it was and knew that the department wanted them to live up to it.

Eric's soft-sell approach caught the attention of those in the police reform world. In 2015, then California attorney general Kamala Harris decided to make PJ training available to officers throughout the state. The California DOJ joined forces with Stockton PD, Oakland PD, Stuart Wakeling's nonprofit, and Jennifer Eberhardt, a psychologist who studies implicit racial bias, to design a one-day PJ course that California cops could put in for and attend. In 2016, the program was expanded to include a "train the trainers" course; departments sent senior officers to learn how to hold PJ trainings in their own agencies. Stockton's experiments were held up as a model.

National attention followed. That same year, Stockton PD was profiled by journalist Tina Rosenberg for a "Fixes" column in the *New York Times*.[16] There, in the country's newspaper of record, was a photo of Eric standing on a Stockton sidewalk in uniform. "Although it was not reflected in the Republican convention that nominated Donald J. Trump for president last week," Rosenberg wrote, "Americans have been experiencing a rare moment of bipartisan convergence on the toxicity of maximum-force policing. Procedural justice has become one of the most important strategies for changing direction—perhaps *the* most important." And when it came to procedural justice, Rosenberg said, Stockton was a leader.

Eric was invited to speak at conferences. He became an executive fellow at the National Policing Institute, a nonprofit whose goal is to improve policing through research. He was asked to apply for chief positions at other large agencies.

Eric took the acclaim in stride. He remained focused. He believed that keeping crime in check and building bridges to the community were his calling. When he wasn't at his desk answering emails or writing memos or reports, he was meeting with his team or community groups or deep in discussions with the city manager. He gladly accepted the accolades he received as a tribute to the good work of the department.

Soon after, the perception of positive developments in Stockton received striking confirmation. In 2017, the Urban Institute once again surveyed residents of some of the poorest neighborhoods in America. As they'd done in 2015, researchers asked questions designed to gauge people's impressions of the legitimacy of the police and the criminal justice system. They found that in Stockton, police legitimacy increased between 2015 and 2017 while it declined in other cities after the unrest in Ferguson. In 2015, only 25 percent of participants thought Stockton police usually or almost always treated people with dignity and respect. Two years later, that number had risen to 46 percent. Likewise, the percentage of disadvantaged Stockton residents who said they trusted the police almost doubled, to 41 percent. When participants were asked in 2017 how much they agreed or disagreed with statements like "The police department holds officers accountable for wrong or inappropriate conduct," or "The police department is responsive to community concerns," or "The police department prioritizes problems most important to your community," they gave Stockton PD higher marks than in the 2015 study, with levels of agreement rising 10 percentage points on average, such that about a third of residents held favorable views of the agency.[17] These numbers left considerable room for improvement, but they represented an unequivocal shift over a short period of time.

Michael Fitzgerald, the retired newspaper columnist, saw Eric as someone who had tried to chart a completely different course for Stockton PD. According to Fitzgerald, Eric knew that the two most important things he could do would be to reduce gun violence and promote reconciliation between the community and a police department that had too often mistreated it. "Only a real leader can tell police in so many words that they're racist and they have to change," Fitzgerald observed. Trust-building workshops, community meetings, procedural justice training, hiring a new generation of officers—they had all moved the needle. "Change is happening in this town," he said.

6

EBK

When Detective Irshad Mohammed arrived at the Holiday Plaza strip mall on East March Lane late in the afternoon of May 1, 2019, he realized he had his work cut out. Home to Nu Smile Dental, Salon Lety, Thrifty Wash, Qiang's (a Chinese bakery), a Domino's, a liquor store, and a tire and smog place, Holiday Plaza was known to Stockton police as a hangout for the Northside Gangster Crips—NSGC—one of the city's largest Black gangs.

NSGC had been around since the 1980s. A 1988 article in the *New York Times* explained how the Los Angeles–based Crips had been expanding their territory northward, to Stockton and other cities, as they sought new markets for crack.[1] By 2019, nearly all the guys who'd been active in the original incarnation of NSGC had aged out, or were lifers locked up in prison, or were dead. But a younger crew kept the gang alive as it splintered into subsets with names like Bianchi 500 (after a road that runs parallel to March Lane) or the Tribe. Sometimes NSGC subsets feuded with one another. Other times they got along fine. The feuding seemed to have subsided in recent years, which might explain why NSGC had fallen to seventh or eighth place in Stockton PD's continuously updated ranking of gangs by the frequency of their involvement in shootings.

Irshad was a homicide detective, not a gang cop, but he knew enough about NSGC to take special note of what the officers at the Holiday Plaza, including Drake and his CRT colleagues, told him: that Ronald Celestine, a thirty-four-year-old OG with an "NS"—Northside—tattooed on his shin, had been shot in the head near the Smog Station. Gasping for air when the first police units arrived, Celestine was whisked away by ambulance but died. Who would want to kill an older guy from a group that was no longer at the forefront of Stockton's gang wars? Save for one Spanish-speaking witness who gave a vague description of the shooters and their car, almost no one the police contacted in the area admitted to having seen anything.

IN HER 2015 BOOK *GHETTOSIDE*, journalist Jill Leovy drew attention to a neglected aspect of racial injustice: police do a worse job solving murders when the victim is Black than when the victim is white.[2] According to a *Washington Post* analysis of homicides committed nationally in the last decade, the police made an arrest in 63 percent of cases involving white victims, but in only 46 percent of cases where the victims were Black—a difference that takes on much greater significance when you consider that Black Americans comprise just under half of all homicide deaths.[3]

Leovy cited research showing that the reduced likelihood of arrest in Black murder cases contributes to the high rates of homicide seen in segregated, low-income Black neighborhoods. In such neighborhoods, a few deeply troubled souls—their perspective shaped by what the criminologist Elliott Currie calls "a particularly toxic array of adverse circumstances" stemming from racial and economic marginalization—come to believe their chances of getting caught are so low that they might as well handle conflicts with deadly violence before someone else does the same to them.[4]

Ghettoside followed intrepid LAPD homicide detectives determined to bring every murderer in the city to justice. But their determination faced limits. Witnesses or tipsters were often reluctant to come forward because they didn't trust the police or didn't think the cops could protect them from the criminals they were snitching on.

Procedural justice promises to help police departments overcome these limits, lubricating the flow of information between the police and groups that distrust law enforcement. Was it fulfilling this promise in Stockton?

• • •

Two weeks before the Ronald Celestine shooting, CRT members assembled in the SEB for a midmorning briefing. Jason Underwood ran through the day's announcements. In the afternoon, the team would break from their work to watch Drake throw out the first pitch at a University of the Pacific Tigers baseball game, an honor he received for being Officer of the Year.

"You do know how to throw a baseball, don't you?" joked Dan Velarde.

"Yeah, I can throw!" Drake replied. "Duh."

Jason mentioned that a movie theater in town would be giving away free tickets to first responders for a special showing of *Avengers: Endgame*. Officer Anthony Perry was excited: his kids were Marvel fans. Perry, as everyone called him, was new to CRT but not to the department. Older than most of the other officers, he'd received commendations. The year before, he'd improvised a tourniquet out of an extension cord to save the life of a shooting victim. He'd also sustained smoke inhalation injuries when evacuating elderly and disabled residents from an apartment building that had been set ablaze.

Dan, a quick-witted team veteran and go-getter who grew impatient when too much joking got in the way of work, started scrolling through his phone. "Antoine Carter got shot last night in Oakland," he said.

"Huh," said Drake.

Carter was a member of the Eastside Crips, a Stockton gang. It didn't shock anyone on CRT to hear that he'd been shot; he was the subject of an ongoing investigation by gang detectives and the San Joaquin County District Attorney's Office, which suspected him of sex trafficking. Drake filed the information away and began rolling his shoulder to warm up his throwing arm.

Later, out at Klein Family Field, he did fine. His pitch was a little high and outside. Most of CRT was there cheering him on. Jason Underwood looked awkward as he squeezed close to the team for a photo under a Stockton police recruiting tent beside the bleachers.

The team ate fish tacos and went back to work. Pretty soon, Dan and Perry came over the radio. They'd stopped a blue Infiniti by the P-2000 Super Store in Normandy Village Center, a strip mall on the north side. They said there was a gun in the car, and they were holding the three occupants at gunpoint. They needed backup. Drake hit the lights and siren and began racing to the mall, the SUV clanging as it went over speed bumps.

Before he reached the store, Drake heard, "Code 4." Everything under control. He pulled up. It was twilight but hot. Drake's SUV was panting, and the air smelled like brakes. Dan and Perry had the occupants of the car they'd stopped, high schoolers, in handcuffs. The kids weren't combative. If they were upset or scared at being detained, they hid it well. Mostly, they seemed bored.

There was no gun, it turned out, just a transparent extended magazine with fifteen rounds on the floor in the back, next to an empty plastic water bottle and some black-and-white flip-flops. Transparent extended magazines are a thing among gang members and wannabes in Stockton, who think it's cool to show everyone the bullets sticking out of the stock of their weapons. The driver, a rail-thin Mexican American teenager wearing a black baseball cap, plain white T-shirt, baggy gray sweats, and black Nikes, freely admitted that the magazine was his, even though California law makes it a misdemeanor for anyone under eighteen to possess ammunition. The cops wrote him a ticket, towed his car, made a speech about the dangers of gang life.

It's doubtful whether anyone on CRT gave another thought that day to the shooting of Antoine Carter. He'd been with his girlfriend and suspected "bottom bitch"—the prostitute in charge of the others in his sex trafficking operation—when he was struck by gunfire. The injuries weren't life-threatening, and Carter wouldn't tell Oakland police what had happened. But for the past few months, detectives and the DA's office had had Carter's phone tapped. On an open line, they actually heard him being shot. In the days following the shooting, they intercepted text messages he sent telling his associates who he thought was responsible: a guy in a group called EBK.

• • •

For his book *Ballad of the Bullet,* sociologist Forrest Stuart immersed himself in the lives of young Black men from Chicago's South Side attempting to make it in drill music.[5] "Drill" is slang for shooting someone, and "drill music" is gangster rap taken to the extreme, with lyrics revolving around guns, gangs, drugs, defending your turf, killing your rivals, showing heart, and surviving the streets. To explain the music's origins, Stuart offered some social context. Young men of color growing up today in poor neighborhoods are doubly disadvantaged. Educational opportunities and jobs that pay living wages are scarce. Meanwhile, street gangs—which historically provided a stable, if risky, pathway for some to earn cash, secure protection, gain respect, and experience a sense of belonging—aren't what they used to be.

In the crack cocaine era, the large gang families that controlled wide swaths of Chicago's inner city, like the Gangster Disciples or Latin Kings, developed a corporate structure. To facilitate the efficient movement of product, a hierarchical organization emerged that saw kingpins on top directing operations while the leaders of neighborhood sets served in effect as branch managers. Lower-level employees did the grunt work: cooking crack, packaging rocks, slinging them on corners, threatening whoever owed the gang money. This structure wasn't without its problems; many gang members had a hard time taking orders.[6] But if you were a young guy willing to do that grunt work, there was money to be made.

When the crack market collapsed, owing to a proliferation of new drugs, the corporate model collapsed along with it. Law enforcement expedited this change, as prosecutors brought racketeering charges against the kingpins. Suddenly everyone needed a new hustle, and without leadership from on high, different sets of the same gang began experimenting with various illicit ventures. Some got into the crystal meth trade, for example; others began robbing fellow drug dealers. The set leaders who planned these ventures gained power, and gang families were transformed into loosely organized federations, with some sets breaking free altogether and going their own way. For young men starting out, this meant uncertainty. If your neighborhood set was successful, you could be, too. If not, you were out of luck.

Faced with these circumstances, Stuart found, many guys—especially those who didn't have the stomach for serious crime—sought a different path. They got into drill music, recording videos on their phones and posting them to YouTube or other social media in the hope of becoming internet stars and getting money that way. But to make a name for themselves, rappers still needed a gang affiliation, and they had to play the part of thugs, even if that's not who they were. For the young men Stuart studied—some of whom, apparently, were quite talented—drill music mostly went nowhere. They earned a pittance. And it subjected them to danger, as the claims and challenges in their songs and on social media posts sometimes led to real-world violence.

In 2018, people who were following the drill music scene in Stockton caught wind of a group calling themselves EBK Hotboiiz. The initials stood for Everybody Killa. With a charismatic kid named EBK Young Joc as their front man, the Hotboiiz released music videos to YouTube with titles like "Sicknen" and "Blue Faces." At one level, the videos were pure teenage bravado. They featured the group smoking pot, showing off handguns, cash, and liquor, and rapping about women and shooting people. Below the surface, the raps narrated pain: the anguish of losing loved ones to violence; loathing and fear of the police; the challenge of trying to be someone when everything conspires against you. Thizzler.com, a Bay Area rap, hip-hop, and R & B website, wrote of the Hotboiiz that they "embody the violent energy of Stockton's underground rap scene . . . They say they'd do you grimy, and you believe it."[7]

EBK wasn't just a rap group, though. It was an actual street gang. Its members were a few years younger, on average, than Antoine Carter and the Eastside Crips. One EBK Hotboiiz video, "EBK Anthem," begins with a shot of the street sign for a particular block of Nightingale Avenue, a row of single-family homes guarded by chain-link fences and pink apartment complexes behind a market. There'd been gangs on that block since forever. What was different about EBK was that its members included anyone down for the cause, whether they came from north or south Stockton; whether they claimed Crip, Blood, anything. EBK was a mash-up.

• • •

WHEN A CALL HAD COME in about a shooting at the Holiday Plaza, Drake and Perry were three minutes away, working a car together. Even though Perry had almost fifteen years' experience on Drake, as a CRT rookie he was the newbie, expected to do menial tasks like booking property into evidence and logging into and out of the computers in the SUV. He didn't object. CRT was a stepping stone for officers into gang investigations. After a while, some of the cops he worked with would rotate off the team, others would come on, and then they'd be the newbies.

On arriving, Drake and Perry saw the victim lying in one corner of the parking lot. Another man, Black and in his thirties with dreadlocks, was standing over him. The man kept crying, "Ron! Ronald!" Perry asked him the victim's name, and he wailed, "Ronald Celestine!"

A second, much younger man wearing a blue T-shirt and jeans was stomping around. "Fuck!" he yelled. He was beside himself. He threw his cell phone on the ground, breaking it into pieces before walking away through the lot.

Cops flooded the strip mall, along with Stockton fire department paramedics. While Perry stayed with the victim, Drake called to the younger man to stop. Potential witnesses to shootings don't get to walk away. But the man kept going, yelling that he had nothing to say.

The dirt field immediately north of the parking lot is part of a dried-up old waterway that extends north and east to the Camanche Reservoir, a recreational area in the Sierra foothills stocked with trout that feels worlds away from Stockton's problems. The man was now storming through the field, Drake calling after him the whole time. Drake could see Alex Guerrero on the other side, near an apartment building where he'd gone with Jason Underwood to look for witnesses. He radioed for Alex to stop the man. Alex and a nearby patrol officer cut him off and found the man still irate. When Drake caught up to them, they were asking him to have a seat in a patrol car. He refused. Drake tried to talk to him, but the man, Dante, who also belonged to an NSGC set, continued to yell. Then he spit in Drake's face. Dante got taken to the ground quick. Drake was a genial guy, but he wasn't that genial.

A teenage girl in a pink shirt and sandals ran up to the cops. "Don't touch my brother!" she screamed.

Another patrol officer told her to stay back. "Don't you touch me either," she said, slapping his hand away. The officer grabbed her. She struggled, and the cop took her to the ground, too, with Alex's help, putting his knee in her back as he tried to get her handcuffed. The girl was all of thirteen years old, a middle schooler. It wasn't a good look.

Once the girl relaxed, she told the cops that she and Dante had a brother, twenty, who'd been arrested the year before, charged with homicide in the death of a sixteen-year-old. Nor was he the only person in the family locked up; her father had been in prison since she was four years old. She didn't know why the cops were after Dante now, but he was the one sibling she had left.

Drake asked Dante to give a statement, but he denied knowing anything about the shooting. The cops called Dante's mom so that they could issue a citation and release his sister. The mother said Dante was on parole and that was why he'd been scared of the cops. But he'd been doing better lately. He had a child and was keeping his head down. Dante and Ronald Celestine were cousins, she said.

• • •

IRSHAD MOHAMMED DIDN'T EXPECT TO become a homicide detective so early in his career. An eleven-year veteran of the force, he was from South Sacramento. After college, he worked with kids in group homes before getting hired by Stockton PD, where he spent six years on patrol.

In a sense, Stockton's bankruptcy was his gain. The senior officers who took early retirement when the department was forced to trim back included a cadre of detectives. That created openings in the investigative ranks. Irshad was brought on board and spent three years investigating child abuse and sexual assault cases, commuting from Sacramento so he could maintain a mental boundary between his home and taxing work life. He was recruited into robbery/homicide by supervisors impressed by his tenacious performance in the family crimes unit.

In the Celestine shooting, Irshad didn't have much to be tenacious with. Dante had pretty obviously witnessed what happened, but he was keeping quiet. The witness with dreadlocks who'd called Celestine's name told police that he was hanging out, smoking a cigarette, when two men opened fire. He'd taken cover by ducking behind a parked car and for that reason didn't get a look at the shooters or the vehicle they escaped in. The Spanish-speaking witness, for his part, said that he'd seen two Black men in their twenties walking in the parking lot when a silver or gray Toyota with tinted windows and a spoiler drove up. He couldn't remember what the men had been wearing. All he knew was that they'd whipped out pistols and started shooting, firing eight or nine rounds in the direction of the Smog Station. Then they ran to the Toyota and jumped in the back seat. The car sped away.

Irshad's clues thus amounted to a vehicle description and a recollection of the two shooters as Black men in their twenties. He got nothing from the store cameras in Holiday Plaza. He spent the days after the Celestine murder asking witnesses for more information, examining Celestine's arrest history and his contacts with the police, scouring social media trying to figure out who might have a beef with him.

• • •

After Antoine Carter's shooting in Oakland, Stockton gang detectives began looking more closely into EBK. They'd heard about it before, from social media. But they didn't know about the connection between EBK and the Eastside Crips, or what exactly EBK was up to; new groups form often, and police intelligence is imperfect. The specific EBK gang member that Carter thought had shot him couldn't have done it; he was on electronic monitoring and hadn't been anywhere near Oakland. But the detectives discovered that EBK was involved in an array of other criminal activities.

According to the district attorney's office, the gang's front man, EBK Young Joc, played a pivotal role in starting the group. EBK Young Joc's real name was Jalique Moore. His older brother, Kevin, was with the Westside Bloods before he died at the age of twenty-two, shot by someone in the same gang. Kevin was the first rapper in the family, and Jalique cited him as his inspiration. EBK formed after Jalique and his younger brother moved across town to Nightingale Avenue and took to hanging out with a new crowd.

The gang got into some bad stuff. Stockton detectives alleged that human trafficking for sexual purposes was one of EBK's major business operations. Through social media or friends of friends or at parties, the guys would allegedly meet and start sweet-talking girls, explaining how much money they could make, how they could access the high life, if only they'd be willing to turn a few tricks. Detectives claimed the guys would then bring the girls to cities where johns had more disposable income: San Jose, Oakland, Tucson, Las Vegas. Sometimes two or three guys would go together, each working four or five girls. They'd spread the word in advance and rent a block of hotel rooms. They'd party with the girls; booze and drugs would loosen them up. According to police, the guys would make thousands of dollars in a night, with only a small fraction going to the women. The next morning they'd drive back to Stockton.

The detectives couldn't be sure, but they thought that the shooting of Antoine Carter had something to do with EBK competing with Eastside Crips for control over girls or territory. But they believed that EBK had its hands in other things, too, from running guns to stealing from legal marijuana processing facilities to transporting undocumented immigrants on behalf of coyotes.

The detectives picked up chatter indicating that the Eastside Crips were planning to retaliate. After doing some surveillance, they had CRT stop a car with four Eastside Crip members in it, along with three guns. The guns were confiscated, and the expected retaliation never occurred.

• • •

THREE DAYS AFTER RONALD CELESTINE was shot, a group of friends and family gathered at the Holiday Plaza for a vigil. They were there to remember and celebrate Celestine's life. They brought votive candles, creating a memorial where he'd fallen. There were tears and speeches.

Then shots rang out, a lot of them. Bodies dropped, and a car squealed away. Minutes later, police cruisers came streaming from every direction. When the cops came to a halt at the strip mall, they found five people down, a mass shooting. Four of the mourners would survive their injuries. The fifth, Benny Lott, Celestine's cousin and fellow NSGC member, died after being rushed to the hospital. Also at the scene was Dante.

This crime and the Celestine murder must have been connected. But how?

After the vigil shooting, the streets started talking. Most of those attending the memorial, even the surviving victims, wouldn't divulge much information, but grandparents and aunts and uncles began asking questions and passing along tips to the police.

A name made its way to Irshad's desk: JR, Jimmy Richards. An EBK guy. He was there for the Celestine shooting, tipsters said.

Dante, who'd been at both shootings, surely knew something. Pressed by one of Irshad's partners, he cracked, identifying Richards as the getaway driver outside the Smog Station. Social media accounts in Stockton lit up with younger NSGC members saying they were now out to kill EBK. And Irshad heard rumors of a possible motive: the morning Celestine was killed, Dante and someone from EBK had gotten into a fistfight.

He began to piece it all together. Celestine, Lott, the others at the vigil who'd been hit—none of them was the intended target. Dante was. In the first shooting, Dante had been huddled with Celestine and his buddies when shooters began firing at him from a distance. The shots missed their mark, which wasn't uncommon in gang shootings since most gangsters were more bullet sprayers than marksmen.

They went back to try again when they learned that Dante would be attending the vigil.

That level of violence and follow-through made no sense as retaliation for throwing some punches. But it wasn't the pettiest motive for a homicide Irshad had seen.

Dante knew he'd been the target all along. No wonder he was grief-stricken and irate. No wonder he smashed his phone in anger.

Irshad was able to get a lead on the car as well, the gray Toyota. It belonged to one of Jimmy Richards's girlfriends. Ballistics tied some of the shell casings from the Celestine shooting to other shootings—nonfatal—that had taken place near where Richards lived. A warrant was issued, and Richards was arrested in Las Vegas. After another wiretap, Stockton police rounded up additional EBK members, charging them with human trafficking, gun crimes, and other offenses.

Richards had been identified as the driver in the Celestine case, not a shooter. Interrogated by police, he copped to his role. But he refused to say who on his crew had pulled the trigger. After more investigation, Irshad and the DA's office figured out who the shooters probably were, but without Richards's testimony, there wasn't enough evidence to charge them, much less get a conviction. Nor was law enforcement able to conclusively tie EBK to the earlier Antoine Carter shooting in Oakland.

Nevertheless, with Richards in custody, and EBK's operations disrupted, violence fell that spring, while Stockton's homicide clearance rates remained on the upward trajectory they'd been tracing for the past few years. In Stockton—anywhere—that was a win.

How much of the outcome in the Celestine case could be attributed to procedural justice? The cops who'd stopped Dante and his sister, including Drake, didn't seem to be practicing the philosophy at the time. Yet Kevin Rooney, the deputy district attorney who oversaw the EBK investigations, believed that procedural justice had made a difference. While PJ wasn't apparent in every encounter between citizens and police in Stockton, Rooney had seen more of it of late, even from the action-oriented gang cops. He was convinced that when, in general, police show respect, that breeds trust, and trust yields cooperation from the community—

which is what had led to the identification of JR. It's possible, of course, that the tip would have come in anyway without procedural justice. A gang war had erupted, and the community needed it to stop. Then again, in cities where departments haven't put in the effort to build trust, deadly feuds can break out without any informants stepping forward.

Other evidence lends credibility to the idea that procedural justice formed part of the ambient background for solving serious crimes in Stockton. A survey of five hundred Stockton residents carried out in October 2020, the fall after George Floyd's murder (when trust in the police was low nationally), found that a large proportion—81 percent—said they would be very or somewhat likely to provide information to police to help find a suspect; perceptions of the respect shown by the department were correlated with readiness to share information.[8] This is consistent with the fundamental insights of procedural justice. And it fits with a 2019 study that found positive interactions between police and the public in New Haven, Connecticut, to increase trust and residents' willingness to cooperate to solve crimes.[9] In Stockton, some people still wouldn't talk to the cops. But that the PD was trying to do better led others to feel comfortable cooperating.

Irshad Mohammed's attempts at connecting with the families of his victims, in the Celestine case and others, helped too. Stockton homicide detectives made their own death notifications, meaning that they were the ones to knock on the door to inform families that their loved ones had been killed. While offering his deepest condolences, Irshad would stress that solving the crime might require that the family work with him to generate leads. In the immediate aftermath of a murder, when people are consumed by shock and grief, they don't have the mental or emotional resources to do anything but cry. But Irshad believed that if one is kind, respectful, and compassionate—which is what procedural justice demands of detectives no less than of patrol or gang officers—chances are, in due course, the family would become your ally.

• • •

THERE WAS PROVEN POTENTIAL BUT also significant limitations to Eric Jones's incremental, one-step-ahead approach to reforming police culture. Beyond the benefit that procedural justice offered to investigators, consider police use of force: in theory, procedural justice should decrease the amount of force used by a department. If suspects in criminal cases feel that they can trust the police and that they'll be treated fairly, they should be more likely to cooperate and less likely to resist arrest. And officers committed to respectful treatment of citizens should do everything in their power to secure cooperation without using violence.

Some of this theory was borne out in Stockton. In 2017 Eric revised the department's use of force policy, informed by procedural justice principles. The new policy mandated that officers attempt de-escalation, if the circumstances allowed for it, and imposed restrictions on when officers were permitted to shoot at vehicles. Whether due to that revised policy or to the officers' growing commitment to procedural justice or both, police shootings fell 80 percent. *80 percent.*[10] While Stockton police were killing four people a year from 2014 to 2016, in the period 2017 to 2020, it was more like one or two.[11] Even one person killed exceeds the zero deaths we should strive for (and it's important not to read too much into short-term trends), but this was a change in the right direction.

In most cities, police shootings are rare events. It's harder to evaluate more routine uses of force or to measure whether Eric's PJ work was generating progress on this front. The department didn't maintain good records on nonlethal use of force before Eric took over. In two years for which data are available, 2017 and 2018, Stockton officers resorted to force during an arrest around 15 percent of the time.[12] Metrics aren't standardized across police departments, so comparisons can be apples and oranges, but on its face, that number is higher than at other urban agencies. The most common type of force used in Stockton was a restraint system called the Wrap, which allows cops to subdue prisoners who are kicking or flailing without hog-tying them or dangerously placing them on their stomachs for extended periods of time. Procedural justice hadn't produced a community of individuals happy to cooperate in their own arrests.

But groups monitoring Stockton PD began detecting fewer incidents of abuse. Bobby Bivens, who served as president of the Stockton NAACP for nineteen years, thought there was no question but that the police department had "improved over time." Since Eric had taken over and gotten behind procedural justice, Bivens said, "Police violence against citizens has been reduced, even though we still have incidents." He recognized that Eric was serious about reducing that violence more and holding officers accountable in circumstances where they had betrayed their oath to protect and serve.

Procedural justice, especially when paired with implicit bias training, is also intended to address racial disparities in policing. How was Stockton PD doing there? Of the nine people killed by Stockton police since 2016, six were Black men, 66 percent. Eric knew that was a terrible statistic.

More quotidian police behaviors were equally telling. In the first three months of 2020, Stockton PD made 10,745 vehicle stops for traffic infractions—about 120 a day; 27 percent of the drivers stopped were Black, yet Black people comprised only 12 percent of Stockton's population, and 24 percent of Black drivers had their cars searched, compared to 19 percent of Latinos, 16 percent of Asians, and 13 percent of white people.[13] This racial skew has remained consistent since before the procedural justice training was implemented, implying continued racial profiling by some Stockton officers. (Factors other than profiling can contribute to racial disparities in vehicle stops; police deployment patterns, for example. Likewise, disparities in searches may be tied to racial gaps in arrest histories, as drivers with records arouse police suspicions.)

Black Stockton residents resent being pulled over so frequently. Wilisha Beatty-Cherry, whose father was killed by the police in 2002, recalled an incident where she and her husband went to dinner with their three sons. Her two older boys, teenagers, decided to take a separate car. On the way home, her sons were stopped for some minor equipment violation. Concerned for their safety, Beatty-Cherry and her husband pulled over, too. Moments after the first police SUV hit its lights, a second SUV arrived. Then a third. Then a fourth. Four police vehicles for a routine traffic stop is a belligerent posture. Nothing happened to her sons, though they were shaken by the encounter in light of the family's history. But what if Beatty-Cherry hadn't been there to smooth the situation over? The question keeps her up at night.

Eric was disturbed by these unchanging patterns. But he was unsure what to do about them. He fretted over policy changes that might make a difference—such as prohibiting pretextual stops (where an officer stops a car for a traffic or equipment violation, when the real goal is to investigate the driver for criminal activity) or scaling back hot-spot policing of minority neighborhoods. Eric worried that ending pretextual stops would hinder the department's ability to seize guns, which was critical to his strategy for reducing violence. Unbiased officers stop cars on pretext, too, sometimes on the basis of good intel that might fail to meet the standard of probable cause. As for hot-spot policing, many Black Stockton residents told Eric that they wanted *more* police officers patrolling their neighborhoods, not fewer.

While there's far more work to be done in leveling treatment toward Black civilians, the 2020 survey of residents suggests that Stockton PD has made progress in the equitable treatment of Latinos and Asians. They hold views of the police department, including about its fairness, that are barely distinguishable from those of white non-Latinos, something that likely wasn't true twenty years ago. One reason is that Eric and his team did a much better job recruiting Latino and Asian officers than Black police. By 2019, 31 percent of Stockton officers—those below the rank of sergeant—were Latino, while 9 percent were Asian. Yet only 3 percent were Black, no more than was the case when Jesse Smith was hired in 2013. Although the social science on police demography isn't settled, there's good evidence that Black and Latino officers make fewer stops and arrests for petty offenses, and use force less, especially when dealing with people of color.[14] So Eric had made inroads with diversity, but if he'd hired more Black cops, racial disparities in police treatment of citizens might have narrowed further. (Recruiting more Black officers wasn't as easy as making the decision to do so. Eric was competing for law enforcement talent with every agency in Northern California. All were hoping to diversify, and most paid better than Stockton. The PD's less-than-stellar reputation might also have dissuaded Black applicants.)

It's not trivial that leading figures in Stockton's Black community felt they had a friend in Eric and that dialogue with the police department was possible. They believed that Eric's command staff was trustworthy and that the foundation had been laid for more change in the years to come.

This was the view of Black faith leaders Eric would meet with, and of Harry Black, who became Stockton's city manager and Eric's boss. A data guy committed to equity, Black knew that Stockton PD was nowhere close to perfect. But he was convinced that the will for change was there and that the department was now acclimated enough to procedural justice so officers wouldn't stand in the way of reasonable policy shifts leading to greater fairness for all of Stockton's residents.

Could procedural justice really be so advantageous? Beginning in 2017, a team of criminologists tested the hypothesis that procedural justice training improves officer behavior and produces better outcomes for the community. With the cooperation of police in Tucson, Arizona, Cambridge, Massachusetts, and Houston, Texas, the researchers first identified forty high-crime blocks in each city. Half were randomly chosen to receive policing based in procedural justice, the other half standard policing. A small number of patrol officers assigned to those blocks were selected to take part in the experiment, with half given a five-day procedural justice training similar to that offered in Stockton and the rest continuing to police as they normally would. Researchers riding with the officers in both the treatment and control groups observed their behavior for about nine months, and households on the blocks were surveyed before and after about their perceptions of the police.

The results were remarkable. Officers who received PJ training "were significantly more likely to give people voice," "show neutrality," and "demonstrate respectful behavior." They also made fewer arrests. Citizens living on the blocks where those cops policed noticed less harassment and use of force. Additionally, those blocks saw a 14 percent reduction in crime compared to ones that received standard policing. The study strongly suggests that Stockton's generally salutary experience with procedural justice was no fluke.[15]

• • •

ERIC'S IMPLEMENTATION OF PROCEDURAL JUSTICE reforms made a real dent in Stockton's policing culture. The change could sometimes be hard to spot. In 2020, seven years after the program was introduced, there still weren't that many Jesse Smiths in the department, cops who lived and breathed procedural justice. Although Eric and others thought that half or more of Stockton's officers were committed to PJ, Jesse saw himself as much more of a rarity in terms of policing philosophy and practice. This was a source of irritation to him, as was Eric's slow pace of change. Jesse wasn't happy about the shortage of Black officers, either.

But if officers like Jesse Smith weren't the norm, officers like Drake Wiest were becoming common. In many ways, they were traditional crime-fighting cops. Yet their aggression was tempered by basic human decency fostered by working in an agency that hammered home the message that all citizens should be treated with respect. Cops like Drake might not be procedural justice enthusiasts, but they'd absorbed its most important lessons.

Given how bad things had been in Stockton before, this change wasn't insignificant. Wilisha Beatty-Cherry was so intrigued by the department's trust-building work that she'd agreed to lead some community workshops with Captain Scott Meadors. Unexpectedly, the two became close friends. She readily admitted that her work with him might have influenced her views of Stockton PD. Nonetheless, "progress has been made in Stockton," she said. "I'm not going to front like I don't see it."

PART II

LONGMONT

7

BELONGING REVOLUTION

In a small classroom with hardwood floors and a globe light hanging overhead, ten participants in the study group pushed their desks together to form a circle. The youngest was in her forties; most were retirement age. All were white. Fleece and sincerity abounded.

At the front of the room sat a man who was glossier than the rest. Mo Siegel was the founder of Celestial Seasonings, the tea company, and he was growing more frustrated by the minute at the lack of tech support at Naropa University, the Buddhist-inspired liberal arts school in Boulder where the group was meeting.

"I am so sorry," Mo said to the people who'd joined the group on Zoom. "There was supposed to be somebody here to help us with the computer, and they didn't show up. So we sound like we're in a tunnel."

The group had assembled, as it did nearly every week, to discuss *The Urantia Book*, a spiritual tract with Christian undertones. The book, which runs two thousand pages, supposedly records the words of divine celestial beings who inhabited the body of a Chicago businessman in the 1920s. All night, the businessman would talk religion in his sleep. William Sadler, a psychiatrist, came to investigate. Sadler maintained a side business debunking occultists. But as he listened to the words coming from the "mysterious sleeper," he became convinced that they were a revelation. He hired a stenographer to record what the sleeper was saying and asked his acquaintances to submit clarifying questions he would pose to the man while he slumbered.

Religious studies scholar Brook Wilensky-Lanford describes the resulting *Urantia Book*—"Urantia" means "Earth," in the book's made-up vocabulary—as an "alternative Bible with the flavor of science fiction and the ethic of progressivism."[1] With its talk of angels, multiple universes, and other civilizations, the book is engaging and eccentric enough to have found a place in Boulder's New Age scene in the 1960s and 1970s.

On this evening early in 2020, the group planned to study portions of *The Urantia Book* about the life and times of Jesus. Someone read a passage aloud describing a trip Jesus took to Jerusalem with his family when he was twelve, where he witnessed preparations for the Passover feast and asked Joseph "why the heavenly Father required the slaughter of so many innocent and helpless animals." A woman with a gentle voice ventured a comment. "It struck me how upsetting it must have been for Jesus to see those animals get slaughtered," she said. "Nobody wants to see an animal suffer."

Carol Engel-Enright was quick to reply. She was about to retire from a teaching career at Colorado State University and was seated next to Mike Butler, her boyfriend, the public safety chief for Longmont, about fifteen miles from Boulder. "I raised my kids on a working farm, and we raised our own meat," she said. "I think everybody who went through the ancient system had gotten pretty used to blood and sacrifice. We still kind of do it in our society around the barbecue grill."

As Carol spoke, Mike beamed. He was sixty-seven, tall and lanky, with a longish neck, straight white hair that fell wherever he combed it, and black glasses. He had on jeans, a polo shirt, and a brown leather jacket, his signature style. Mike was on the verge of retirement, too. An unlikely figure as a police chief, Mike had, over the course of twenty-five years, endeavored to create a progressive police department in Longmont that served the public good, inspired by a philosophical and sociological theory of justice, but also by his admiration for the loving, forgiving God of Urantia.

Carol had come into his life seven years after the breakup of Mike's longtime marriage. She was no hippie. She believed in business and capitalism and the Republican Party. But like Mike, she was open, a seeker. Though her kids had grown up on land near Hygiene, Colorado, she'd given birth to her last child in a house in Boulder previously owned by Stephen Stills of Crosby, Stills, Nash & Young, with an aboriginal medicine woman in attendance.

After her husband was killed in a car crash in 2017, she and Mike had found each other. "My darling," he called her. She thought of him as a visionary. In the new house they'd bought together at the edge of Longmont, smooth jazz playing from the built-in speakers, Mike kept a high-powered telescope and a collection of camera fittings. He planned to take up astrophotography in his retirement, capturing image after image of the heavenly realm that had given his life purpose and meaning.

• • •

THE LONGMONT SAFETY AND JUSTICE CENTER, which houses the police department, the administrative offices of fire, the city's Office of Emergency Management, and the municipal court, is in the center of town. It sits right off Main, a busy commercial street anchored by Italianate-style brick buildings that date to the late nineteenth and early twentieth centuries, when Longmont's economy was ranching and sugar beets. Constructed in 1993, the Safety and Justice Center blends old and new, its façade brick and stone, concrete and glass. The building has a quirky architectural feature: accessing the front doors requires walking through a large unenclosed cylindrical area, resembling an observatory without finished walls or a roof. The 153 cops on the Longmont force have never been sure what the cylinder symbolizes, if it symbolizes anything at all. A radar dish maybe, in homage to the fact that Longmont is home to an FAA facility that monitors planes flying over an enormous stretch of airspace in the American West? Or perhaps the circle represents openness, inclusiveness, community?

The messaging coming from Mike's office was clearer. Some chiefs surround themselves with flags or SWAT paraphernalia or collections of police challenge coins, imprinted with the logos of different departments. On the wall behind his desk, Mike chose to display a photo of a lighthouse next to one of his favorite inspirational quotes, lines often attributed to Ralph Waldo Emerson but actually an adaptation of the work of a Kansas woman named Bessie Stanley who won an essay contest in 1905: "Successful is the person who has lived well, laughed often, and loved much, who has gained the respect of children, who leaves the world better than they found it, who has never lacked appreciation for the earth's beauty, who never fails to look for the best in others or give the best of themselves."

Born in 1952, Mike was raised in Perry Township, Ohio, outside Massillon, south of Cleveland. His dad worked for Eaton Manufacturing Company making nuts and bolts for the auto industry. His mom was a nurse. Both were active in church, a plain-vanilla congregation that read the Bible literally. "If a man cause a blemish in his neighbor; as he hath done, so shall it be done to him; Breach for breach, eye for eye, tooth for tooth." But also: "Inasmuch as ye have done it unto one of the least of these my brethren, ye have done it unto me."

Mike was a strong student. He graduated high school at seventeen and started college at the University of Akron. He planned to major in engineering—"Choose a lucrative career," his dad would say—but he also loved physics, chemistry, anything science. One semester he took an elective course taught by Joseph Lentini, a former Massachusetts cop who'd worked as a detective on the Boston Strangler case. (In the 1960s, eleven women in the greater Boston area were sexually assaulted and murdered, most if not all by a serial killer.) Lentini was a captivating storyteller. So much so that, hearing him describe his experience on the force, Mike began to imagine himself as an investigator. He asked Lentini to go for coffee. "I'm interested in law enforcement," Mike told him.

Accountability had been big in Mike's family. If you do something wrong, own it. Perhaps that's why criminal investigations appealed. Finding the culprit meant tracking down someone who refused to be held accountable.

Lentini suggested that Mike switch his major and encouraged him to consider a career with the FBI, the big leagues. Mike formulated a plan. He and his wife had gotten married right out of high school. The couple needed money, so Mike quit the University of Akron and put in for a civilian FBI position. The Butlers decamped to the DC area around his twenty-first birthday. When he wasn't providing site security at FBI Headquarters, he could be found taking classes at the University of Maryland (where he'd transferred, changing his major to behavioral sciences).

After graduating, Mike applied to become an FBI agent and was inching his way closer to the top of the hiring list. But he started having second thoughts. Because of Watergate, information had come to light about the bureau that wasn't flattering. Also, many of the agents he was getting to know weren't happy with their jobs and were counting their days until retirement. They were bureaucrats, essentially—not the exciting life Mike had pictured when he was taking Joseph Lentini's class. These agents would work one tiny aspect of a case without having a sense of the whole.

In his free time, Mike was a hiker. As a kid, he'd dreamed of being a forest ranger, living in a ranger station, elk and deer his best friends. One summer he and his wife took a vacation out to Colorado. They fell head over heels for the mountains, the sky, the spirit of the place. Mike saw that Boulder PD was hiring. Maybe that's where he'd find his vocation. Boulder took him on as a police officer in 1978, and the couple bought a house in Longmont, where prices were cheaper.

Boulder was something of a cultural mecca. Mike loved being a cop there—never a dull moment. Soon after he was hired, he befriended a higher-up in the department who assigned him as personal driver to Robin Williams and Pam Dawber. The two would come through town for occasional on-location shoots of the TV show *Mork & Mindy*, set in Boulder, which played off its reputation for weirdness. Dawber was gorgeous, Williams a nonstop hilarity machine who'd have to be dragged off the dance floor at two in the morning. (Mike was too starstruck to suspect that drugs could have been part of that picture.)

Mike relished his interactions with Boulder residents, the relationships he built. An artist named Terry Kruger who did police sketch work introduced him to *The Urantia Book*. The book's message—that there's a spark of the infinite in everyone—moved him like nothing else ever had.

By 1990, Mike had risen in the ranks to become Boulder PD's second-in-command. His job was fulfilling, but what he most wanted was to lead, to take charge of a police agency and make it a source of community uplift. He applied broadly for chief positions—Kirkland, Washington; San Marcos, Texas. His wife kept telling him that if he waited, Longmont would open up. In 1993, it did.

• • •

DEMOGRAPHICALLY SPEAKING, THERE'S NOTHING UNUSUAL about Longmont; it looks a lot like the state of Colorado. The city is 68 percent white, 24 percent Latino, 3 percent Asian, and 1 percent Black. (The Centennial State's Black population is somewhat larger, at 5 percent, concentrated in Denver and Aurora.) The average age of Longmont residents, 38.1, approximates the state average of 37.1. Longmont's median household income is $79,000, compared with Colorado's $75,000, and 44 percent of people living in Longmont have a bachelor's degree, which is high when set against the US average of 33 percent but on par for well-educated Colorado. One of out every ten Longmont residents lives in poverty—also true for the state.

Average as can be. That's why what Mike pulled off there is so noteworthy.

On becoming chief, he got to work on three main things. First, restorative justice. In 1996, two peace activists, Beverly Title and Lana Leonard, teamed up with him to create an alternative to incarceration for some of the city's criminal offenders. Restorative justice, modeled on Native American principles, steers wayward individuals into a community-run program where—if the victims of crime are willing—the offenders are brought face-to-face, in a circle, with everyone who's been impacted by their bad choices. The offenders are asked to reflect on what they did and why, and on the harm they'd inflicted. They're asked to apologize. Often there's an educational component and restitution. In Longmont, the entire process is facilitated by volunteers. If offenders see the restorative justice cycle through to the end, they're not prosecuted, serve no jail or prison time, and keep their records clean.

Mike became intrigued by restorative justice as soon as Beverly Title told him about it. He'd looked on with horror at the nation's—and Colorado's—prison boom of the previous twenty years. With crime soaring and the public clamoring for action, politicians had lengthened sentences for violent, property, and drug offenses. To constrain the leniency of judges, they imposed "mandatory minimums" and "three strikes and you're out" laws. They made it harder for parole boards to grant prisoners early release. The result was predictable: the prison population exploded. New facilities were built all over the country to deal with the overload. In the early 1970s, about 200,000 Americans were in state or federal prisons. By 2009, when the prison boom peaked, that number stood at more than 1,600,000, giving the US the highest incarceration rate of any country in the world.[2] If you include those in local jails, the total number of people behind bars today exceeds 2 million. (It's worth mentioning that the incarceration rate, calculated in relation to the total US adult population, has edged downward over the last decade.)[3]

Mass incarceration, Mike believed, was both a moral failing and ineffective public policy.[4] America's prisons were brutal. And without rehabilitation—which few prisons were offering—prisoners would often reoffend upon release. Those who didn't faced discrimination and daunting prospects in the labor market. Wouldn't it be better, Mike imagined, if at least some offenders in Longmont were offered the chance to make amends and find their way back into the good graces of the community?

The contemporary restorative justice movement can be traced to a program that developed in Ontario, Canada, in the 1970s, after a probation officer there came to the view that no one would benefit if two teenage vandals were imprisoned.[5] US reformers then took up the cause. Howard Zehr, a Mennonite activist and academic, argued in an influential book that Americans were looking at criminal justice through the wrong "lens," and that the country's reliance on incarceration was "out of step with our Christian roots and even with much of our own history in the West."[6] While procedural justice (as practiced in Stockton) is concerned with fair and equitable behavior by agents of the law, restorative justice asks how citizens who've broken the law might repair the damage they've caused, including moral damage.

Restorative justice wasn't a panacea; Mike realized that. Sometimes people are too dangerous to remain at large and need to be incarcerated. But he felt strongly that everyone has gifts to give the world and that those gifts are squandered when human beings are locked in cages.

So he built out formal connections between the Longmont police department and the nonprofit that Title and Leonard started, the Longmont Community Justice Partnership. Unlike other communities with restorative justice programs, where typically cases are referred by the district attorney's office *after* an arrest, in Longmont, police officers can make such referrals *instead* of effecting an arrest. For all the downsides of police discretion, an upside is that the police are within their rights to not arrest an offender if they think that justice would be better served through other means (except when it comes to domestic violence, where arrest is mandated by state law). Longmont cops mostly direct juvenile cases to restorative justice, grateful that they don't have to slap handcuffs on every kid they encounter who shoplifts a cheap piece of jewelry or is caught spray-painting graffiti on the walls of the long-abandoned Great Western Sugar Mill. But the officers also refer adults in cases where it seems like someone took a temporary wrong turn in life and might be set back on track. Since the program started, more than six thousand Longmont offenders have wound their way through the restorative justice process, with only about 10 percent of young participants reoffending. Randomized, controlled trials in the UK and Australia have shown that offenders subject to restorative justice are less likely to commit future crimes than those who are arrested, incarcerated, and released. Victims who take part in restorative justice circles often have better outcomes, too, such as fewer symptoms of post-traumatic stress disorder.[7]

Interest in restorative justice has been burgeoning, although statistics on its use are scarce. A survey conducted more than twenty years ago by the Department of Justice found about 290 "victim-offender mediation" programs, a category that includes restorative justice.[8] Since that time, funding for restorative justice nonprofits has expanded; "45 states and the District of Columbia," according to legal scholar Thalia González, "have codified 'restorative justice' into their juvenile and/or adult criminal justice systems"; restorative justice principles have been incorporated into school disciplinary proceedings (though there are still around seventy thousand arrests on school grounds annually); and progressive prosecutors in several large cities have expressed their support.[9]

In many American jurisdictions, no legal barrier exists to police departments doing what Mike did: diverting offenders to a restorative justice nonprofit in lieu of arrest. Realistically, however, it would be difficult to sustain a program like the one in Longmont without cooperation from prosecutors; support from the local political establishment; a nonprofit that could be trusted to run the programming well; and clear rules governing eligibility, to ensure that dangerous offenders don't remain loose and that biases don't enter into police decision-making about who they deem suitable for referral.

When Mike first pushed his department toward restorative justice, officers pushed back. Some threatened to quit; they thought the approach was a joke. A few actually did quit. Others stayed but tried to undermine the program by referring offenders who they expected to prove incorrigible. The joke was on them. More often than not, restorative justice worked as promised, inducing offenders to change and helping victims achieve closure. Longmont's violent and property crime rates were above the Colorado average when Mike took over the department; those rates fell to below the statewide average. While it's difficult to determine how much of this decline, if any, was due to restorative justice, the trend suggests no inherent trade-off with public safety. On the Longmont force, converts were won.

Mike's commitment to restorative justice grew as well. Besides its intrinsic merits, he came to think of it as a way that police departments "might disassociate themselves from the criminal justice system." The unsoundness of that system was becoming more apparent to him with each passing year.

In keeping with this opinion, the second big thing Mike did was reorient Longmont PD around a "harm-reduction" approach to drug use. During his time in Boulder, Mike had come to regard the war on drugs—the nationwide attempt to stamp out narcotics use by subjecting manufacturers, dealers, and users to criminal prosecution—as a complete failure. You could arrest and imprison all the dealers you wanted; others would take their place. Drug addiction is a medical condition linked to mental health and socioeconomic factors; it generates near constant demand. Rather than try to arrest our way out of the problem, Mike thought, what if cops partnered with social services to treat addiction and ameliorate its underlying causes, and focused on making sure that drug users caused as little harm as possible to themselves and the community?

Longmont PD didn't stop its drug enforcement altogether. There were still raids at seedy motels on north Main Street and stops for minor traffic offenses where the real aim was a fishing expedition for narcotics (or so it seemed to attorneys in the Boulder office of the Colorado State Public Defender). But the department devoted less energy to these efforts than other agencies, spending its time on programs like LEAD, Law Enforcement Assisted Diversion—a Seattle-based model where cops identify people who they think have committed crimes because of substance abuse, sending them out of the criminal justice system and into treatment services—and CORE (Crisis, Outreach, Response, and Engagement), which puts mental health clinicians in cars with specially trained police officers and paramedics to deal more effectively with those in crisis, drug-related or not.

Mike was in a good place to enact programs like these requiring cooperation among city agencies. In 2008, Longmont's fire chief retired. Mike and his boss, the city manager, thought it could make sense for the sake of efficiency to consolidate the police and fire departments under one administrative roof. Mike was tasked with leading both organizations; though his main expertise was in policing, henceforth he'd also be in charge of Longmont's fire and EMS services. That's when his official title was changed from chief of police to chief of public safety, a designation that meshed with his multidisciplinary thinking.

Mike's third move was to make community involvement a centerpiece of the PD's work. Police departments everywhere seek community partnerships, whether it's beat cops attending neighborhood watch meetings, school resource officers doing drug education in the classroom, or chiefs soliciting input on policy. Mike saw another function for the police: encouraging residents to get involved in local affairs. Citing political scientist Robert Putnam, Mike called it "activating social capital."[10] He was concerned that American citizens had become disconnected and isolated, holing up in their houses when they could be working together to make their neighborhoods better places to live. Cops were out in those neighborhoods every day. Perhaps they could nudge people into donating some of their time to worthy community organizations and projects.

ON A SUNNY, BRISK WEEKEND morning, Mike was strolling through St. Vrain Village, a mobile home park next to the railroad tracks abutting St. Vrain Creek, an offshoot of the South Platte River. Well-kept trailers, with fences and front gardens, were arrayed along outspread streets. Longs Peak, the tallest mountain in Rocky Mountain National Park, loomed over the skyline, offering a stunning, serene view even to Longmont's poor.

Two weeks earlier, there'd been a murder in the trailer park. A twenty-nine-year-old suffering from schizophrenia allegedly killed his brother's dog. Then, according to police, he chased his brother outside onto the street and killed him, too, stabbing him in front of a witness. Mike decided to walk St. Vrain with Dan Benavidez, a sprightly eighty-one-year-old former city councilman and one of his best friends, to take the pulse of the neighborhood after the murder, reassure residents, and encourage them to volunteer in the community. This week it was St. Vrain, but Mike and Dan had done some two hundred similar walks in other parts of Longmont.

Dan had been working to improve Longmont since the 1960s, when it was practically a different town. Historically, there'd been a large Ku Klux Klan presence in Colorado, and Klavern 2 in Longmont was particularly active, with parades and cross burnings. In 1923, the Klan took over city government, with the mayor swearing allegiance and Klansmen winning a majority of the seats on the city council. Their reign was short-lived—voters booted them out four years later because of administrative incompetence—but it was a tense time for Latinos in Longmont, mostly ranch hands, sugar beet workers, and their families.[11]

Racism continued to thrive when Dan, a radar technician born in Colorado, returned with his wife and daughter after a stint in California for a job at what's now called the Denver Air Route Traffic Control Center. A house on the west side of Longmont near the golf course seemed perfect for the family, but the realtor demurred, telling them "their kind"—Mexican Americans—belonged on the east side. Dan went to talk to the landlord; he would be a federal employee making good money, and he was a veteran. The landlord was willing to take a chance on Dan, he said, on the condition that he pay monthly in cash. "If you mess up, out you go." Dan rented the house, but the incident stung. It would spark a lifetime of anti-racist activism and public service.

Dan began paying close attention to the police department in 1980, when a young white cop shot two Latino men following a traffic stop. The men had been with some friends on their way to pick up ice after a wedding when a drunk member of their party—not Latino and not shot—yelled from the car window that the cop and his partner were pigs. The police stopped them and pulled out the wise guy. Juan Louis Garcia and Jeff Cordova, both twenty-one, stepped from the car to aid their friend. A fight ensued. In a struggle for one of the officer's guns, Garcia and Cordova were killed, Cordova shot in the back as he was running away.[12] Many Latinos in Longmont were outraged by the senselessness of the shootings and their echo of the town's history of racism and abuse.

In the face of calls to burn the city down in response, Dan helped form an advocacy organization called El Comité. Among its goals were changing the police department through anti-bias training and hiring Latino officers. The notion that it was important for Longmont PD to foster a positive relationship with the city's Latino community was thus already part of the conversation by the time Mike became chief. But Mike would lead the department past what Dan thought possible.

As he walked through St. Vrain Village, Dan, with a gray mustache, wore jeans, tennis shoes, and a zip-up jacket over a collared shirt that read "Belonging Revolutionary." The "belonging revolution" was a phrase he and Mike had coined. Longmont's Latino population was a mix of families that had been in the US for generations, like Dan's, and newly arrived immigrants from Mexico and Central America, not all of whom were documented. Dan wanted to make sure that everyone who wound up in Longmont knew that they were valued members of the community; that they belonged; and that they had full access to city government, whatever their immigration status. Mike wanted the same.

They spotted a man, probably in his twenties, wearing a plaid bathrobe and slippers. Wan and balding, with a goatee, he had let his dog out in front of a white-trimmed mobile home. Despite the cold, flowers were blooming in pots next to the driveway.

"How are you?" Dan called out. "Do you have a moment for the chief of police?"

"I'm Mike," said Mike, extending his hand. "What's your name?"

"Andrew," said the man.

"This is Mike Butler. He's the chief of police for the city of Longmont," Dan announced.

"And this is Dan Benavidez," Mike said. "Dan and I walk neighborhoods most Sundays, and we chose your neighborhood today."

"That's cool," Andrew replied but in a worried tone.

"I'm not here on official business, like to investigate anything. I'm just here to figure out how people are feeling about the neighborhood, the community. And to make an invitation to people as well. That's what this is about," Mike said. He'd uttered these words thousands of times but always tried to make them sound fresh. "Do you live here?" he asked Andrew.

"Yeah."

"How long?"

"Well, my uncle used to live here; he passed away. I've been through quite a bit."

"Talk to us about that, Andrew," Mike said. "Talk to us about what you've been through." (Later, reflecting on the day, Mike would write in his journal that "we discover the abundance and intimacy of our neighborhoods not only when our gifts are acknowledged, but also when our sorrows are revealed.")

"He passed away, and then my mom passed away as well," said Andrew.

"Oh gosh," Dan murmured. "I'm sorry."

"She got ran over, hit by a car. Then I took over the trailer. I haven't been here for too long, but it seems like it's been doing pretty good. With all the crime, it used to be pretty bad around here."

"There's been a lot of attention paid," Mike said, "but there's also been a lot of community work done. The community, the residents have really stepped up." He was referring to neighborhood meetings the police had arranged after receiving calls about drug activity and theft in the trailer park. In those meetings, residents had pledged to do a better job looking out for one another.

Andrew paused for a few seconds. "Well, I definitely see a change."

"So you feel safe here?" Mike asked him.

"Yeah, except for the raccoons."

Mike and Dan laughed. Mike asked Andrew about his job and learned that he was employed by a restoration company that cleaned homes and businesses after fires or major water leaks.

"What's your take on local police and fire services?" Mike asked.

"I haven't really run into them," Andrew answered.

"So, I've got an invite for you, Andrew," said Mike. "I'm always looking to call people to see if they can be helpful on things. We've got issues going on in this community. We've got a low crime rate, but we also have issues like people struggling with homelessness, people struggling with addiction."

"Yeah, actually, there's this person down there, he always yells. He lives under the bridge." Andrew pointed in the direction of the railroad tracks.

Mike asked a few questions about the man and jotted down notes before returning to his appeal. "Here's what I'd like to be able to do, Andrew. I'd like to be able to call on you somewhere down the road and have you participate with helping some people. I don't know what kind of time you have, but I believe our community has to participate a lot more, and I believe our community has a lot more to offer. Public safety can do a lot, our service providers can do a lot, but we really need our community. Are you open to me calling on you later?"

"Yeah, sure," Andrew said.

• • •

Restorative justice, harm reduction, community involvement: these were the pillars of Mike's stewardship of Longmont PD. He'd made countless smaller-scale policy changes to the police department as well, all important. He'd restricted when and how officers could use force (framed by the philosophy that citizens were to be treated as "extended family," the policy was that force was to be used only as a last resort); limited the circumstances in which they could initiate vehicle pursuits (only for violent felonies); imposed new training requirements with a focus on de-escalation; created a civilian panel to review complaints of police misconduct, which were rare; changed the department's priorities when it hired recruits (preferring people with emotional intelligence and some life experience, making college education mandatory, disqualifying anyone with a personal history of violence).[13] But none of these things fully captured Mike's contribution.

When social science was in its infancy, in the mid-nineteenth century, scholars sometimes used the term "ethos" to describe the overall character of a society or group. In 1957, anthropologist Clifford Geertz, trying to clarify the phrase, defined "a people's ethos" as "the tone, character, and quality of their life, its moral and aesthetic style and mood."[14]

Mike Butler brought a new ethos to the police department, a new character and tone. He liked to say that when someone calls the police—or has the police called on them—what they usually need is a neighbor, friend, coach, social worker, psychologist, minister, or ambassador from the city able to connect them with the appropriate municipal service. He wanted the men and women of Longmont PD to be those neighbors, friends, and coaches when no one else was available. It was the role he himself had tried to play, as a street cop in Boulder and as chief in Longmont. Mike hoped that if he embodied the virtues he held dear, the officers who worked for him would follow suit and come to recognize a distinctive Longmont way of policing—one that prioritized humaneness and social responsibility.

Did every officer become invested in that ethos? Of course not. But it was palpable in the hallways and offices of the Safety and Justice Center and palpable on the streets of Longmont.

8

I WILL BE HURTIN'

Eddie was in middle school but seemed more like a child in an adult body. At fourteen, with cherubic cheeks and luxuriant curly brown hair, he was five feet eight and approaching two hundred pounds, the physique he was getting used to barely contained by his long-sleeve beige camo shirt and baggy black jeans. Eddie lived with his grandfather and two younger siblings in a rented condo in Longmont. He'd been living there a while, having been cycled in and out of foster care. That was because Eddie's mother was mentally ill and on drugs; she couldn't keep a roof over her kids' heads.

Eddie's grandfather was trying to become the children's permanent legal guardian, but there'd been a hitch. Two, actually. During its investigation, Boulder County Housing and Human Services learned that the grandfather occasionally whupped the kids to punish them. Caseworkers needed to determine if this meant a spanking, which was allowable under Colorado law as long as it didn't result in physical injury, or a beating, which was not. Also, in an interview, the grandfather allegedly volunteered that decades earlier, he'd molested a stepdaughter who was living with him. He expressed contrition and said he'd learned the error of his ways. He'd never dream of repeating the behavior with his grandkids, he insisted. But if there was any risk, Housing and Human

Services couldn't sign off on the permanent guardianship—and would have to remove all three children immediately and place them elsewhere, most likely with yet another foster family.

On a Friday afternoon, caseworkers planned a visit to the condo to investigate further. They asked for a Longmont police officer to meet them there in case things became heated. They didn't have a good read on how the grandfather would react when they told him they'd need to interview the kids. Eddie, for his part, had inevitably had some anger episodes and was big enough that the caseworkers, one of whom was disabled, didn't feel completely safe around him. Officer Vijay Kailasam was dispatched.

Some cops dislike child welfare calls, thinking they're not real police work, but Vijay—six feet four and barrel-chested, with a closely cropped beard—lived for them. When he was eleven, he'd had an experience that left a deep impression. He grew up forty-five minutes from Longmont, in Greeley. Vijay's parents were Indian immigrants. His father was a doctor, an allergist, while his mother stayed home to take care of him and his two sisters. One day, his oldest sister had a breakdown. Vijay had been an anxious child anyway, prone to panic attacks, but his sister's crisis sent him into a tailspin. He refused to go to school or even leave the house.

Finally, his mother had had enough. "You have to go to school, or I'm getting the police involved," she told him. Vijay called her bluff, and she called his.

Two Greeley police officers showed up, the two coolest guys he'd ever seen. They didn't try to strong-arm him; they took their time and talked to him, listening and giving him a different perspective. They told him what a hard time they'd had in their youth and reassured him that he'd find a way to work through whatever was going on. It hadn't mattered that they were white and that Vijay and his family were among the only Indian Americans in town. The cops spoke a language Vijay could relate to: they welcomed him into a fraternity of men who could acknowledge emotional pain.

Grown-up Vijay, a hunting, fishing, pickup-truck-driving country music fan with a sizable gun collection—an Indian cowboy, his sisters called him—hoped to become a K-9 or SWAT officer down the line. In the meantime, he was always on the lookout for the opportunity to be the coolest cop some kid had ever seen.

• • •

WHEN HE GOT TO THE condo, Vijay learned that the two main caseworkers assigned to Eddie and his siblings were delayed at the office and wouldn't arrive for almost an hour. They'd sent their colleague, a thirtysomething white man with a shaved head, to begin the interview. He knocked on the door holding a legal pad. Vijay—uniformed—hung back, about twenty feet behind him. It was Human Services' case, not his. His job was to stay out of the way unless needed.

In Boulder County and throughout the US, the police and child welfare authorities work closely together. Describing police involvement in child welfare, criminal justice scholar Frank Edwards notes that the police "conduct front-line surveillance of children for signs of abuse and neglect," reporting what they observe to child welfare agencies (as do teachers, medical professionals, and others); such agencies "conduct joint investigations with police"; "many police departments have . . . special units directed at child abuse and neglect"; and "police themselves handle noncriminal maltreatment investigations in some jurisdictions."[1]

Given these connections, inequities in one institution often carry over into the other. In her 2002 book *Shattered Bonds: The Color of Child Welfare*, law professor Dorothy Roberts pointed out that at that time, Black children were massively overrepresented in foster care—a staggering half of foster kids were Black—and that "once removed from their homes, Black children remain in foster care longer, are moved more often, receive fewer services, and are less likely to be either returned home or adopted than other children."[2] Since 2002, those disparities have declined, but they haven't been eliminated. Today, Black children make up 23 percent of those in foster care, still an overrepresentation since Black children are only 14 percent of the child population. As to why, critics like Roberts argue that the structural racism evident in policing also influences how child welfare agencies make their decisions. Moreover, police may be more likely to report Black families to child welfare authorities or to initiate what Edwards calls "crises of care" by arresting Black parents. (In Colorado, Latino children are overrepresented in foster care as well.)

Yet no one doubts that some kids, regardless of race or ethnicity, are at risk from their caregivers. Child welfare agencies investigate abuse or neglect allegations concerning about 7.9 million children annually. Approximately 650,000 of these children are found to have been mistreated, although the true scope of the problem is larger as many cases go unreported or slip through the investigative cracks. On average, 5 children die each day because of abuse or neglect.

Too often, child welfare agencies have failed to protect vulnerable children, or they have suspended or terminated parental rights on the basis of insufficient evidence or without adequately weighing the long-term harm that foster care placements may cause. Nevertheless, the prevailing assumption in policy circles is that if such agencies didn't exist, or if their operations were curtailed, child abuse and neglect would rise. And though the presence of the police can sometimes inflame tensions during investigations, policy makers generally also assume that without the cops there to provide backup, child welfare agencies would be toothless.

When the caseworker knocked, Eddie came to the door. His grandfather had run to the grocery store with Eddie's sister. They'd be home any minute, he said. A birdfeeder with chimes was suspended from the eave, but the air was still and the chimes silent.

The caseworker asked Eddie if they could talk while they waited. "All right," said Eddie, his hands thrust in his pockets.

"There was a concern that your grandfather was abusing you guys or neglecting you," the caseworker said bluntly. "I was wondering if you had any concerns about that."

"I wouldn't say he'd been, like, abusing or any of that," Eddie replied.

"What would you say?"

"Well, they did tell us to quit whupping them, we did that. Last time my brother and sister got whupped, 'cause I never do, was months ago."

"Do you have worries about your little brother and sister?"

"Well, I worry about how my mother will become if she gets them again. I'm hoping my mom can clean her act up and pull herself together, but honestly I don't see much hope for that."

The caseworker scratched on his legal pad. Eddie talked slowly, deliberately. From his mouth to the legal pad to the ears of a family court judge. It was a heavy load for a fourteen-year-old to bear.

"Do you have any worries about the little ones being touched inappropriately?"

"Maybe being hit but touched, no. I've never seen or heard of that happening."

"When you say hit, what does that look like?"

"Well, maybe being hit on their bottom because they've been bad. Which is very rare because most of the time nowadays we just send them to their room."

The caseworker asked if he could speak to Eddie's brother. Eddie said OK and invited him in, but Vijay piped up: "We'll talk to him out here. Just because you're not old enough to give me consent to come inside."

"Paul 305, status check?" Vijay heard on his earpiece.

"I'm Code 4, thanks," he answered. "No need for status checks."

• • •

VIJAY'S PATH INTO LAW ENFORCEMENT had been circuitous. After high school, he worked for a couple of years at a cattle feedlot in the Greeley area before entering community college. High school had been challenging for him academically and emotionally, and he needed time to get his head screwed on straight before returning to a classroom. He kept working once he finished his associate's degree and transferred to Colorado State. During the school year, he sold shoes at an athletic footwear store. Over the summer, he worked construction. To the disappointment of his father, Vijay never developed an interest in medicine. School bored him, except for some econ and criminal justice courses.

In 2010, he entered the police academy. In most states, there are two ways to become a police officer. You can enroll in a police academy on your own dime, and then once you finish, apply to various departments and hope that one hires you. Or you can get hired by a department as a recruit and have them pay your way through the academy. Thinking it would increase his chances of getting a job—because a department wouldn't have to shell out the money for six months of paid training—Vijay chose the first option. He soon realized that his timing was off. He had been slow to finish his bachelor's degree. Near the end of his time in college, he started dating his future wife, Meghan, whom he'd known since childhood. Meghan was about to finish med school. The next step in her career was a residency, and there was no guarantee she'd get one in Colorado, the only state in which Vijay would be eligible to work as a cop.

Sure enough, she was offered a great residency back East, at Penn State. Vijay followed, with a plan mapped out to return to Colorado when her residency was done. The question was what he'd do for work until then.

In Hershey, where Penn State's medical campus is located, he could have used his degree in economics to land a middle-management position of some sort, preparing charts and graphs in a cubicle. He chose to take a job in car sales. He found it satisfying to connect with customers even if they came from different backgrounds than his—and in small-town Pennsylvania, they almost all did. Selling cars, Vijay learned the importance of listening to people, to what they wanted, to their stories of having gotten ripped off, or treated well, the last time they came into a dealership. He learned the value of slowing down with a sale. Doing things right.

A few years later, he and Meghan decided to move home, and Vijay sent his resume to police departments up and down the Front Range. From Fort Collins to Colorado Springs, business was going like gangbusters: aerospace, biotech, energy, light manufacturing, marijuana. People were moving from California, New York, Illinois, wanting jobs in a place where their families could prosper, spread out a little, and breathe the mountain air. Tract homes and generic apartment communities were sprouting overnight. It seemed like every police agency was hiring.

When Longmont called, Vijay discovered he was a natural fit. It was

2018, and he was in his early thirties. He wasn't a kid anymore. He'd dealt with some serious stuff in his life and had come out the other side. He was educated, but he wasn't only smart on paper. He'd spent years working in jobs that put a premium on people skills. He wanted to become a police officer to protect and help, not to lock up as many "scumbags" as possible. On its end, Longmont PD prized maturity and sound judgment in handling cases over racking up arrests or dominating suspects. The officers interviewing Vijay saw him as a kindred spirit. Mike saw him as a kindred spirit.

Vijay's basic training certification had expired, so Longmont sent him through the academy a second time, now at the department's expense. There's been a great deal of discussion lately about how short and deficient US police training is compared to that offered in other countries.[3] Indeed, Vijay's experience of attending the academy again (effectively doubling the length of his basic training) was a boon. He got a useful refresher on criminal law. For the practical side of the job—arrest and control, firearms, defensive tactics, pursuit driving, de-escalation—more hours of training meant greater mastery.

Once Vijay was sworn in, he spent four months in field training, riding with senior officers who showed him how to take what he'd learned in the academy and apply it to the world he'd encounter as a cop. Those officers taught him about Longmont PD's policies and procedures. Most important, from his field training officers, Vijay soaked up the Longmont ethos that Mike had tried to develop: Citizens are extended family. The use of force is a last resort. Everyone has gifts to give the world.

• • •

THE GRANDFATHER ARRIVED IN A pickup truck with Eddie's sister before the caseworker got very far in his interview with the brother. Vijay met him in the parking lot of the complex. The grandfather, who was Mexican American, was carrying a gallon of milk in one hand, plastic bags of groceries in the other.

"Hey, Martin, right?"

"Yeah."

"I'm here with DHHS. They're here to speak with the kids."

"Who?"

"The kids."

"Oh, OK."

"How are you?" Vijay said to the girl, who was in a pink top that she kept tugging. "You having a good day?"

"Mm-hmm," she said.

Martin made his way to the front door, girl in tow. When the caseworker explained in vague terms why he was there, Martin acted nonchalant. He went to put the groceries away while the caseworker talked to Eddie's brother and then moved on to his sister. Eddie wandered inside.

Once the interviews were done, Martin invited the caseworker and Vijay to take a tour of the condo. It was clean and organized. The little kids shared a room on the top floor across the hall from their grandfather. Eddie slept in the unfinished basement. He joined them as Martin showed the others around. The four of them got to talking about Eddie's mother.

"She struggles with substances?" the caseworker asked.

"I don't know what substance she was on," Eddie said, "but when she was coming down off of it, she was *mean*."

Martin started telling the caseworker his life story: the jobs he'd had, where he'd lived. The caseworker thanked Martin for the tour. He told him that he'd call his colleagues to find out when they'd be getting there. He and Vijay went outside to wait.

Before long, the other caseworkers arrived. Both men were Black, one young, the other older with a pronounced limp. They went in to talk to Martin at his small dining room table while the kids stayed upstairs.

They had no choice but to remove Eddie and his siblings from the home, the caseworkers said, and place them in foster care until they could make a final determination as to their safety. There were too many unanswered questions. Martin wasn't happy about it but told them he understood.

Vijay had been on the call for an hour at this point. He asked if he was still needed; all had been calm so far. The caseworkers said he should stick around for a while longer. They didn't think Eddie would take well to the news that he'd have to up and leave.

They were right. Eddie had overheard bits of the conversation and came down the stairs mumbling, "I don't want to hurt anybody." A switch had flipped. He wasn't the same kid he'd been a few minutes ago.

"Come on, have a seat, Eddie," the older caseworker said.

"I heard something," Eddie replied. "I ain't signing anything. If you have plans to remove me from my grandfather and his household, I will not agree. I will put up a physical fight. I will be hurtin'."

"You won't hurt me, Eddie," the caseworker told him—a statement of fact, not a threat. Vijay was right there to keep the peace.

Eddie began shaking and shifting his weight back and forth and clenching his fists. "I won't hurt you. But if you try to move me from this household, which I've been at for most of my fucking life, I will fuck anybody up!"

"Eddie, relax your hands. Grab a seat, buddy. Take a deep breath."

Eddie sat.

"I don't care if you take my brother and sister. The one person I have lived with for my entire life, you will not take me from him. I will not go willingly. I'm giving you a fair warning."

The older caseworker sat with his elbow on the table and his chin in his hand. "Unfortunately, I've been down this road before," he said. "Um, this can get really unpleasant."

"Oh, I know it can," Eddie said, trying to sound ominous. "And I'm warning you." His threats were delivered with cinematic flair.

"We want to work with you."

"You're not working with me if you're taking me away from my fucking household!" Eddie yelled.

"Well, we don't have a choice."

"I don't give a fuck what your choice is. I'll fucking take all of you with me if I have to." He rose.

"Paul 305," Vijay said over the radio to his dispatcher. "Do you have another unit available to head this way?" He'd been trying to give the caseworkers space to do their thing, but it looked like he might have to step in.

"I know my grandpa's past," Eddie now said. "But I don't give a fuck about it. Because it's in the past. If you can't pull your heads out of your asses, I'm going to fucking hurt you!" Eddie was shouting, but he was crying, too, radiating pain.

"Do you want to sit down and talk about this a little bit more?" the caseworker said.

Eddie regained his composure. "I've been through fucking hell, and I am not going back to one of these shitty fucking holes that you think are so wonderful."

"How do we resolve this?"

"I don't know," Eddie said. "I'm thinking of breaking all your fucking noses. But I'm not doing that because I'm civilized."

"So what do we do?"

"Maybe pull your head out of your ass and notice that my grandpa's not a bad person."

"I never said your granddad was a bad person. OK? We have a job we have to do. You yelling at me, you being frustrated, you being pissed off, it's not going to change that."

"This ain't frustration," said Eddie. He was shaking again. "This is preparing to go to my funeral."

"Would you go to your aunt's?" suggested the caseworker.

"I don't have any family members I like," said Eddie. "I don't want to become any more of a fucking burden."

"Why are you a burden? I've got three kids at home, and they're not burdens."

"You're fucking stupid!" shrieked Eddie. He slammed his fists on the table and stormed toward the kitchen area. That's when Vijay got involved. Kitchens have knives.

"Eddie, hey, you want to come outside with me real quick," Vijay said in a voice that was louder than the caseworker's but not unkind.

Eddie spun around. "I'm not going with you. I'm not going outside," he said, barely able to squeeze the words from his mouth.

"I just want to talk to you outside, man, that's all," said Vijay. "I got no reason to do anything else."

Vijay's assurance registered. Eddie headed out the front door with Vijay following him.

"Take a deep breath," Vijay told Eddie. Connecting with troubled youth, that was his whole thing.

"Deep breaths, through your nose and out your mouth," Vijay said. Eddie did it. De-escalation 101.

"I can't imagine how hard this is for you right now, man. They don't want to do this, but they have rules they have to follow."

"I'm going to show them my rules."

"You don't want to do that."

"What, are you going to shoot me?"

"No."

Vijay's backup, Officer Kurtis Hampton, arrived. A younger white cop, he was wearing a Longmont PD ball cap. Vijay said, "This is my buddy Kurtis."

"What's your name?" asked Kurtis.

"Eddie."

"Eddie, nice to meet you."

"DHHS is moving the kids, including Eddie, and we're not happy with that," Vijay explained to Kurtis.

"That's terrible. I'm sorry to hear that," said Kurtis.

"It's not happening. I can tell you guys that much," Eddie said, trying to catch Vijay's eye.

"I can't imagine what that feels like," Vijay said. "I honestly can't because I've never been there."

"Ripped from the person who's basically your fucking dad. You never had that happen, did you?"

"No, I didn't."

"They're not taking me from my grandpa because he raised me for most of my life. I know he's not a bad person, and I know he's changed. If it wasn't for my fucking grandpa . . . But you don't give a fuck!"

"I do," said Vijay. "That's why I'm here talking to you. I absolutely do give a fuck. I'm here as a sounding board for you right now because I saw what happened inside."

“I’m gonna fucking kill them all,” said Eddie. “If they take me, they’re going to the grave with me.”

“What happens if your brother and sister go, and they need you?” asked Kurtis.

“It’s tough, right?” Kurtis continued. “I’m one of five kids. It’s hard. I feel you on that. Do you like it in Longmont?”

The question was so mundane that it caused Eddie to stop and think for a moment—another effective de-escalation tactic.

“I like it better in Longmont than anywhere.”

“I’ve lived in Longmont my whole life. It’s a good town.”

“Other than the people who live in it,” was Eddie’s retort.

“You spend a lot of time out at Union?” Kurtis asked. Union is a reservoir and nature area.

“Yeah, sometimes,” Eddie said. “I jump the fence and go fishing.”

“Oh yeah?” said Kurtis. “What’s the biggest one you caught out there?”

“Biggest one I caught was maybe half a foot.”

Kurtis excused himself and went inside to speak with the caseworkers.

“I can’t get one fucking break, can I?” Eddie said to Vijay. “I’ve been in a shithole my entire fucking life; you want to take it away?” He suddenly began hyperventilating.

“Take some deep breaths, buddy,” said Vijay. “Grab a seat for me.”

“I’ll stand right here.”

“OK,” said Vijay. He would have preferred that Eddie sit, but he wasn’t going to force it. “Try to lower that heart rate a little bit. I get you’re pissed, dude. I get it.”

“The only thing I know that’s ever been good to me was my grandpa. Because he’s the only person I’ve ever fucking trusted. I’ve fucked up my entire life. . . . I don’t go to fucking school, for fuck’s sake. I hate it. I already learned what I need to be alive.”

“You’re fourteen years old,” said Vijay. “There’s nothing unique about hating school. I hated school, too.”

Eddie leaned against the wall that separated his front door area from his neighbor's.

After a few minutes, Kurtis came back outside.

"So did they run you down on what they're trying to work on for you?" Kurtis asked.

"No," said Eddie.

"That's why I went inside, to get an update," said Kurtis. "They're trying to find a way to let you stay here. Can I offer a piece of advice? Best thing you can do to help that is to try to calm down just a little bit. Because the more escalated you get, the worse it's going to be for them. All I'm doing, all my partner Vijay is doing here, is we're trying to be the middleman. Because we don't have a dog in this fight, do we? I can't pretend to be in your shoes at all. My biggest concern, Eddie, is I don't want anybody to get hurt."

If Mike Butler could have been there that day to see Vijay and Kurtis in action, he would have been pleased. This was the compassionate policing he dreamed of, though he understood that sometimes compassion can only get you so far.

"I'm not someone who's violent. I don't like blood. But if things come to things, I will," said Eddie.

"But see, that's what I'm talking about," said Kurtis. "I'm trying to find a way to get you to stay here, and you're threatening to kill people. I need you to help me help you."

"I know," said Eddie. "I've had the same kind of anger issues all my life."

"Play the game with me," said Kurtis. "Try to work on your breathing. Don't make any threats to these guys."

"I've already thrown more than enough threats to get myself locked up," said Eddie. "Now it's just up to my mind, whatever my mind wants to do."

"Have we not treated you with respect?" asked Kurtis.

"You two have," said Eddie. "These cocksuckers inside ain't done shit."

"Can I tell you where I think these guys are coming from?" said Vijay. "This isn't a permanent thing. It's just so that they can do their investigation thoroughly."

"How are they going to do it thoroughly? They've already been fucking my entire family over for the past few months."

"Let's just have a conversation," said Vijay. "There's no need to yell at me, right? We're cool?"

"Yes, I trust you more than most," said Eddie.

"Well, I appreciate that."

Two other Longmont officers arrived, one a tall, thin bald white man with glasses, the other a white woman with shoulder-length brown hair and a full sleeve tattoo of flowers and leaves.

Seeing the two new cops, Eddie said, "I can't do it," under his breath. He pivoted and made a beeline for the front door. He tried the knob, but Kurtis had made a point of locking it on his way out. Vijay sprang right up but stopped short of grabbing him. "Eddie, you don't want to do that," he said.

Eddie balled his hand into a fist. Kurtis grabbed his Taser.

"Go away, Mr. Midget," he yelled to Kurtis, who was shorter than his colleagues.

"I will tase you, man. I don't want to have to do that."

"Tase me. Tase me. I'm wearing more than enough clothes to fucking stop it!"

The tall officer, who had more years on the job than the others, intervened. "Eddie, you've been talking to my partners. We're going to go out to the hospital." News of the foster care placement had triggered something in Eddie, and he seemed incapable of calming down, no matter how much de-escalation the police attempted. Quietly among themselves on the radio so that Eddie wouldn't hear, they'd decided to take him for an emergency psychiatric evaluation.

"I'm not going back. Last time, I got sent to the goddam psych ward. I'm not going."

"What can we do to get you to cooperate with us?" asked the tall officer.

"Oh, I know. . . . Leave me with my fucking family!"

Eddie was standing inches from his door. The cops took positions around him in case they had to keep him from going inside, where the caseworkers were.

"This pussy thinks he's going to tase me," Eddie said, nervously eyeing them but pointing to Kurtis.

"We don't want to get hurt," said Kurtis.

"A fucking fourteen-year-old is going to hurt you," said Eddie, mockingly. "Fucking pull your head out of your ass."

"You can't threaten people's lives, man," said Kurtis.

"If we take you to the hospital, the doctor's gonna talk with you. If he doesn't see any reason to keep you there, he'll let you go," added the tall officer.

"He will see a reason! I'm violent as fuck right now!" said Eddie.

Just then, Eddie's grandfather opened the door. Eddie seized the opportunity and bolted inside. The tall officer was only one step behind him, Kurtis behind the tall officer, Vijay behind them. The tall officer tried to grab Eddie by one arm, but Eddie pushed him off and struck the officer repeatedly in the chest before running toward the living room area, toward the brown leather sofa where, a day before, he might have hung out watching TV with his brother and sister. The tall officer and Kurtis and Vijay tackled him, knocking the sofa over. Eddie fought back with every ounce of his angry fourteen-year-old being. He rolled forward, crashing into a box of Huggies on the floor that had been converted into a makeshift toy chest. His nose began to bleed.

"Not good, guys!" yelled Martin from the stairwell. "I hope you don't get a choke hold on him."

Longmont PD had a policy prohibiting choke holds, but still, given Eddie's age and how badly the officers felt about what he'd been through, a choke hold would never have crossed their minds. Their aim was to get Eddie's hands behind his back so they could handcuff him. He was determined to keep that from happening and attempted to kick any officers within striking distance of his legs.

"You're not fucking taking me! Let me go! Argh!" Now on his stomach, Eddie tucked his arms beneath him so that the officers wouldn't have access. They managed to pry his left arm out, pulled it behind his back, and got one cuff on.

"Grab this arm," the tall officer said to Vijay, nodding toward the other limb. Vijay opened his extendable baton and placed it in Eddie's armpit area, hoping to get some leverage.

"I'm not doing it willingly unless you fucking let go!" Eddie yelled.

It took them half a minute to get the other arm out and cuffed.

Eddie wasn't giving up and kept kicking. "Let's hobble him," said the tall officer. The female officer took charge, tying straps around Eddie's legs.

"Fucking pussy ass n——!" Eddie yelled, to no one in particular. "I can't fucking breathe!" He let out a series of high-pitched wails.

"There's nobody on top of you," said Kurtis. The cops were sitting on either side of Eddie, holding the cuffs in place at his lower back. It had been such an intense scuffle it was no wonder Eddie felt out of breath.

"I'm going to shoot all of you!" yelled Eddie. "You're all fucking dying!"

"Stop struggling with us. We don't want to hurt you," said the tall officer. They rolled Eddie onto his side to improve his breathing. "Start medical," the tall officer told dispatch.

"Take some deep breaths, Eddie," said Vijay.

"I'm going to fucking kill you, you fuck. You'll be dead in a fucking week. Let me sit on the fucking couch!"

"No, you're under arrest for assaulting a police officer," said the tall officer. It was one thing to be a scared kid and mouth off, another to repeatedly punch a cop. Even in forgiving Longmont, that was over the line, though Vijay and his colleagues would spend the next couple of days debating whether an arrest had been the best course of action or whether something like a restorative justice referral might have been more appropriate.

That's when Eddie craned his neck and tried to bite Vijay, who was standing next to him, on the leg. Vijay snatched his leg away before Eddie could penetrate the skin.

"Don't you fucking bite me," Vijay said.

"That's enough of that," Kurtis said to Eddie.

"Then leave me alone!" said Eddie, who was more sobbing than anything else.

"You don't understand, you're under arrest," said Kurtis. "You've got to stop this."

"My lawyer is going to hear about this!" said Martin from the stairs.

The police kept Eddie on his side in his living room until the Longmont fire department arrived. He refused to calm down, continuing to yank at the cuffs and trying to kick his way through the hobble. Although he was bound for juvie, he'd have to go to the hospital first for that emergency evaluation and for medical clearance, since his nose was bleeding, and he was complaining of breathlessness. To get there, he'd have to be placed on a gurney and tied down with soft restraints, but he was resisting too much for the police and fire—even working together—to get him on the gurney safely. The paramedics administered a sedative, which relaxed him straightaway. The threats stopped pouring out. While controlling Eddie's hands, the cops released the cuffs, put him on the gurney, and secured the restraints. He was wheeled off.

VIJAY, THE INDIAN COWBOY, WENT home that night and cried—for Eddie and his siblings and the cruel hand they'd been dealt in life.

You could say that Eddie's case revealed the flaws in the child welfare system, and you wouldn't be wrong. But the caseworkers did have reason to investigate. You could say that it shows why the police shouldn't be involved in noncriminal matters, especially situations involving kids and mental health. Yet if Vijay and his colleagues hadn't been there, there's a real possibility that Eddie would have assaulted the caseworkers, resulting in injury to them and more serious criminal charges. (Since no one had been injured, a judge decided to send Eddie into a diversion program, which in Boulder County often means community service rather than jail time.) You could say that Eddie's case proves that police reform doesn't work—because, despite the positive changes Mike had made to Longmont PD, the cops' attempts at de-escalation failed. But perhaps they could have succeeded, if Eddie's emotional state had been different that day. As bad as the outcome was, the same circumstance—a teenager threatening to kill social workers and police—handled by a different department and different officers, accustomed to a different culture of policing, could have ended in tragedy.

9

TOY HANDCUFFS

We need bodies upstairs. The cases keep coming, and we're down four or five people at least."

Sergeant Todd Chambers, who supervised the Persons Crimes Unit of Longmont PD's detective bureau, was making an impassioned pitch to Mike and Deputy Chief Jeff Satur during a weekly command meeting. White and middle-aged, Chambers was desperate for more detectives.

Longmont didn't see much street crime. But there were occasional shootings, stabbings, robberies. Child abuse cases and domestic violence never let up. All required investigation, and Chambers reminded Mike, Jeff, and the other members of the command staff that detective work was more time-consuming than it used to be. Suspects now left electronic trails of their whereabouts and activities, recorded in text messages, social media posts, and images captured by doorbell surveillance cameras.

Accessing that trove of evidence took effort. Detectives had to write warrants nonstop and become unofficial members of the Geek Squad, learning the technical ins and outs of new devices every year. If they couldn't figure out how to transfer a video clip from a surveillance system to the PD's cloud-based platform for electronic evidence storage, then it wouldn't get done. So investigations were now extremely demanding.

Which would be fine, if there were enough detectives to do the work. But the unit wasn't anywhere close to full staffing. Chambers hadn't been allowed to hire the people he needed from other units because they were short-staffed as well.

The issue wasn't Longmont's budget; money was available. The problem, as everyone in the room knew, was that in 2020—even before the killing of George Floyd—fewer and fewer qualified people wanted to become cops. Hampering recruitment, in Colorado and nationally, was a tight labor market, meaning good job opportunities outside law enforcement; a distaste among young adults for inflexible shift work; mounting anti-police sentiment; and fear of doing something wrong on the job that would turn one into the next viral video sensation.

Chambers said he understood the difficulties. He knew patrol was hurting. So was traffic. But no matter how you sliced it, he didn't have the staff to keep pace with the current caseload. So solvable cases were going unsolved, and people who'd committed crimes were getting away with them.

"Something's got to give," Chambers said. Maybe patrol could run an efficiency review, to check if they really needed all their officers. Maybe the department could invest in some time-saving technology, like automated transcription for interviews. Transcribing took detectives forever: two, three, four hours a case. Or maybe, against the odds, Longmont PD could move to quickly appoint enough cops to fill out the patrol ranks, allowing the detective bureau to start recruiting again.

Mike thanked Chambers for his presentation. He'd raised good points. Efficiency reviews could be helpful when done right, Mike said, though they were a time suck. The department could look into automated transcription. There were also some new hires on the way. Mike turned to Jeff for an exact count. The number wasn't as large as anyone would have liked.

The staffing circumstances that day may have been particularly dire, but pitches like the one Chambers made weren't unusual. Mike ran a bottom-up police organization, one that valued the views and contributions of each of its members. Except for meetings involving confidential personnel matters or ongoing criminal investigations, regular department meetings were open to everyone on the force. Sometimes as many as sixty people would show up, including the janitorial staff, if the discussion was relevant to them. For people who couldn't attend, minutes were distributed after. Everyone was encouraged to come forward with suggestions and proposals for improving the PD and to weigh in if new policies were under consideration. "We hire the best and the brightest, and we treat them like adults," Mike said. That meant not presuming that the people at the top of the organizational chart knew more or were wiser than frontline cops, the opposite of the hierarchical, chain-of-command model preferred by most police chiefs.

• • •

THE 1970S AND 1980S WERE a fruitful time for research on police culture. Two books from that period, a period formative for Mike's thinking, help explain what he'd tried to accomplish in Longmont.

Working the Street, by political scientist Michael K. Brown, was published in 1981.[1] As a graduate student at UCLA, Brown had commenced a study of three Southern California police agencies: Inglewood, Redondo Beach, and the LAPD. He spent five months riding with officers, observing their behavior, and interviewing them.

The questions Brown asked were devised after thinking about James Q. Wilson's *Varieties of Police Behavior*. It made sense to Brown that policing styles might vary from department to department, but he wasn't convinced that Wilson had conceptualized that variation in the right way. He wondered whether there was more nuance to police culture than Wilson had appreciated. Brown also found it puzzling that Wilson advanced an oversimplified argument about how departments developed their styles—that it came down to the tenor of local politics.

In Brown's view, the defining feature of police work is that the police are empowered to use physical coercion if necessary to get people to obey the law and comply with their requests. The police don't always use force; what matters is that they can.

For scholars like William Westley and Jerome Skolnick, the pioneers of police culture research, the coercive aspect of policing was, in the final analysis, why the public dislikes cops. By contrast, Brown thought the main consequence of coercion was chronic anxiety among officers. The possibility of a fight, even a shootout, is ever present. Add to that the other inherent uncertainties of police work, and the result is a job filled with stress and fear.

Brown argued that the principal aspects of police culture—loyalty to other cops, us-versus-them thinking, a shared belief in the legitimacy of police violence—arose to help officers cope with this anxiety. Were cops unable to count on their colleagues' reassurance that their behavior is justified and that someone would always have their back, they'd quit showing up for work.

Like Wilson, however, Brown believed variation around this cultural kernel was possible. According to Brown, the fact that police officers are granted discretion means that the loyalty and groupthink aspects of their culture are counterbalanced by a tendency that doesn't usually come to mind in connection with policing: individualism. Cops know that their peers will all take somewhat different approaches to handling cases and calls, and they value the freedom that makes this possible.

In police agencies, individualism is what allows cultural variation to take root. Brown's research suggested this variation had to do with how officers understood their jobs as crime fighters. While the police spend only a fraction of their time on criminal matters, "most patrolmen define their task largely as the responsibility for controlling crime."[2] The question was how "aggressive" officers were in going after criminals, "and how selective they were in the enforcement of the law."[3]

Based on his observations of the three Southern California agencies, Brown identified four "operational styles" that officers might adopt. Cops who were highly aggressive and selective about the offenses they went after he termed "old style crime fighters." They spent "most of their free time . . . prowling down darkened streets, often with the car lights out . . . stopping any vehicle or individual that looks even remotely suspicious," the goal to apprehend serious offenders or those likely to commit major crimes.[4] These cops, Brown found, though keen to make arrests, were cynical about the justice system and weren't averse to using violence when dealing with suspects, reasoning that criminals have no rights.

Similar in some respects was the "clean beat crime fighter." Officers of this type were aggressive but not at all selective. As clean beat crime fighters saw it, "an effective patrolman . . . looks for all kinds of violations on his beat, from jaywalking to homicide, and makes as many stops as he can."[5] Brown told the story of a terrible LAPD officer he rode with, a man he called Appleby. This cop drove around furiously stopping drunks, harassing teenage couples in cars, and accosting jaywalking tourists, to no particular end and succeeding only in angering the community.

"Professional style" officers were different. "These patrolmen," wrote Brown, "are legalistic without being rigid." Professional-style officers strove to follow all the policies and procedures of their departments but would "temper" their compliance with "a judicious understanding of the foibles of human nature."[6]

The last group of officers exhibited a "service style": "What distinguishes them from the other three styles is their belief that crime suppression is *not* the most important goal of a police department. They argue that the police should take a positive role in assisting people to solve their problems."[7]

Brown's approach allowed him to measure the proportion of officers in each department who embraced one of these four styles. He found an interesting mix. Not every officer in an agency had the same style. A department's culture of policing was best understood as its mix of operational styles.

As to why particular mixes developed in particular places, Brown acknowledged that local political culture was a factor since it could influence the choice of chief. Even more important was the role of field training officers and sergeants, who socialized the rookies. These often-overlooked figures might pass along the culture promoted by an enlightened leader (as the officers who'd trained Vijay Kailasam had done), or they might promote their own retrograde views, as shaped by a politicized police union, perhaps, or by racial resentment.

Brown suggested other contributing factors. High-crime cities tend to have more aggressive officers and therefore more aggressive policing cultures. Then there is department size: huge agencies like the LAPD include all kinds of cops, leading to a greater diversity of styles. Big departments also tend to be bogged down in bureaucracy, which could produce cynicism, as seen among old style crime fighters.

While Brown didn't address the possibilities for reform, it is reasonable to infer from his book that an ethical, effective police agency would fuse the best elements of the professional and service styles. Such a department would choose and train officers who'd be restrained, conscientious, rule abiding yet flexible, and committed to arresting offenders who posed a threat without neglecting other aspects of their job, including the charge to help people whenever they could. Old style and clean beat crime fighters would be marginalized.

That's one way of thinking about the police culture Mike had tried to nurture in Longmont: his ideal officers were a blend of Brown's professional and service styles, with respect and kindness the glue that was to hold everything together. Vijay Kailasam matched the description. He saw himself as a professional who was duty bound to follow department policy and the law. He was no RoboCop, though. He knew that justice required that he fine-tune his response to the all-too-human contours of different situations. If he had the opportunity to help someone, he would, gladly.

Yet there was another side to Longmont PD, best explained in a second book from the same era, *Policing a Free Society* (1977), by the scholar Herman Goldstein.[8] After working as the executive assistant to O. W. Wilson, Chicago's police superintendent from 1960 to 1967, Goldstein took a position at the University of Wisconsin Law School, where he stayed for decades. In the 1980s and 1990s, he was the foremost architect of "problem-oriented policing," a perspective that encourages the police to reconsider their profession. Instead of merely responding to calls for service, officers should seek out partnerships—with residents, workers at other city agencies, staff at nonprofits—to devise lasting solutions to recurrent public safety problems they encounter on their beats: intersections where pedestrians are often struck by cars, abandoned houses used as drug dens.

To become community problem solvers, Goldstein argued, cops should stop thinking of themselves only as law enforcement officers. And their supervisors should give them enough time and autonomy to work out resolutions to whatever problems they're tackling.

Many chiefs today extol problem-oriented policing. But few heed the deeper claim that Goldstein had developed earlier. On the first page of his book, he argued: "The strength of a democracy and the quality of life enjoyed by its citizens are determined in large measure by the ability of the police to discharge their duties." Not only is it impossible for people to flourish without public safety, Goldstein suggested, but the police are guardians of democratic freedoms. One of their responsibilities is "to protect the very processes and rights—such as free elections, freedom of speech, and freedom of assembly—on which continuation of a free society depends."[9] If the police perform well in this regard, liberty is preserved. If they fail, becoming agents of repression, society becomes undemocratic, and we all suffer.

Goldstein maintained that the American police weren't nearly as wedded to democratic ideals as they should be. No wonder: most efforts at police reform in the twentieth century had the narrow goal of turning cops into professional and successful crime fighters, nothing more. That aim wasn't to be scoffed at. Inefficiency and corruption were bad. But while the country had seen occasional attempts to force the police to abide by the Constitution, there'd never been a major reform drive geared at recasting officers as bulwarks of democracy. "A concern for preserving and extending democratic values" should "be made the ethos of professional police work," Goldstein insisted. We should "be committed—aggressively, overtly, and unashamedly—to creating a system of policing in which this is the foremost goal."[10]

How might such a lofty purpose be achieved? "Upgrading police personnel" would be a start.[11] Goldstein didn't mean (as many had argued for during earlier periods of reform) hiring those who scored best on civil service exams; there was no reason to believe they'd be more committed to democracy than anyone else. Racially diversifying police forces was a laudable goal, but that, too, wasn't enough. Nor was hiring college-educated officers, who might have done only specialized criminal justice coursework that wouldn't prepare them for the moral weight of the job. Rather, chiefs and recruiters should look to a new breed of candidate: individuals with democratic as opposed to authoritarian instincts; those whose first inclination would be to talk things through and to tolerate difference and nonconformity unless they crossed over into behavior that was illegal and actually dangerous.

But for such candidates to find police work appealing, the occupation itself would have to change. For starters, military hierarchy, which reformers had long seen as key to professional policing, should be deemphasized: "The rigid military structure of police agencies," Goldstein wrote, "is not only demoralizing to the officers and dysfunctional in its lack of support for democratic values. It is also wasteful in preventing administrators from taking advantage of the best talent in the agency."[12] Goldstein didn't propose abandoning hierarchy and rank structure entirely, but he thought that departments should move toward becoming more internally democratic.

Along with this, different criteria should be used to evaluate officers; arrests should no longer be the sole metric by which police performance is judged. Cops should be encouraged to explore alternative ways of dealing with people and their conflicts, including methods outside the criminal justice system such as mediation. This would benefit society: arrest and incarceration, though sometimes necessary, are no cure-all for urban ills, and often cause more problems than they solve. Another reason for shifting the focus of police work was that democratically inclined cops would appreciate having an array of options at their disposal, so that they might respond to calls as a broad-minded public would want them to.

Finally, chiefs should use their influence to reshape the culture of policing. "Perhaps more important than . . . administrative devices," Goldstein summed up, "is the need for aggressive advocacy by police leaders of a quality of police service that is more responsive to the diverse needs of the community, that is more sensitive to humanitarian concerns, and that reflects a full awareness of the delicate nature of the police function in a democracy. A skillful administrator who sincerely stands for these things and who manifests his values in everything he does—especially in the numerous opportunities he has for communicating both with his community and with his personnel—has tremendous potential for eliciting support for his values from his subordinates."[13]

Mike Butler was a proponent of problem-oriented policing. Unlike other chiefs who were drawn only to that one aspect of Goldstein's work, however, Mike was taken with the democratic concerns of *Policing a Free Society*. The department he assembled in Longmont and the ethos he evolved were exactly what Goldstein had in mind. Longmont PD was meant to be a police agency that—as Mike said—"encouraged, enhanced, and supported democratic principles and active citizenship in the community." The officers he hired would share that sensibility.

• • •

WHATEVER THE FACTORS DRIVING DOWN police recruitment, they weren't issues for Edna Munoz. Edna, twenty-eight, had known since she was a child that she was going to be a police officer. Maybe it was because she was a natural-born rule follower. Growing up, she'd been bothered when she'd seen kids jaywalk or cheat on a test at school. She'd never tattle or call people out, but she'd always hoped the kids would get caught so they wouldn't break the rules again.

Born in Mexico, Edna spent the first seven years of her life in Chihuahua. Her parents didn't have much money, but when they could afford to buy her a costume for Halloween, she dressed as a cop. One year, as Christmas was approaching, she begged her dad for toy handcuffs. Her parents thought it was adorable.

When the family immigrated to the US, settling in the Denver area, Edna's parents began pushing higher education. Her dad got a manufacturing job with Sealy, the mattress company, while her mom worked in a factory assembling lanyards and was later hired by a commercial bakery. They wanted Edna and her two younger sisters to have a more comfortable life. Edna was smart and motivated. She'd go to college, and then, her parents hoped, she'd become a lawyer or a doctor.

But Edna remained drawn to law enforcement. As she grew older, her parents found this less adorable, more worrisome. Why consign yourself to a blue-collar career if you have other options? Also, Edna was five feet four and skinny as a teenager. How could she possibly catch criminals without getting hurt? Her family was as close as could be, and shuddered at the notion of her in danger.

Edna didn't want to disappoint or upset her parents, but she brushed aside their blue-collar concern. She'd picked up their work ethic and had no problem with long hours or getting her hands dirty. And police officers in Colorado are well compensated.

The size thing, though, that was another matter. She'd had the same thought: How could she, little Edna Munoz, fight a much larger male assailant? Nearly every image of a police officer she'd seen on TV was of a huge buff guy, usually white.

After high school, Edna got a scholarship and went off to Colorado State (the same school Vijay attended). She majored in sociology with a concentration in criminal justice. She took an ethnic studies minor, focusing on Latin American and Caribbean studies, trying to stay open to other things she might want to do, but she kept coming back to policing.

During her studies, she'd occasionally sign up for a ride-along with a Front Range police agency. Being in those patrol cars felt right to her. It might have been the bubble of lawfulness that the cruisers created wherever they went, drivers slowing down, coming to a full and complete halt at stop signs, as though they were sixteen and trying to pass their driver's tests. Or that the cops she rode with were responding to calls from people who urgently needed help, who'd been victimized or felt threatened, who were in the midst of arguments about to spin dangerously out of control.

It was easy to criticize the police, to point out times when they'd mistreated people, especially minorities. Such mistreatment couldn't be ignored. But on the street, Edna perceived the police in much the same way that Herman Goldstein did: as a vital service. Without them, to her mind, citizens' lives would be immeasurably worse.

When she finished her bachelor's degree, she lost her nerve. Maybe her parents were right. Maybe becoming a police officer wasn't realistic. She found a job as a caseworker with human services in Denver doing child protection. After a few weeks of training, she was sent to investigate situations like the one involving Eddie where someone—the police, teachers, a neighbor—believed that a kid was at risk. It was difficult, consequential work. She dealt with children and families at their most vulnerable. Taking kids away from their parents, even temporarily, could cause permanent scars. Leaving them in unsafe environments was surely worse.

Edna learned to be sensitive but firm, to pay attention to what she heard and what was left unsaid. She also learned that social work wasn't for her. She didn't have the training or authority to provide kids with all the protection they needed. Nor was it the job she'd been dreaming of her whole life.

Her parents could tell she was miserable. They encouraged her to quit.

Meanwhile, she moved to a town neighboring Longmont and went for one more ride-along, with Longmont PD. The female officer she was assigned to ride with was Edna's age and no bigger physically. The cop sang the department's praises. There were a bunch of women there, she said, and it was a supportive workplace. She talked about Mike Butler in glowing terms, about his vision for humane policing. Then the officer made a DUI arrest of a big, brawny suspect who wasn't cooperative. With help from another officer providing backup, but so what? For Edna, that clinched it. Maybe I *can* do this, she thought.

EDNA MUNOZ LOVED BEING ON patrol, the job itself and its rhythms and routines. On her workdays, she'd go to the gym, shower, drive to the station, don her uniform and gear, sit through a generally upbeat briefing, and get a car. Most of the vehicles in Longmont's fleet were SUVs. The city sits at an elevation of 4,979 feet, and the SUVs did well in winter driving conditions. They were also easier for officers to climb in and out of a hundred times a day without torquing their backs. But because of her size, Edna would select one of the sedans, moving her seat so far forward that her tactical vest, which resembled the shell of a beetle, almost bumped the steering wheel. After testing the lights and siren, she'd pull next to her personal car and retrieve her rifle from the trunk. All Longmont officers carried rifles in addition to handguns (in case they'd need extra firepower); Edna ported hers from car to car with particular enthusiasm. She looked forward to every training day at the range, giddy at her good fortune for having a job where they paid you to practice shooting.

She'd never shot anyone and hoped she'd never have to. But being proficient with her weapons boosted her confidence. Between her rifle and her handgun, her Taser, her expandable baton, and her months of defensive tactics and de-escalation training, she felt ready for anything. "Paul 309, in service," she'd tell dispatch, flattening her vowels in that Colorado way, a hint of Spanish cadence underneath.

Edna's goals as a patrol officer were several: apprehend people who were breaking the law and who posed a threat to others; send cases to restorative justice as appropriate; assist anyone who needed help; make sure people's rights were protected; serve as a liaison to the Spanish-speaking community; be a role model.

On patrol, you never knew what would come your way. One evening, about a year after Edna finished field training, she was out by a Walmart when she saw a Chevy Trailblazer roll into an intersection and stop. She hopped on the radio and said she'd be checking a stalled vehicle, a roadway hazard. From nowhere, a young man ran up to the front passenger door of the Trailblazer, yelling and apparently trying to pull the passenger out. Edna had no clue what was going on. Was it a medical emergency? Was the man attacking someone? The Trailblazer was so filled with stuff that Edna couldn't see much through the windows. She flipped on her emergency lights and sprang from the car. She started asking questions of the man, telling him to talk to her, but he ignored her.

An older woman, in her fifties, emerged from the Trailblazer and inexplicably began fixing her hair. The young man wanted her to leave with him. Edna asked them both to sit on the curb. "No," the woman said. "I need to get my shit out of the car. I'm going."

Edna saw the driver's door open a crack. She told the driver, a man who was around the woman's age, to step from the car. She got all three to sit, and it became clear that this was a family conflict. The driver, who was the woman's boyfriend, began raising his voice, saying that the young man, the woman's son, had attacked him. He stood up; the son stood up. They started yelling, about to come to blows.

Her Taser at the ready, Edna calmed them. None would say much about what had transpired, but witnesses approached Edna. They'd seen the Trailblazer whipping through the Walmart parking lot, the woman's legs dangling from the passenger side window. Investigating more, Edna learned that the woman and her boyfriend had been living together in the vehicle, which is why it was chock-full. They'd been passing time with the woman's adult son when they got into an argument. The boyfriend wanted to take off with the woman. She refused. When the son came to her defense, the boyfriend picked up a metal pipe and chased him before pulling the woman into the Trailblazer, grabbing her by the hair as she tried to escape, and speeding away. She managed to reach over and shut off the ignition, causing the Trailblazer to glide to a stop in the intersection.

Edna arrested the man for domestic violence, kidnapping, and menacing the son. She ran his name and discovered he had a warrant for beating and trying to kidnap the same woman a few months earlier. Handcuffed inside a patrol car, he kicked and screamed, so much so that the officers assigned to assist Edna had to take him directly to the Boulder County Jail, bypassing Longmont PD's booking area.

The Trailblazer incident gave Edna serious credibility with the other officers on her shift. Edna felt good about herself, too. She'd turned a roadway hazard into a violent crime arrest. More to the point, she realized that helping women who were victims of domestic violence—a group historically neglected by law enforcement—was something she cared about very much.

10

VICTIM WHISPERER

Mike Butler believed Sandie Campanella to be the best domestic violence detective in the state of Colorado. On a Wednesday in October, Sandie—a wiry, white fifty-five-year-old with brown hair in a pixie-style cut and a penchant for beaded necklaces—made her way to an apartment complex in north Longmont.

Around noon that day, Officer Al Baldivia had been dispatched to check on a woman and her infant. The woman had sent an alarming text message to a friend. Her boyfriend had a history of attacking her, and she and her friend had code words they could use if she was in danger. Her message had read, "apartment."

The friend rushed over. The boyfriend had left already. The woman's face was swollen, she was bleeding from her lip, and she had red marks on the side of her neck. The friend encouraged her to call the police, but she didn't want to. Her friend said that she'd call, then.

"No, don't call," the woman begged.

"He's going to kill you."

"I know," she said. "He told me he would."

After the friend left the apartment, she dialed 911, telling dispatchers she thought the woman, named Lisa, might need medical attention. Baldivia couldn't get an answer at the door when he knocked, so he and his backup asked the manager of the apartment complex for keys. As they pushed the door open, they saw Lisa coming up the stairs inside. She was wearing a camouflage hoodie and held a baby in her arms.

When Baldivia asked what happened, Lisa began sobbing. She didn't want to talk. "It will just make things worse." She did tell Baldivia that she had no money, her car had broken down that morning, and she was getting evicted. The apartment was littered with half-packed moving boxes.

That's when Baldivia called Sandie. She was known in the department as a victim whisperer. Sandie could get women to talk when other officers couldn't. She'd been passionate about domestic violence cases ever since the early 1980s, when a close friend was assaulted. Sandie, Sandie's first husband, her friend, and the friend's husband—the attacker—had been in the army together, stationed in Germany. Sandie was serving as a linguist for military intelligence, her job being to translate East German radio intercepts.

One night while Sandie's husband was on duty, her friend came over. She was crying and looked as if she'd been used as a punching bag. Sandie drove her thirty minutes to the nearest American military hospital, where a female army doctor, a major or a colonel, examined her and asked how she'd been injured. Sandie's friend wouldn't say; she stared at her hands. Sandie relayed what she'd been told: that the friend and her husband had spent the day before drinking at a wine festival, and he attacked her when they returned home. Sandie expected the doctor to get on the phone and order the husband to be taken into custody. But the doctor said, "Sadly, he is outside my chain of command. I have no authority over him." That pissed Sandie off. Where was the feminist solidarity?

The next morning, they reported for duty, Sandie's friend wearing too much makeup to cover her bruises. When she stepped out for a moment, the platoon leader, a first lieutenant, asked the same question as the doctor: What happened? Sandie told him and asked what he planned to do about her friend's husband. The first lieutenant chewed on that one, and then he put on his hat. "Well, he's not in my platoon," he said and left.

Sandie was again indignant, but at her friend's request, she stopped talking about the assault. The army's callous response and the savagery of her friend's husband, a man Sandie had once found charming, stayed with her.

As a domestic violence detective, Sandie would explain to victims that unless they gave a statement, the chances were unfortunately high that their attackers would attack them again. This time they'd survived. Next time they might not. Your life is precious, Sandie would say. Your abuser might have told you otherwise, but the fact is, you matter. Talk to me so that I can take him into custody and get you out of danger.

These days, almost all police agencies in cities with populations over 250,000 have specialized domestic violence or family violence units, but fewer than half of smaller departments do. Longmont had no such unit when Mike Butler became chief in 1993. Two years later, the state of Colorado enacted a tough domestic violence law. Police in the US had long treated domestic violence in the same way as the army lieutenant of Sandie's memory: for the most part, they ignored it, unless the victim's injuries were severe. They might tell an enraged, intoxicated husband that he should find another place to sleep for the night. They might suggest to a wife with a swollen lip that she should consider looking for another husband. But rarely would they make an arrest. Many cops thought of fighting between intimate partners as a private affair within the bounds of normal.

In the 1970s and 1980s, victims' rights advocates demanded change. Domestic violence was widespread and could be deadly. They wanted to see consequences, and a well-publicized experiment carried out in Minneapolis showed that men were less likely to reoffend if they were arrested.[1]

In response, a number of states passed laws mandating that police officers make an arrest when there was any visible sign of injury in a domestic violence case. Colorado was stricter, mandating an arrest if the responding officer had probable cause to believe domestic violence had occurred, whether or not there were visible injuries. The state also broadened the definition of violence to include any criminal act meant to intimidate, such as a threat of violence.[2]

Many domestic violence cases in Colorado still went nowhere. Responding officers might make an arrest, but their reports would be skimpy. While a detective would follow up in the most serious cases, that detective rarely specialized in domestic violence and couldn't do the kind of investigation needed to secure a conviction. Domestic violence cases are unique in that usually there's no question of whodunit. You know who. The question is, how do you prove it? This requires getting victims—who've already been abused or violated by someone they trusted—to trust you, a stranger, enough to tell you the whole story, or at least as much as necessary for a successful prosecution. But victim whispering was a skill that grizzled, general-purpose detectives didn't have.

In the 1990s, domestic violence flared in Longmont. The city saw a rash of domestic homicides. Even in cases that weren't fatal, injuries to victims were grave. No one knew why. Mike recognized that this was the most serious crime problem Longmont faced at the time. When people considering a move there asked him whether the city was safe, he'd say, "It depends who you live with."

To Mike, violent domestic partners displayed weakness of character and emotional immaturity, which he presumed was rooted in childhood trauma, mental illness, drug or alcohol abuse, or a feeling of failure or rejection. The victim became a convenient scapegoat. Mike believed, further, that no one with a well-developed sense of compassion or mutuality would ever strike a person they claimed to love out of anger. In this way, domestic violence betrayed spiritual emptiness.

While therapy or a journey of self-discovery might help an abuser manage their rage and pain, Mike thought that the community could take steps to address the problem of domestic violence as well. He and Mary Kopman, who ran Longmont's safe shelter, came up with the Longmont Ending Violence Initiative (LEVI), which raised awareness of domestic violence through school and community presentations and ribbon-wearing campaigns, and served as an informational and service hub for victims.

Longmont PD would also have to do more. Colorado's mandatory arrest law meant that Longmont cops couldn't divert domestic violence cases to the restorative justice program if they wanted to. (And many victim advocates argue that such cases aren't appropriate for restorative justice, as the key to a woman's safety may be to prevent future contact with her abuser.) For the department to ramp up its enforcement efforts, patrol officers needed better training in conducting their initial investigations so that they wouldn't botch an arrest by not knowing how to interview a victim or locate witnesses. Improved detective work was another must.

In 1995, Greg Malsam, an energetic day-shift patrol officer, went to one of Mike's weekly command meetings and gave a data-backed presentation on how many domestic violence cases fell apart due to a lack of timely follow-up. He got Mike's attention. Malsam volunteered to take charge of the department's follow-up when he wasn't handling other calls. A few years later, as LEVI was being rolled out, Malsam persuaded Mike that two officers should be assigned specifically to domestic violence. That two-person, uniformed unit was later absorbed by the detective bureau. Sandie joined in 2010, after Malsam had rotated off to auto theft.

At the north Longmont apartment, Sandie introduced herself to Lisa—or rather reintroduced herself. They'd talked once before. Four months earlier, a different case with Lisa as the victim had landed on Sandie's desk. Lisa, who struggled with drugs, was with the same boyfriend, the father of her child. He'd strangled her until she blacked out. When Lisa came to, she told her mother, who called the police. They arrested the boyfriend, and it fell to Sandie to contact Lisa and get more of a statement. But Lisa wouldn't talk. She minimized the incident and wouldn't let Sandie photograph her injuries.

That time, Sandie hadn't been able to get through to her, which wasn't uncommon. Domestic violence victims often won't call the cops. In the event that someone does call, victims generally say as little as possible. Later, they'll often recant any incriminating statement they may have made. This is for all sorts of reasons: fear of retaliation, economic repercussions for them or their children, a misguided sense of loyalty to their abusers, even love. Until a victim is ready to say enough, there may be little the police can do. Given the severity of this particular attack—a strangulation—Sandie felt frustrated she couldn't convince Lisa that the time to say enough was now. The boyfriend spent three months in jail while the DA's office tried to get its case in order, using as evidence the information Lisa had shared with her mother and other witnesses. He accepted a plea for second-degree assault and was released shortly thereafter. Although the court imposed a no-contact order, he went right back to Lisa, claiming to have changed. She welcomed him. She loved him. She wanted him to be her family.

Now in her cluttered living room, Lisa acknowledged Sandie. They sat in the middle of the mess, Lisa on a chair, Sandie on a stool, their knees six inches apart. Sandie asked what had happened that morning, but again Lisa wouldn't say. She kept clearing her throat and seemed to be in pain when she turned her head.

All she would offer was that she hadn't seen her boyfriend in a while. Before they got together, she revealed, she'd been married—to her boyfriend's brother, who had custody of her other children. They'd had a life. She'd managed a small business, and they'd owned a home. But her ex-husband had beaten her, and his brother had been the one to defend her.

Becoming more talkative, Lisa told Sandie a story so far-fetched it could only have come from desperation. Her boyfriend and her ex-husband were physically indistinguishable, she said. Today, one of them—she didn't know which—came over and began yelling, calling her an ugly slut. They wound up in the bedroom, where the man, whichever brother it was, hit her over the head, pinned her to the floor, and punched her arm. But she couldn't say who did it because it could have been either of them.

In her book *No Visible Bruises: What We Don't Know about Domestic Violence Could Kill Us*, journalist Rachel Louise Snyder notes that for victims of domestic abuse, it can often feel as though "a bear is coming at you."[3] If a bear is coming at you, you'll do anything, say anything, to get away. If you're convinced that the only thing that will get you killed is telling the truth to the police, then no lie, no matter how outlandish or implausible, is off-limits.

Sandie nodded slowly. She told Lisa that she saw marks on her neck. "Those are the kind of marks people get when they're strangled," she said. "I'm worried about those marks."

She asked Lisa to describe the sensations she'd experienced during the attack. Sometimes you can coax a statement out of an uncooperative victim that way. In describing the feel of her injuries, a woman might inadvertently say who was responsible, even while trying to protect her abuser. Sandie had never tried this tactic before, but she needed to throw a Hail Mary pass.

Lisa admitted that she'd been strangled; she couldn't recall if it was with one hand or two. She didn't think she'd gone unconscious, but she remembered everything looking black and starry. She told Sandie that she remembered her attacker saying, "I should have let my brother kill you when he had the chance"—but that statement could have been made by either man.

Crying, Lisa said that she should have never left her ex-husband. There was now no question in Sandie's mind that the boyfriend, not the ex-husband, was responsible.

Sandie was genuinely worried about the marks on Lisa's neck. She'd read about cases where a victim was strangled for a short time and seemed OK until a few hours or days later when her throat would swell so much that she stopped breathing. While the two were talking, Sandie saw the marks get darker and darker, which freaked her out.

Sandie asked whether Lisa would come with her to the hospital to be checked. "I'm worried about your health and well-being," she said. "And you've got a baby that's counting on you." If the doctor said she was fine, Sandie would drive her right back to the apartment. Sandie offered to help with her broken-down car; a service manager at an auto dealer did free work for domestic violence victims.

Lisa agreed to go, and they put a baby seat in Sandie's detective car. At the emergency room, the doctor was concerned about the swelling on the side of Lisa's neck and sent her for a scan, which revealed that her right carotid artery had been torn. She spent the next three days in the hospital on anti-clotting medication, a medical team monitoring her for signs of stroke. Had Sandie not brought her in for treatment, she could have died.

The baby slept in the hospital room with Lisa, and Sandie visited every day. As they talked, Lisa opened up about her meth and alcohol use, how she'd been homeless for a time after her divorce. She made clear how deeply she loved her kids. Lisa could be rude and off-putting, but Sandie came to adore her and thought of her as a force of nature. They became increasingly friendly in those hospital conversations—and Lisa conceded that her boyfriend was the attacker. She and Sandie exchanged cell numbers and began a text conversation that would continue for two years. It continued as Sandie listened to recordings of jailhouse phone calls in which the boyfriend confessed to the attack. It continued as Sandie tried to help Lisa get custody of her three other children, and during the time when Lisa lived out of her repaired car, Sandie working to secure housing and job interviews for her, therapy, and rehab. The exchange continued even after the boyfriend, confronted with Sandie's investigative prowess, pled guilty to first-degree assault and was sentenced to more than twenty years in prison.

• • •

SANDIE HAD HER EYES ON Edna Munoz from the first time she saw her at work. In Longmont, domestic violence detectives offer training for new patrol officers. Edna stood out from the other rookies: she was the only one taking notes. Later, as Sandie reviewed Edna's domestic violence reports from her patrol shifts, she was blown away. They were detailed and well written. Evidence collection had been handled properly. Edna treated the cases with the seriousness they deserved.

When Edna put in for detective and was promoted in November 2019, she met with Sandie to discuss the pros and cons of domestic violence investigation compared to other assignments. Sandie gave her best sales talk. The most gratifying aspect of the job, she said, is that, if everything goes well, you get to guide victims from a dark place to a better future. "Knowing and working with all these remarkable women in their most dire situations can be an amazing, beautiful experience," she told Edna. Domestic violence detectives aren't therapists or social workers, but they can be life changing for women who have no one else to turn to. DV cases also have a rewarding crime-prevention angle: if you're able to get a conviction, you know that you're keeping a victim from being attacked again, as the most serious offenders—like Lisa's boyfriend—don't stop.

The Boulder County District Attorney's Office gives an annual award to an officer who has shown distinction in their service to domestic violence victims. The award, named for Beth Haynes, a twenty-six-year-old cop with Boulder PD who was killed in a shoot-out with a domestic violence suspect, was given to Sandie in 2011; she received special recognition from the award committee again shortly before she and Edna spoke. Those were two of the proudest moments in her career, she told her.

On the flip side, she said, if you make a mistake in an investigation—mess up an interrogation or warrant, delay following up for a few days or a week because you're behind with your caseload, don't return a text right away when it's midnight and you've put in ten hours already—someone could die. The hours were insane, the pressure ridiculous.

Edna was in. Since starting at Longmont PD, she'd become a total workaholic. If you dangle an all-consuming, important job in a workaholic's face, she's going to take the bait. Sandie was no dummy.

As a new detective, Edna would work a diverse set of cases to learn the ins and outs of the craft. But mostly she'd be apprenticing with Sandie Campanella. Edna hung her uniform in her closet and went shopping for professional outfits. Her parents could relax a little; no more street patrols. Maybe the caseload would be more manageable than Sandie had described, she thought.

• • •

In March 2020, Vijay Kailasam and his wife got sick. They had fevers and body aches for eight days straight. There were fewer than three hundred confirmed COVID-19 cases in Colorado at that time. They both tested negative, but months later, Meghan, now established in her career as a pathologist, would come up positive for antibodies. She could have been exposed to the virus at her job, although pathologists have little patient contact. More likely, Vijay got it while on duty. COVID hit law enforcement hard.

In New York City, an epicenter, nearly five thousand NYPD members had contracted COVID by the end of April, with thirty-seven losing their lives. At one point, almost 20 percent of the department was out on sick leave. Police case rates were also punishingly high in Seattle, Chicago, Detroit. Soon every department and sheriff's office in the country was feeling the pain. Some agencies were diligent about trying to slow the spread of the virus. Many weren't.

Longmont PD did its best to keep its cops and the citizens of Longmont safe, yet its response was imperfect. The department made personal protective equipment available but, according to some officers, was slow to secure an adequate supply. Officers had to skip work if they had any symptoms. Indoor roll call was initially canceled and then started up again; cops wore masks and tried to socially distance. At first detectives were asked to work from home, but then they were told to come back. The department ordered officers to stay out of people's houses unless absolutely necessary. The Boulder County Jail stopped taking arrestees unless they were charged with very serious offenses, since COVID could spread like wildfire inside. Longmont cops adjusted by writing more tickets. Restorative justice went virtual. On the other side, when the SWAT team held an active shooter training for the department at its range in east Longmont, masks weren't required though dozens of cops were squeezed in for the classroom portion while lanes on the range were so close together that officers could smell each other's funk, as Sandie Campanella put it.

Vijay had a good idea where he contracted what he was pretty sure was COVID. A week before, he'd been dispatched to check on a homeless man who had called 911 saying he was feeling unwell, with fever and nausea and a cough. The fire department asked the police to respond first—maybe they thought he would be combative. Vijay found the man and gave the green light for the paramedics to come in, noticing that they had way more PPE than he did. He went back into service wondering if he'd be OK.

It didn't help that Longmont PD was in the middle of a leadership transition when COVID struck. In February, one month before the pandemic got really bad, Mike had announced his retirement. No one had thought that police or fire services would fall apart without Mike. As deputy chief, Jeff Satur had long been in charge of day-to-day police operations, and he would continue doing his job, as would his counterpart in fire. But with COVID at hand—a crisis that would disproportionately affect EMS—the time didn't seem right for a vacancy at the top or a full-fledged search for Mike's replacement. The city manager asked him to push back retirement a few months, and Mike agreed.

But while Mike remained in command officially that spring, he seemed, to some of his officers, to have one foot out the door. They didn't feel his presence as much as they used to. That made it harder for the PD to tackle the organizational inertia that every police agency faced responding to COVID. The avuncular Jeff Satur, who'd gone to high school in a town near Longmont, initially thinking that he'd be a military pilot, was a great cop and tactical leader. He'd been a detective and commander of the detective unit and had almost two decades of experience on Longmont's SWAT team, where he specialized in the deployment of less-lethal munitions. But he didn't pretend to have Mike's charm or vision, and he wasn't necessarily the type to tell his officers that they needed to completely rethink policing until the virus was defeated.

• • •

Sandie Campanella was annoyed by what she saw as the department's inconsistent COVID protocols. But as the pandemic wore on, she and Edna Munoz found themselves so crushed by the rise in domestic violence that she didn't have the energy to mount an internal protest.

As with all crime, the causes of domestic violence are both individual and social. Some people are predisposed to assaulting their intimate partners; they have experiences and traits that make them so, whether it's exposure to domestic violence as children or rage and control issues. A change in societal circumstances can also cause upticks or downturns in the rate of violence at home.

When governments around the world imposed lockdowns to control the spread of COVID, victim advocates began worrying. The lockdowns led immediately to mass unemployment. Unemployment benefits and government relief packages would mitigate this stress, but the fear was that, in the interim, domestic violence would increase as unpaid bills led to arguing and fighting.

On top of that, COVID forced drug and alcohol treatment centers to close. As addicts relapsed, some with diminished access to product (the flow of heroin and other narcotics dwindled as international borders were sealed), it stood to reason that their intimate relationships would be disturbed. The lockdowns also turned homes into pressure cookers. People were cooped up 24-7 with their partners, children, and extended family. That could only make abusive relationships worse.

In Longmont, domestic violence reports actually slowed at the start of lockdown. Victims are hesitant to call the police under normal circumstances. During COVID, the last thing anyone wanted was to summon exposed frontline workers.

That wall of silence soon began to crack. Edna and Sandie met every week on Zoom to review new cases, and as they tallied reports in the spring and summer of 2020, they kept reaching new record highs. The two of them together were now handling an average of one hundred cases every month, which was way more than they could cope with, even with both working sixty hours a week. The cases were damn serious. In the span of three weeks, they caught two unconnected assaults where the weapon was a machete and the victim nearly died.

Sandie had no choice but to plunge Edna into the deep end. In other circumstances, she might have assigned her the basic cases and helped her work her way up. But Sandie didn't have the bandwidth to manage all the heavy cases coming in, which ran the gamut from premeditated assaults to creepy ex-boyfriends attaching trackers to their ex-girlfriends' cars to monitor their moves. So Edna took half. She wasn't one to shirk.

As Edna worked her cases, she made sure to learn from Sandie. She'd listen to recordings of Sandie's victim interviews, paying close attention to how she gained trust, how she walked the fine line between investigator and friend. Edna took notes on those recordings, comparing them to Sandie's notes to see where she might improve. She also listened to Sandie's suspect interviews, noticing which interrogation techniques Sandie used at what point and when she backed off. When Edna drafted warrants, she'd ask Sandie to correct them, saving the corrections so that she could study them until she learned to produce documents that would be legally unassailable.

Sandie and Edna were good cops. But they were good cops in Mike Butler's department. Longmont PD might not have had a domestic violence unit were it not for Mike's concern with the issue and his management style, which rewarded Greg Malsam's initiative. That Mike made the department a relatively supportive place for women encouraged Edna to join. (And may have improved things in its own right. According to legal scholar and former DC police reservist Rosa Brooks, "Studies show female officers are significantly less likely to use force than male officers, more likely to display empathy and more likely to de-escalate fraught encounters."[4] In 2020, just under a quarter of Longmont cops were women, about twice the national average.) Sandie's above-and-beyond dedication to victims, whatever else they were dealing with in their lives, had also developed and flourished in the department's progressive cultural environment.

DV investigations during the pandemic were different from normal. Edna and Sandie relied much more on phone interviews, though sometimes there was no choice but to go talk to a victim, suspect, or witness in person. And they knew that most of the people they'd arrest would be let out of jail quickly; for the time being, the court system would be operating at greatly reduced capacity and at a glacial pace.

All the same, the experience Edna gained working the onslaught of cases was invaluable. Because of COVID, she saw more in six months than the average DV investigator would see in a year. Edna had always wanted to be a busy law enforcement officer assisting victims and bringing wrongdoers to justice, and now she was. She enjoyed being busy, but sometimes, understandably, she felt too busy. She and Sandie devised strategies to manage stress. On Edna's days off, Sandie would email her reminding her to "stay green"—to not work if at all possible, to spend time with friends or family. Edna would do the same for Sandie. Did either of them actually stay green? No. But it was nice to have a sister-in-arms telling you that you were supposed to.

Edna was in awe of Sandie. And the feeling was mutual, tinged only with the slightest hint of jealousy on Sandie's part. Edna was so young and energetic and focused. If Sandie had started her law enforcement career as early as Edna had, who knows what heights she might have reached? To Sandie, Edna seemed like a younger, better version of herself. Mostly, though, Sandie was bone proud of her apprentice and proud to have had a hand in shaping the career path of a woman who seemed destined to become a law enforcement star.

• • •

HOW, OVER THE DECADES, HAD Mike Butler been able to establish such an unusually positive culture and set of working practices in the Longmont police department?

Part of the answer is favorable circumstances. To say that Longmont PD had a service style, as James Q. Wilson in *Varieties of Police Behavior* understood the term, doesn't capture what was special about it. But Longmont officers did see service to the community as among their most important tasks, and it's possible—likely even—that the community's emerging suburban vibe contributed to this. Longmont's transition into a suburb accelerated on Mike's watch: the city housed a growing number of workers who were priced out of Boulder or commuted all the way down to Denver. Outside of a few pockets, Longmont wasn't a particularly wealthy suburb, and given the size of the Latino population, it was fairly diverse. But, contrary to stereotype, suburbs don't have to be wealthy or homogeneous. And more and more across the country, they're neither.

As Wilson recognized, many suburban municipalities try to attract and retain residents by offering efficient, responsive city services. In one New York town Wilson studied—Brighton, a suburb of Rochester—"the service orientation of the police" was supported "by the attitude, widely shared among the officers, that this is what the community expects of them."[5] A similar dynamic in Longmont may have made the rank and file more open to Mike's reforms (the initial resistance to restorative justice notwithstanding): he often framed his policing philosophy as a way to better serve the community. At the same time, though Longmont wasn't wealthy, its flush tax coffers—a function of rising property values—meant that the department could offer enough in pay, training, and benefits to attract top-notch, well-educated, community-minded cops like Vijay, Sandie, and Edna.

There's no evidence to suggest that progressive cities have better police departments, on average, than conservative ones, but Longmont's political orientation may have also factored into Mike's success. Colorado, formerly a Republican stronghold, has become a decidedly purple state, with Democratic politicians and liberal causes gaining ground. This change has been attributed to many things but perhaps none so much as the economy: jobs in tech, finance, and business and professional services are now more numerous than jobs in Colorado's traditional mining, ranching, agricultural, and forest sectors. Tech and finance require educated workers—and given the lay of the political land today, those workers tend to vote Democratic. Colorado's tourist and recreational economy is also booming, creating a workforce with incentives to protect the environment, a Democratic cause. Add to that people moving to Colorado from other, more progressive states, like California, and an expanding minority population. It's a recipe for political realignment.

Not all cities in Colorado moved in lockstep with this change, but Longmont did, aided by proximity to Boulder's progressive, environmentally conscious political culture. While every mayor of Longmont from 1989 to 2011 was a Republican, subsequent mayors have been Democrats or independents.

Longmont isn't Boulder. It's more pragmatic and pro-business. Residents point out that while the Boulder city council is preoccupied taking stances on global issues—as when, in 2016, it established itself as the sister city to Nablus, Palestine—the priority in Longmont is good local governance, such as blazing-fast broadband provided by the city's power and communications utility.

Still, Longmont's shift leftward probably made it easier for Mike to find allies for building a progressive police agency. The city was more conservative when he began making changes to the department in the 1990s; he was able to garner support anyway by appealing to practicality and common sense. But it would have been harder for him to make a sustained case for restorative justice or get his cops on board with easing up and practicing some version of loving-kindness had Longmont been a Bible Belt community pulled into the orbit of the populist right, with its demand for a retributive version of law and order. In a similar vein, Mike's message of inclusion, developed with Dan Benavidez, wouldn't have resonated in a town seething with anti-immigrant sentiment. If you're trying to shift the culture of a police agency, it helps if people in the community—politicians, business leaders, regular folks—can see their values reflected in the changes you want to make.

One of the factors identified by Michael K. Brown could have contributed to Mike's success as well: Longmont PD's size. An organization with 153 cops isn't an unwieldy bureaucracy, and that limited officer cynicism while allowing relations of personal trust to form between Mike and his officers. This was key. Cynicism is particularly poisonous, and trust particularly important, if a chief wants to achieve a transformation in cops' understanding of their jobs. An upshot is that it may be easier to achieve culture change in midsize or smaller police departments, contrary to the view held by some police reformers that larger, well-resourced agencies are the most malleable.

In these ways, the decks may have been stacked in Mike's favor. But there are many communities that resemble Longmont—suburban, liberal leaning, medium-sized—where the police department lacks the ethos of Longmont PD. So what made the difference?

Herman Goldstein wrote that "the police administrator is a much more important figure in the overall structure of government than is commonly recognized."[6] A good police chief needs "more than traditional managerial skill," Goldstein contended. "He must be aware of the need for change and committed to achieving it. He must be open, challenging, curious, and innovative." He also needs "a masterful capacity to relate well to the various elements that comprise his community . . . and an equally effective ability to relate to his own personnel, eliciting their best performance and coordinating their efforts toward his preestablished goals."[7] That was Mike: open, challenging, curious, innovative. He was able to articulate a compelling philosophy of policing and wind it through the entire organization so that, for many cops, it became second nature. Able to inspire his officers, he was willing to recognize and value their creativity and ingenuity. And he could work collaboratively with community members.

Contemporary sociologists Jal Mehta and Christopher Winship presented a relevant concept: moral power.[8] Why are some politicians, social movement leaders, and executives adept at making meaningful change, while others are stymied? Circumstances do matter: change is easier to bring about in some settings than in others. No less important, though, is how good leaders are at persuading people to follow them, which is where moral power comes in.

Moral power, according to Mehta and Winship, is whether a person, "by virtue of his or her perceived moral stature, is able to persuade others to adopt a particular belief or take a particular course of action."[9] Specifically, it is "a function of whether one is perceived as morally well-intentioned, morally capable, and whether one has moral standing to speak to an issue."[10] Moral power is different from charisma or social skill (which Mike had, too). The question isn't whether you're captivating or able to read a room; it's whether you appear to embody virtue.

Mike rarely discussed his spiritual beliefs at work; he was a public servant who hewed to the separation of church and state. But it would have been clear to anyone who had a conversation with him that he was driven by a moral calling. Nearly everyone in the PD had experienced an encounter with Chief Butler that left them feeling like he was a big-picture thinker impelled to make the world better and whose ideas merited close consideration, no matter how out there they might have seemed at first.

One Longmont cop, Stephen Desmond, told a story that's widely circulated in the Safety and Justice Center. It might have been apocryphal, but that didn't matter because it spoke to how Mike was perceived. One day, Stephen's buddy was running radar. He clocked a car going eleven miles over the speed limit and made the stop. When he walked up to the car, he saw that he'd pulled over Mike Butler. His buddy made a joke. "Hey, who do you think you are, the chief?" and waved him off. But Mike insisted that he receive a ticket. He'd broken the law, and he should get the same punishment as anyone else. That happened two other times that Stephen knew of. That was integrity for you. That was moral power.

PART III

LaGRANGE

11

RAISING THE CAIN

Bat, come here and talk to me. Where'd he hit you at?"

"Right here on my face, broke my glasses."

In hilly LaGrange, Georgia, a former mill town an hour southwest of Atlanta, Corporal Robbie Hall, forty-seven, had arrived at a small, run-down, one-story house—more of a shack—on a street that dead-ended into the woods. It was early evening in winter, already pitch-black and raining.

Bat, the woman who'd called the police, was fifty going on eighty. Life had not been kind to her. White, maybe five feet two, and gaunt, she had weathered, leathery hands with oversized silver rings and bulging, inflamed knuckles. Her lips were chapped to the point of bleeding, and she wore black pants and a brown coat that smelled of body odor and beer. A long tangle of blond hair cascaded down from beneath a dirty white New Orleans Saints baseball cap, an ode to her Louisiana roots. She had on Buddy Holly–style black glasses, but the left stem was missing so they were askew on her face. She leaned on the hood of Robbie's car, trying to hold herself up and catch some warmth.

"Tell me what happened today," said Robbie, in a lilting west Georgia accent. "Both y'all been drinking, right?"

"I got me two forties. He drinks that liquor. You know I don't drink no liquor. Anyway, I got home before he did, we been down looking in dumpsters. He come home, he want to get all smack mouth with me. I told him, 'Bitch, I'll knock your eyes out, go ahead and swing at me.' So he swung."

"You told him to start swinging?" Robbie asked.

"Well, he said he was gonna hit me! Look, I love the little no-dick bastard. But that motherfucker ain't gonna hit me. I'm gonna hurt *him*."

Just shy of six feet, Robbie, also white, had neatly trimmed brown hair and compact metal glasses that were beginning to accumulate drops of rain. His dark blue uniform was completed by a clip-on tie. LaGrange police chief Lou Dekmar believed that ties communicate professionalism, which he considered as important in a town of thirty-one thousand as it was in a metropolis.

"Where was y'all when you squared off?" Robbie inquired.

"We was in the living room," said Bat.

One of Robbie's colleagues, a newish cop named Jessica Tomlinson, a tall single mom who used to be a detention officer working the jails, came to provide backup. She, Robbie, and another guy on the day shift, Ryan Cadenhead (whom the cops called Clark Kent on account of his square jaw and right-parted salt-and-pepper hair), ate breakfast together most mornings.

"Was anybody in there with you?" Robbie asked. He was hoping for a witness. Bat was not the most reliable complainant. Her real name was Betty, but she insisted people call her Bat to show respect for her toughness and willingness to go batshit crazy on you. She'd only been out of prison two months after her latest sentence for aggravated assault. Her MO was to get drunk, get into fights with the men in her life, and then stab them. In the last few years, she'd racked up over a hundred contacts with the LaGrange PD.

Bat cocked her head. "Was there anybody in there with us? Shit, who else you think gonna live with Joey?"

"So what'd he hit you with, his fist?"

"Nah, I think it was a two-by-four."

Robbie had been a policeman in LaGrange for twelve years. Before that, he worked as a sheriff's deputy in Columbus, Georgia, which is next to Fort Benning, the army base. He'd grown up there. After graduating high school, a bunch of his friends went into the military, but Robbie wasn't the saluting type. The "yes, sirs" and "no, sirs" that rolled freely out of his mouth reflected Southern geniality more than martial spirit.

He got a job with the railroad, working his way up from conductor to engineer on freight trains. Some people think of railroading as an exciting life, a new city every day. Robbie hated it; he was never home to see his kids. His first daughter had come when he was twenty-five, his second three years later. Those girls meant the world to him.

Considering what else he could do, Robbie realized that law enforcement was in his DNA. Both his grandfather and uncle had served as cops. His uncle, who'd been with LaGrange PD, encouraged him to start with the sheriff's department so that he'd gain some jail experience. If you can learn how to do well inside, his uncle told him, how to talk to people who've gotten in trouble, you'll be ready for the street.

Robbie stayed with the sheriff's until he and his first wife divorced. Alimony and child support were expensive, and LaGrange PD paid better, simple as that.

After a year on the job, Robbie was one of the first LaGrange officers to become Crisis Intervention Team (CIT) certified. The police deal with many people in the throes of mental health crises. CIT-certified officers take a forty-hour training course where they learn to recognize the presence of mental illness, de-escalate situations that involve the mentally ill, and work with other service providers such as clinicians. The program started three decades ago in Memphis after police killed a man who was stabbing himself with a butcher knife and coming at the officers. If they'd had different training, they might have been able to talk him down and spare his life.

Robbie's sister, now deceased, was born with spina bifida and had spent her childhood in a wheelchair. He'd always been drawn to helping people with disabilities. In his youth he'd thought that school bullies who picked on special ed kids deserved a place in hell. He was well suited for CIT, but it was no shield against police work chipping away at his own mental health.

Not long after the training, Robbie was dispatched to a shotgun-style house. The mother of a man in his forties had called. When Robbie arrived, she was sitting on the porch. Her son was bipolar and schizophrenic, she said. She was afraid he was going to hurt himself but was scared to go inside.

Robbie waited for backup. He noticed that the house smelled of gasoline. The mother said that her son kept his lawnmower and gas in the back room. Plenty of people do that if they don't have a garage or garden shed, so Robbie didn't think too much of it.

He and the other officer entered the house, going from room to room calling the man's name, their guns unholstered just in case. The man didn't answer. There was only the back room left.

As the officers proceeded down the long hallway, the gasoline smell grew stronger. When Robbie reached the door, he peered around an inch at a time, a technique the police call "slicing the pie." The man came into view. He was sitting on a chair, gazing downward, an old metal wash bucket at his feet. The gasoline odor was overwhelming. Robbie knew right away what was in that bucket.

The man slowly looked up. Then he lit a match, tossing it in Robbie's direction.

"It was probably the closest to death I'd ever been," Robbie later said. His daughters flashed before his eyes. A voice in his head boomed at him, "Get out!" He bolted. When he reached the front door, he screamed into his radio, "Fire, gas, help!" and kept running.

The house didn't blow up. After a five-hour standoff with the SWAT team, the man was taken into custody and transported to the hospital. The fire department had been called in, and the fire marshal told Robbie there hadn't been enough oxygen in the room for the gasoline to ignite. If the window had been cracked a quarter inch, the outcome would have been very different.

Robbie could joke about the incident, but he flinched every time someone lit a match. He'd never forget the look on the man's face, a look that said, "I'm going and I'm taking you with me." It had wormed itself into Robbie's mind, into his nightmares. He tried to not let it temper his instinct for compassion.

ROBBIE WAS MORE SYMPATHETIC TO Bat than some of the LaGrange officers. He knew her story. Once, when she was riding in the back of his car, she told him that the first man she'd ever cut was her stepfather after he'd molested her. As a young woman in Baton Rouge, she'd been a stripper. Robbie thought it was clear that her violence toward men was a result of the abuse she'd suffered. But that didn't help him know how she might turn her life around. Send her to a domestic violence shelter? She'd threaten half the women in there. Find her a job? Most of the time she was barely coherent. Try to get her more welfare benefits from the state? If that was possible, she'd drink the money away—and she had no interest in getting sober.

Mean as Bat could be, Robbie worried about her. She'd only been staying with her boyfriend, Joey, a few weeks. Other than that, if she wasn't locked up, she was homeless, passing her nights under a bridge down by the Food Depot.

Robbie had been worrying about people a lot lately. Maybe it was because he was getting older and had been through some things himself. When he gave out speeding tickets, he worried whether the driver could afford the fine. When he arrested someone for drug possession, he worried whether it would help the person get clean. He fretted over his daughters, adults now. He worried about the mentally ill in LaGrange who had no one to care for them.

AS BAT WAITED BY THE cruiser with Jessica Tomlinson, Robbie went into the house. Joey sat smoking a cigarette in the dark. He, too, was emaciated and looked to be about the same age as Bat. The utilities had been cut, and the only light came from Robbie's flashlight and the tip of the cigarette when Joey took a long drag. Robbie asked Joey his version of events.

"Bat been out rumming and bumming," said Joey. "Doing her thing. She got about three forties and got drunk and come home raising hell."

"So what happened when she started raising the Cain?" asked Robbie.

"Same old shit. She started swinging, and I started ducking."

"Did you hit her?"

"No."

"How'd her glasses get broke?"

"Man, she broke 'em falling down drunk. They already been broke for days!"

Outside again, Robbie took photographs of Bat's face and hands. Other than the glasses, he couldn't see any evidence that she'd been struck. Given Bat's history, and that she seemed way drunker than Joey, Robbie thought it as likely she'd been the one to attack him. He decided to write up the incident as what's called in Georgia an "affray"—a mutual fight—and to separate Bat and Joey for the rest of the night rather than charge either of them.

Bat was OK with that. She'd begun to calm down. She told Robbie she'd sleep on a neighbor's couch, then changed her mind and asked for a ride to the Food Depot.

"You're gonna stay under the bridge tonight? I don't know if somebody else is down there or not," said Robbie.

"I don't care if they are, they ain't gonna mess with me," said Bat.

"All right," said Robbie, hesitating. Before putting her in his car, he asked, "You ain't got any guns or knives on you?"

"Youngen, that's about the stupidest question," Bat replied. Jessica patted her down and pulled a switchblade from her pocket.

They dropped her by the Food Depot and watched her shuffle off into the bushes, shoes muddier with every step. "Good ol' Bat," Robbie said ruefully, as he drove away.

ROBBIE HALL TOLD PEOPLE HE liked his job. Each day, each shift, the universe, or God, sent him to deal with a random assortment of calls. Some were humdrum, like a logging truck broken down on the hill by picturesque Lafayette Square, blocking traffic. Some were bizarre: an odor so noxious emanating from a guest room of the Great Wolf Lodge after a family checked out that the cleaning staff fainted. (Hair dye, most likely.) Some calls were terrifying, others tragic: a twenty-year-old who hung himself in a closet with a dog leash because he was having issues with his girlfriend. In a moment, any call could turn violent. The human condition in all its pain and glory was Robbie's to observe, to witness. Occasionally he would have the chance to really help someone. Police work was rarely boring, that was for sure. It was more interesting than driving a freight train or being a mail carrier, which is what his dad had done for thirty years.

• • •

LOU DEKMAR WASN'T FOND OF the phrase "police reform." As he was cooking dinner for family friends who had come to stay, retirees from Wyoming, he argued that reform is something you do if there are big problems that need fixing. That might be true for a few departments, he said. But overall, police in the US were doing much better than the media gave them credit for.

It was 2019, and Lou, sixty-four, trim and graying, was coming off a yearlong term as president of the International Association of Chiefs of Police, an elected position and an honor for any police leader. His visitors were Republicans, as was he, and he'd been impressing them with stories of arranging for President Trump to speak at the IACP convention in Florida. But as past president of the association, he had more than stories at his disposal. He had numbers, and, as he saw it, they were evidence of an effective institution.

More than 61 million Americans have contact with a police officer in any given year, he said. Only 2 percent of those contacted have force used against them, or are threatened with force, and that includes arrests of dangerous suspects. The media focuses much of its attention on lethal force, Lou noted, dishing up some roasted salmon he'd prepared, along with avocado salad and grits; his wife, Carmen, usually the chef in the family, was at work. While it's true that the police kill more than a thousand people annually—a number Lou knew was too high—all but a relatively small fraction of those cases involve people who are armed.

Lou's comments echoed public opinion polls that year, which showed that more than half of Americans had confidence in the police. Crime was way down from previous decades, a testament, Lou claimed, to smart policing strategies. Bottom line, he told his friends, the country doesn't need police reform so much as efforts by departments to build upon the already generally excellent policing services they offer.

Lou was making a vigorous case to his guests, but he was a bit of a contradiction. He could sometimes sound insensitive to the reality of what it's like to be policed, particularly for people of color, many of whom would dispute his positive characterization of the profession. Yet he was widely admired in LaGrange for his leadership on civil rights issues, and his understanding of race had recently deepened. Ultimately, his actions spoke louder than his words. The fact is that he'd reformed the heck out of LaGrange PD.

Lou was born in New Jersey, in a town called Franklin. His father dropped out of school in the sixth or seventh grade, later joined the navy, and then found factory work in Roxbury Township at the Hercules Powder plant, an explosives and munitions manufacturer, where he made nitroglycerin and dynamite. Lou's mother was a housewife.

When Lou was five or six, his parents divorced. Although the family had roots in New Jersey—his grandparents on both sides were Hungarian immigrants recruited to work in the area's zinc mines—Lou's mother decided to relocate. She was drawn to the Pacific Northwest, so she and her three children moved to Oregon, the Willamette Valley, where she remarried, her new husband a mechanic.

Lou grew up in the 1960s and early 1970s near Salem. He was a Boy Scout and member of Future Farmers of America. He can still recite the FFA Creed (as he learned it, before it was revised in 1990): "I believe in the future of farming, with a faith born not of words but of deeds." In high school, he joined a Search and Rescue Explorer post run by the Marion County Sheriff's Office. He and his fellow Explorers trained in search and survival tactics and assisted the deputies when a hunter or hiker got lost in the mountains, putting their scouting skills to the test. For Lou, it served as his introduction to the world of public safety.

In his senior year of high school, as the war in Vietnam was coming to an end, Lou and a few friends decided to join the service, aiming to take advantage of the GI Bill. His parents couldn't really afford to pay for college. At seventeen Lou enlisted in the air force, where he became a military police officer. He was sent to an air base in Cheyenne and in 1974 underwent training at the Wyoming Law Enforcement Academy, where he studied side by side with nonmilitary personnel. Then he was reassigned to a base in England.

Lou enjoyed the challenge of police work and the moral strenuousness he found it to require, so when his tour of duty was finishing, he began applying for similar jobs back in Wyoming. He took the first position he was offered, as an officer in Douglas, current population 6,351, town motto "Home of the Jackalope." After a couple of years, he moved to the Converse County Attorney's Office, where he spent almost a decade as an investigator, dealing with cases of incest, molestation, and sexual assault, as well as the occasional homicide—including one where a doctor was charged with killing his wife by injecting her with a lethal dose of migraine medicine. Lou's work was crucial to the case, and the doctor was convicted of first-degree murder.[1]

While employed full-time, Lou would drive several days a week to Casper, where he was studying for his bachelor's degree in justice administration at a branch campus of the University of Wyoming. He got married. He and Carmen had a son, with plans to have another child soon. Ambitious, he thought about higher-level law enforcement jobs. An investigator's position with the Wyoming Attorney General's office would require constant travel around the state. He'd never see his family.

Another channel was becoming a police chief. If there was one thing that truly bothered him, it was unprofessional police departments, those with lax standards that couldn't deliver security or equal justice to the citizens they served. Equity before the law was particularly important to Lou, perhaps because of a family story that his grandmother had often told him and his siblings. The zinc mine where his grandfather worked had a poor track record for safety. One day there was a cave-in, and his grandfather was killed. His grandmother, a devout Catholic, had three young children, one of them a daughter with polio. She and her husband had purchased a company house. Not long after the funeral, men from the mine came by to evict her.

Lou's Hungarian grandmother took a stand. She might not have had money or an understanding of American law, but she knew right from wrong. She fought the men off, promised to find a way to make the payments, and went to work cleaning houses, toting her disabled child around with her in a wicker basket.

The law should have shielded his grandmother, Lou always thought. The mine should have been required to operate safely, and after the accident, the company shouldn't have been able to threaten her. While another person might be inspired by such a story to pursue a career as a lawyer, suing irresponsible corporations, Lou drew the lesson that society and its institutions were obliged to treat all people fairly. Applied to the police, this means that anyone needing their aid should receive the same level of service and protection regardless of income or ethnicity or race or creed. Some of the sheriffs and chiefs Lou encountered as an investigator weren't running their agencies this way; as a police chief, he would be in a position to insist on it.

But most departments in Wyoming were so tiny that if Lou were to become chief, he wouldn't have much to sink his teeth into. Douglas PD, where he started his career, had thirteen cops; there were fewer than fifteen hundred police officers in the entire state.

At a twelve-week training he'd attended at the FBI National Academy in Quantico, Virginia, Lou befriended a guy who worked for the police in Macon, Georgia, and told him the department was hiring. Why not apply and let us send you through the police academy? (Georgia cops call it "mandate school.") After you serve for a while, you can look around for chief's jobs in the area, his friend said. It's a good life down there, with plenty of issues to tackle.

So that's what Lou did. He and his family moved to Georgia in 1987, his wife happy to get away from the snow.

Macon PD was a huge change. In Douglas, he'd worked with only a few other officers. As an investigator, his backup had been a sheriff's deputy who was sometimes an hour away. Macon, by contrast, was running thirty, thirty-five cars a shift.

He also learned that the department had a reputation. One day Lou pursued a car outside the city limits. He arrested the driver, a Black man, handcuffed him, and put him in his cruiser.

"When are you going to do it?" the man asked.

"Do what?" said Lou.

"Beat me up."

"Huh?" Lou said. "Nobody's going to beat you up."

The man didn't believe him. "Everybody knows when you run from the police, when they catch you, they beat you up."

Lou found the statement strange; he hadn't seen his new colleagues beat anyone. Had he not witnessed the abuse? Or did the man's perception of the department reflect its past more than its present?

Following through on his plan to climb the ranks, Lou moved next to the police department in Perry, a little farther south, taking a job as captain. He stayed almost four years while pursuing a master's degree in public administration.

His first chance as police chief was in Morrow, a suburb of Atlanta. Four years later, in 1995, he became chief in LaGrange, after the Morrow city manager moved there. LaGrange today is 52 percent Black, 39 percent non-Latino white, and on the periphery of the flourishing "New New South," with a median household income (in 2021) of only $37,000. Predominantly a blue-collar community, LaGrange's largest employers include Milliken & Company, which produces textiles, carpet, and industrial fabrics; Sewon America, an auto parts manufacturer; and a Walmart distribution center. LaGrange also has a small business and professional class. But 25 percent of residents live in poverty—almost double the Georgia average—with a high concentration in the Black population.

When Lou took over, LaGrange PD was a mess. Shortly before he was hired, the district attorney's office dismissed hundreds of felony arrest warrants because the police refused to send over files, presumably because the cases were so weak. The department did a terrible job maintaining control of evidence. Officers were undertrained and poorly equipped.

The department was facing lawsuits from arrestees who claimed their civil rights had been violated and from Black and female employees who were alleging discrimination. A cop in the drug unit was being investigated for assault. Nudie calendars were tacked to the station walls.

In a classic paper, the sociologist Alvin Gouldner drew a distinction between two types of workers in bureaucracies.[2] Some are "locals." Laboring at the same organization for years, they're so steeped in its ways of doing things, in its norms and values and practices, that they can't imagine anything else. Other workers are "cosmopolitans." They've spent their careers moving among different organizations and have a wider range of knowledge and experience. Cosmopolitans also pay attention to what's happening in their field nationally, reading trade publications and attending conferences, so they tend to be up to date on new developments.

Lou was a cosmopolitan. He'd done law enforcement in the military and had worked for six different agencies in two states. He'd studied at the FBI National Academy; he read. He'd seen good and bad policing. When he got to LaGrange, he cleaned house.

While working for Perry PD, Lou had gotten involved with an organization called CALEA, the Commission on Accreditation for Law Enforcement Agencies. CALEA will accredit a police department—certify that it's being run professionally—if the department aligns its policies and procedures with those that CALEA experts from law enforcement and academia deem best practices.

CALEA accreditation is voluntary. It's an arduous, multiyear process; only about 5 percent of law enforcement agencies bother to go through it. For those that do, their success is a point of pride. Departments still tailor their policies to local circumstances, but accreditation means that the agency, no matter how small or geographically remote, is operating to national and international specifications, from training to use-of-force policy to investigative procedure. There's not much evidence to show that CALEA agencies use force less often, solve more of their cases, or draw fewer citizen complaints. But reform-minded chiefs can use the process of accreditation as an opportunity to overhaul their departments. "CALEA says we have to do it this way" generates less resistance from stubborn cops than "I say we have to do it this way."

Lou had introduced CALEA in Morrow. Now, with his boss's continued support, he set about securing accreditation in LaGrange, which required remaking the PD top to bottom. A few officers—Black and white—were sympathetic to Lou's plans; they'd been trying for years to improve the agency.[3] They became fellow travelers as Lou rewrote policy, mandating de-escalation, banning ticket fixing, and instituting college requirements for promotion. He upped field training for new recruits and in-service training for current officers. LaGrange cops receive eighty hours of in-service training per year, four times more than the state requires. He demanded professional conduct, equal treatment, and respectful communication, even prohibiting officers from talking to citizens while wearing sunglasses for fear it would send the wrong message. In Lou's first nine months on the job, the department conducted fifty-four internal affairs investigations, finding almost half the cases to have merit. Lou fired cops who'd committed ethical breaches or policy infractions. This was easier to do than it would have been in other departments because the LaGrange police weren't unionized. Georgia is one of only four states that prohibit collective bargaining for police officers. Without a union, there was no convoluted disciplinary procedure Lou had to follow and no powerful interest group to reckon with.

With backing from the city manager and city council, Lou invested in new equipment and technology, including dashboard cameras for cruisers and, later, body-worn cameras. (The department was an early adopter of both.) He increased police salaries so that he could recruit officers with more skills and experience. He got his cops used to documenting everything with reports because police conduct and behavior matter, and records should be kept.

Four years after Lou became chief, LaGrange PD was CALEA accredited, and it's been reaccredited every three years since, the CALEA logo displayed on patrol cars. LaGrange's eighty-five officers say that they work to a higher standard than their peers in surrounding agencies. Sometimes young cops will join the department and find that it's not for them. The rules are too strict, the paperwork burden too heavy, Lou's Catholic conscience—which permeates the culture of the agency—too severe. These young cops never last very long in LaGrange, where officers are randomly monitored to ensure compliance with departmental policies, to the point where they fear getting their pay docked if they're caught on camera so much as swearing. Others thrive in the regimented environment.

Officers who stay believe the benefits of Lou's leadership are clear. From 1995 to 2019, violent crime in LaGrange fell 50 percent. Although that drop was in line with national trends, given the high poverty rate it's not implausible to think that the city could have remained a crime outlier had Chief Dekmar not reformed the department. Over the same period, LaGrange PD investigated seventy-nine homicides, solving 84 percent of them, a solve rate well above the national average. LaGrange officers use nonlethal force a little over 1 percent of the time that they make an arrest, which is very low in comparison to other agencies, while the department's long-term rate of police killing is also below average. (Two fatalities during Lou's tenure.) In terms of accountability, the department typically receives around sixty complaints per year, finding fault with officer behavior in more than 20 percent of the cases (compared with the national average of around 12 percent of complaints sustained). Since LaGrange PD responds to over fifty thousand calls for service annually, this means that only about a tenth of 1 percent of calls result in a complaint.

Not everything was encouraging. The city has no property tax. In an unusual arrangement, a large source of its revenue is a city-run utility that provides electricity, gas, and water to households and businesses. But about $1 million each year (out of a total revenue of $109 million) comes from municipal court fees, including steep fines for traffic offenses like driving without a license. LaGrange PD often sets up traffic checkpoints (which it deems important for safety), the tickets issued generating that revenue. Until recently, LaGrange residents who couldn't pay their fines had their utilities cut off, in what attorneys for the NAACP and other advocacy organizations called a violation of the Fair Housing Act. An NAACP legal complaint charged that 90 percent of those threatened with utility cuts were Black, reflecting greater poverty as well as the fact that Black drivers in the city are stopped more often than white drivers, relative to their population share. (This disparity is much smaller than the average in other municipal agencies, however.) In 2020, the city settled a lawsuit and agreed to repeal its policy.

The department also fell short when it came to recruiting a diverse workforce. LaGrange's racial demographics are similar to Atlanta's: in both cities, there are more Black than white residents. But while a majority of Atlanta cops are Black, only 15 percent of those in LaGrange are. The reasons for this are complex. The metro Atlanta area is booming, and many young Black men and women from LaGrange have relocated there. Educators speak of a failure in LaGrange's de facto segregated school system, noting that while it prepares some Black students for college and professional careers, it does little to prepare others for skilled blue-collar or civil service employment. Lou's command staff is largely white, which may send the discouraging message that there's a glass ceiling in the organization for Black cops. The department has a long-standing policy of giving bonuses to employees who refer applicants for police officer positions, a practice that unwittingly produces a disproportionately white hiring pool given the racial makeup of the agency and that social networks tend to be segregated by race.[4] In pockets of the Black community in LaGrange, there remains, as well, a deep wariness of the police.

Despite these challenges, Lou thought the changes he'd made had affected public perceptions; that the department was generally seen to be turning over a new leaf.

Then, one day in 2012, a LaGrange PD captain, Andree Robinson, stepped into his office.

"You're not going to believe what I heard in the hallway," she said.

The third-floor hallway in the station is decorated with historical memorabilia: black-and-white photos of buttoned-up cops from the 1950s in front of lumbering police cars with wings, like something out of *The Andy Griffith Show*. There's the entire department posing on the stairs of an older, now defunct police station, not a single non-white face in the group, and handwritten arrest ledgers from the 1940s showing people taken into custody for offenses such as “drunk,” “stabbing,” and “wife whipping.”

Two elderly Black women had been visiting when Andree, who’s also Black, saw one of them point to a picture and say, “They killed our people.” Neither she nor Lou had any idea what the women were talking about.

12

AUSTIN CALLAWAY

Sergeant Robert Moore, one of Robbie Hall's close friends, was sinewy, built like a competitive cyclist. A former Army Ranger, now an internal affairs investigator for LaGrange PD, Robert had won the title of Georgia's Toughest Cop three times (1999, 2000, and 2002) in the state's Police and Fire Games, beating out a field of competitors at a grueling obstacle course, run, and shooting competition. After that, he took up a new sport: Brazilian-style jiujitsu.

Brazilian jiujitsu was developed in the 1920s and 1930s. Minimizing the use of throws, it focused on taking opponents to the ground and grappling and using leverage to defeat them. The style caught on in Brazil and came to the United States in the 1970s. Soon enough, there were more jiujitsu schools scattered across the country—in strip malls and repurposed commercial spaces—than there were Brazilian steakhouses.

When Robert got a group of friends together to begin jiujitsu training out of a defunct elementary school, Robbie Hall was among them. He'd never been a big fitness guy. He hated lifting weights and couldn't run because of shin splints. He met his second wife, Tina, at Country's Barbecue where she worked (located a few blocks from the police department) because he went in there regularly for lunch. Country's had an outrageously good barbecue pork platter. But after Robbie turned forty, he decided it was time to start taking better care of himself and jiujitsu sounded like it could be fun. A few sessions in, he was hooked. In high school, Robbie had been on the wrestling team. Rolling around on mats with his friends and getting a sweat going made him feel young again. It reduced his stress. Jiujitsu also promised to help him on the job.

After a few years, Robert Moore opened a jiujitsu training academy in LaGrange, which he called Invictus Combatives, after the poem, "Invictus," by William Ernest Henley: "In the fell clutch of circumstance / I have not winced nor cried aloud. / Under the bludgeonings of chance / My head is bloody, but unbowed." Robbie and the others from Robert's informal training group now had a more official place to work out. Radio traffic permitting, LaGrange officers were allowed to extend their usual thirty-minute lunch break to an hour if they used the time to exercise. Robbie still ate at Country's occasionally, but the dojo became his new lunchtime hangout. He'd park his cruiser out front, lock his gun belt in the trunk, and walk in to spar with whoever might be around.

• • •

EVERY TIME HE HIT THE mat at Invictus Combatives, Robbie contemplated the adversaries he might face at work. He and Robert Moore talked about how they'd use jiujitsu to respond to a punch or grab or knife thrust, and they'd rehearse their response over and over until it became instinctual. In this they weren't alone. Whether or not they're martial artists, most cops think and talk incessantly about the dangers of the job.

Policing *is* dangerous. In 2020, for example, about one out of every twelve police officers nationwide was assaulted, with a third of them sustaining injuries. Forty-six officers were killed. Each year, another sixty officers, on average, die in motor vehicle accidents while on duty.

Yet policing isn't on the top ten list of most dangerous lines of work, unlike accident-prone occupations such as logging, fishing, roofing, garbage collection, or driving a truck. Policing has also become safer over time, a result of less violent crime, improved ballistic vests, seat belt policies, and the like. Although lethal assaults on officers spiked in

2021—a worrisome exception to this trend—in more typical years, it's a bit of a puzzle why cops devote quite so much mental energy to the possibility of peril.

To understand the phenomenon, sociologist Michael Sierra-Arévalo spent several years riding with patrol officers in three large cities, which he called Elmont, West River, and Sunshine.[1] A common theme in all three departments was the cops' obsession with danger. Their fixation exceeded what previous generations of police scholars had observed and led them to embrace a warrior mentality more appropriate for soldiers than local law enforcement.

Seth Stoughton, a law professor and former police officer, described the key features of this mentality in a 2015 article.[2] Stoughton wrote that "under the warrior worldview," officers see themselves as "locked in intermittent and unpredictable combat with unknown but highly lethal enemies." Believing that "hypervigilance offers the best chance for survival," these cops "learn to treat every individual they interact with as an armed threat and every situation as a deadly force encounter in the making."[3] Cops who think of themselves as warriors don't just embrace standard officer safety techniques, such as never standing directly in front of a door when you knock (in case the person inside starts shooting) or holding their flashlights in their non-gun hands. They're on guard at every moment, which means viewing citizens (especially in tough neighborhoods) as enemy combatants. At the root of the warrior mentality, argues Stoughton, is fear. This is what was drilled into me all those years ago at the Sacramento police academy; that, and the injunction to be ruthless in pursuit of those who'd broken the law.

Others writing critically about policing today, like the *Washington Post*'s Radley Balko, trace the genesis of a warrior mentality among cops to the increased availability of surplus military hardware, the preferential hiring of veterans, the way in which politicians frame the job as a war (on drugs and on crime), and the entrepreneurs who've profited by offering military-style training to law enforcement.[4] Sierra-Arévalo's take was different: his study examined the relationship between perceptions of danger and the collective memory of police organizations.

Collective memory is an important area of research.[5] Distinct from individual memories, collective memories are the official or unofficial stories of the past told by groups, institutions, even nations. Sociologists assume that you can't explain how groups understand the past simply by looking at historical events. History can be told from multiple points of view, and collective memories commonly diverge from the historical record.

So sociologists study the social processes that lead groups to have the collective memories they do and the consequences of those memories. Was July 4, 1776, "the greatest single day for human liberty in the history of the world," as the editors of the conservative magazine *National Review* declared?[6] Or "were our democracy's founding ideals . . . false when they were written," as journalist Nikole Hannah-Jones wrote for the *New York Times*' 1619 Project, an initiative that recast the nation's true founding, metaphorically at least, as the arrival of the first slave ship from Africa?[7] Which understanding of history Americans believe has great bearing on the country's politics, hence the political, cultural, and academic battles to orient the nation's collective memory toward one or the other of these narratives.

Police departments can have collective memories, too. In the three agencies Sierra-Arévalo studied, he discovered a culture of "commemoration": how the departments and individual cops routinely memorialized officers who'd died in the line of duty.

Funerals are the most obvious place where that commemoration occurs. But Sierra-Arévalo looked past the obvious, noting the shrines to fallen colleagues displayed in police stations, like the one at the entrance to Elmont PD with a caption that read, "Above and Beyond the Call of Duty: Dedicated to the courage and sacrifice of the officers who gave their lives in service to the community of Elmont."[8] Fallen police are discussed frequently in training classes. Trainers praise their sacrifices while pointing out tactical mistakes they may have made. Cops wear black bands across their badges in honor of the deceased, and not only for those in their own agencies, but sometimes for officers they've never met, from departments in other states.

Sierra-Arévalo appreciated the motivation for honoring them

and the sociological functions such rituals serve, including fortifying bonds among cops and linking policing with sacred values, but he argued there was a cost: when so much collective police memory involves recalling the murder of comrades, the threat of danger comes to take center stage in police culture, pushing cops toward their fear-based warrior mentality.[9]

That mentality doesn't have much going for it. There's no evidence it has contributed to safety in policing. It may make policing *less* safe: jumpy, hair-trigger cops cause situations to escalate needlessly. A warrior mentality also alienates the community, which puts everybody at a disadvantage. Perhaps, Sierra-Arévalo speculated, redirecting some of that commemorative energy would open up space for a new mentality to take hold.

• • •

In the gift shop of the Troup County Archives and Legacy Museum, a bookshelf holds lush photographic histories of the area: *Treasures of Troup County*, *Travels through Troup County*, two volumes in the *Images of America* series.[10] Concentrated on LaGrange, the county seat, these histories tell the story of a community with all the peculiarities, charms, and faults of the old South being wrested into the modern era.

According to the books, settlers—their racial identity unspecified—began arriving in the early nineteenth century, claiming land that had been sold to the US government by the Creek Nation and then given away by the state of Georgia. These settlers built grand plantations and cleared plots for family farms. Early planters grew "wheat, barley, rye and oats," with "cotton becoming 'king'" later on.[11] LaGrange—named after the French estate of the Marquis de Lafayette, who ostensibly said that west Georgia reminded him of home—emerged as a prosperous commercial and cultural center, with a number of plantation owners deciding to live in town rather than the countryside to take advantage of offerings like LaGrange Female Academy, one of the earliest schools for women in the South. Imposing Greek revival mansions sprang up. In a sign of the town's status in antebellum Georgia, the first speech delivered in the state arguing in favor of secession was given by a

LaGrange minister (although pro-Union sentiment in the area was also strong). Troup County contributed twelve companies of soldiers to the Confederacy.

By the early twentieth century, LaGrange had transformed into a mill town. The community was already home to industrial concerns: an ironworks, a sash and blinds factory. Now it retooled for large-scale manufacturing. Many people played a part in this, but none would prove as decisive for LaGrange's history as Fuller E. Callaway. A minister's son, Callaway started a department store and mail-order business before turning to cotton milling (and a host of related business ventures). Callaway Mills expanded into one of the most successful textile mill operations in the country, with production continuing into the 1950s and beyond under the direction of Fuller's sons, Fuller Jr. and Cason. In the process, the family amassed a fortune.

The Callaways, we learn from these histories, gave their employees comfortable homes with vegetable gardens and access to pastureland. They started a night school. They supported cultural and recreational activities. They donated to LaGrange College, the Methodist liberal arts institution that LaGrange Female Academy had become. They were LaGrange's leading family and benefactors.

The books are right to note the Callaways' influence. They were part of a distinctive pattern of social organization that arose in many Southern mill towns: paternalism. As sociologists Michael Schulman and Jeffrey Leiter explain, "Early mills in the U.S. South were situated in geographically isolated towns, where the labor force was white, unskilled, and recruited from the farm population. Workers, many of them women and children, were often members of the same family or kin. . . . The mill was central to village life, providing housing and welfare activities and sponsoring community organizations. The dominant ideology within the mill village portrayed owners and workers as bound together in a 'white family.'"[12] This arrangement was paternalistic in that owners presented themselves as fatherlike figures, providers as well as authorities.

While mill owners may have had altruistic motives for setting up such a system—Fuller Callaway Sr. once said he was in the business of "making American citizens and running cotton mills to pay expenses"—they also had economic incentives: the investments they made in the town and in their employees enhanced productivity and reduced turnover. Owners hoped, too, that the benefits would forestall any possible advances by labor unions. According to one historian, Callaway Sr. reasoned that since "his employees were already provided with everything they needed and could reasonably want as . . . part of the cooperative scheme to keep the mills running well and the employees happy," unions should have little appeal.[13]

For all the historical detail in the gift shop books, some elements are more visible than others. The books mention the role of enslaved people in the development of Troup County but don't discuss it nearly as much as they should, perhaps because pictorial evidence was harder to find. The horrors of life on plantations—which historians such as Edward Baptist have argued should rightfully be called slave labor camps—are minimized.[14] There's little on the exploited Black tenant farmers and sharecroppers who provided much of the backbreaking labor for cotton production until mechanical harvesters came into widespread use in the 1950s. The books are silent on the fact that the Callaways were staunch segregationists, like most Southern whites of the day (and many outside the South). The mills themselves were segregated for decades, Black workers relegated to menial jobs. One family philanthropy, the Callaway Educational Association, maintained what were, in effect, separate recreational facilities and swimming pools for LaGrange's white and Black children all the way until the early 1990s. Fuller Jr., who set the course for that philanthropy until his death in 1992, is reported to have said that his real belief wasn't in segregation but in slavery, while Bo Callaway, a politician, Fuller Jr.'s nephew, and Cason's son, helped spearhead the effort in the 1960s to revive Georgia's Republican Party in reaction to northern Democratic support for integration.[15]

Notably, the books don't mention Austin Callaway.

After Captain Andree Robinson told Lou Dekmar about the conversation she'd overheard in the third-floor hallway, he began doing some research. He knew about police shootings that had occurred on his watch. What had happened prior? Looking for older documents, he googled "police kill Negro in LaGrange" and found a digitized October 1940 edition of *The Crisis*, the magazine of the NAACP.

Its news brief stated that on September 8, 1940, a Black sixteen-year-old named Austin Callaway had been lynched. Callaway had been arrested by LaGrange police for attempted assault on a white woman and was placed in a jail cell. That night, six masked men barged in and demanded that the jailer turn Callaway over to them, which he did. The men then drove Callaway out of town and shot him.

Aha, thought Lou. This must be what the women were referring to. To get more information, he looked through old LaGrange PD files. But he couldn't find an arrest record for Callaway or an incident report for the abduction or killing, though other records from the period were well preserved. Nor could he find any evidence that the police chief in 1940, J. E. Matthews, had opened an investigation into Callaway's death. He did discover that after the murder, the Troup County grand jury issued a recommendation: get better locks for the jail. Clearly, there'd been some sort of cover-up.

A few years after Lou made these inquiries, LaGrange residents Bobbie Hart and Wes Edwards started their own research. Bobbie and Wes knew each other from Alterna, a local faith-based group that promoted social justice and immigrant rights. Bobbie, who is Black, had spent most of her life in LaGrange. Wes, who is white, had been raised in southern Georgia, moved to New York to get a PhD in public policy from Cornell, and had a career in civil rights and affordable housing advocacy before relocating to LaGrange to be closer to his doctors at Emory—for health problems—and to his Columbus-based parents.

Every year the Alterna group read one or two books that spoke to issues of mutual concern. In 2015, they were making their way through *The Cross and the Lynching Tree*, by theologian James H. Cone. Cone drew connections between lynchings and the crucifixion of Jesus. "During the lynching era," Cone wrote—1880 to 1940—"the lynching tree joined the cross as the most emotionally charged symbols in the African-American community—symbols that represented both death and the promise of redemption, judgment and the offer of mercy, suffering and the power of hope."[16]

Cone's book stirred strong emotions in Bobbie and Wes. Bobbie, who believed that her own grandfather had been murdered years earlier while working for the railroad, had a personal connection to America's shameful history of racial terror and violence. Wes, for his part, was driven to try to understand how people of strong Christian faith could take part in such unspeakable acts.

As they prepared for their discussion of the book, Bobbie and Wes—and Anton Flores-Maisonet, a Latino activist who'd founded Alterna—began wondering about the history of lynching in LaGrange and Troup County. They stumbled across the name Austin Callaway. Since Lou had first become interested, a law student working with Northeastern University's Civil Rights and Restorative Justice Project had written a paper about the NAACP's involvement with the Callaway case.[17]

In the NAACP archives, the student had found a letter written a month and a half after the lynching by L. W. Strickland, the pastor at LaGrange's Warren Temple, a Black church. Strickland had written to Thurgood Marshall, at that point an attorney with the organization, to request help investigating Callaway's murder. He told Marshall that authorities in LaGrange were turning a blind eye. The NAACP was in the midst of a nationwide campaign to end lynching—more than four thousand Black people had been killed in the South in the previous half century. In December 1940, it planned to take part in a conference at the Tuskegee Institute, where the goal was to arrive at a precise definition of lynching and lay the groundwork for more effective advocacy. Among other things, the NAACP was attempting to persuade Congress to pass an anti-lynching bill. It was vital that the group get a handle on any new incidents.

According to the law student, Callaway's case helped convince the NAACP of the need for a broader definition. Increasingly, the NAACP believed, lynchings were no longer public spectacles but rather secretive affairs carried out in the shadows, such as the fate that had befallen Callaway. Or so it appeared.

Despite her many years in LaGrange, Bobbie Hart had never heard of Austin Callaway. There are both white and Black Callaways, probably connected through slaveholding, so it didn't strike Bobbie as strange that the young man who was lynched had the same last name as LaGrange's most powerful family. With the seventy-fifth anniversary of Callaway's death coming up, the Alterna folks decided to put together a memorial service. On September 8, 2015, a small group made a pilgrimage to Liberty Hill, the rural area out of town where Callaway was shot and left for dead. They wanted to pay their respects, pray for him, and ask for forgiveness for his murderers. For Bobbie especially, to be Christian meant to forgive.

After the memorial, however, Bobbie and Wes were troubled by how little they knew. Who was Callaway? Who'd killed him and why? What was the true nature of the police department's involvement? Other historical reports claimed that Callaway was taken from his jail cell around midnight, after the officers on duty had left the station to respond to a fire at a fertilizer plant. How would the men have known to come to the jail just then unless they'd been tipped off or the fire had been set deliberately, as a distraction?

One way to answer these questions, Bobbie and Wes thought, was to ask the community for relevant family history and lore. They hoped that this approach would not only reveal facts about an injustice shrouded by the passage of time but would make the community stronger by drawing residents into a common project. They named their effort Troup Together.

Wes wasn't from LaGrange and had no family stories to contribute. But he was a trained researcher and could help on that front. He began showing up at the Troup County Archives, looking for background on Austin and for any new details about the murder. He pored through old school records, police files, court documents, and left empty-handed. It was as though the town had erased the young man's existence.

• • •

Every month the mayors of LaGrange, Hogansville, and West Point (the two other incorporated parts of Troup County) would meet for lunch with the chair of the county commission. In January 2014, Jim Thornton, LaGrange's new mayor, began urging his colleagues to work on healing the racial rifts that beset the county. A white Emory Law School graduate, Thornton spoke with new urgency about the issue after the unrest that summer in Ferguson. Under Lou's leadership, LaGrange PD strove to respect civil rights, which put it light years ahead of Ferguson PD. But west Georgia had an extreme history of racial injustice. Troup had been the fifth-largest slaveholding county in the state. Significant disparities remained between Black and white residents in education, income, and health. And everybody over a certain age remembered those segregated swimming pools. Who was to say underlying racial tensions couldn't spark a conflagration, as they had in Ferguson?

Since the early 1990s, Initiatives of Change, a national nonprofit based in Richmond, Virginia, had been running a program called Hope in the Cities. The program aimed to foster interracial trust and communication through workshops and facilitated dialogue sessions. Thornton, a moderate Republican, convinced the other mayors to send a two-person delegation to Richmond to check it out: the Reverend Carl Von Epps, a pastor and businessman who represented LaGrange in the Georgia State House, and Ricky Wolfe, who'd recently stepped down as county commission chair. They came away from their trip impressed. Hope in the Cities seemed to have made progress in Richmond. They were also struck by the Reverend Sylvester Turner, the nonprofit's thoughtful and methodical director of reconciliation programming; and by Cricket White, his co-facilitator, who purposefully played the part of the "HSWW"—the "high-strung white woman"—as a counterpoint to Reverend Turner's more pastoral style. Hope in the Cities was hired to run workshops in Troup County, and the first LaGrange trust-building session was scheduled for March 2015. Thornton asked Lou Dekmar to take part.

"I'd really rather not" was Lou's response. He'd participated in racial sensitivity training in the air force in the early 1970s and in some of his earlier police jobs. He thought it was a waste of time. Better to just do the right thing than pussyfoot around a major social divide.

Thornton told Lou he wouldn't insist that he go, but he encouraged him to take a closer look at what Hope in the Cities was up to. Once Lou did that, his curiosity was piqued. The program wasn't sensitivity training; nor was it merely trying to teach a different vocabulary. It aimed to stimulate what Rob Corcoran, Hope in the Cities' founder, called "honest" and "productive conversation" about race, history, and public policy.[18] The program's working assumption was that too often racial matters go undiscussed for fear of causing offense or creating misunderstandings. Yet if people from different backgrounds could be put in situations where they might feel comfortable enough to speak openly about their lives, the chances are that they'll find common ground.[19] There was a no-nonsense quality to the Hope in the Cities model that appealed to Lou. He changed his mind and participated in the workshop, then kept on participating as more were organized, all under the watchful eyes of Reverend Turner and Cricket White. The workshops were attended by over four hundred people. When they concluded, Von Epps and Wolfe arranged monthly breakfast meetings so that the conversations could continue. Dozens of Black and white Troup County residents would gather over eggs and coffee to hear presentations by speakers and reflect on the points raised, "enough capital having been built" from the workshops to allow for "discussion, not debate," as Reverend Turner put it.

It might seem odd that a small town like LaGrange could sustain interest in an interracial trust-building project. But LaGrange residents talk of an uncommonly cooperative community spirit, despite the racial disparities and the social distance that separates many Black and white households. According to John Tures, a political science professor at LaGrange College, that spirit is evident in "a St. Patrick's Day festival, a Christmas parade, a dozen or more civic events . . . Not many towns this size could support . . . places where games are set up for kids to come, where church groups meet to write thank-you letters to hospital workers for their COVID-19 service, where the rec centers are flooded with community baseball, and where each church seems to have a Scout troop."

Some of this cohesion is due to the presence of the college; the social fabric of college towns tends to be tightly knitted. But it may owe more to the ambiguous legacy of the Callaway family. The Callaway Foundation, the family's current philanthropic arm, with an approximately $200 million endowment, funds a variety of local institutions that bring people together. Sweetland Amphitheatre, for example, which opened in 2016 with an adjacent park, hosts concerts and community events, transforms into an ice rink in winter, and reflects a partnership between the foundation and the city. That partnership is rooted in the paternalism ushered in more than a hundred years ago by Fuller E. Callaway Sr. His mills are gone, but an ethic of civic-mindedness—finally broadening to include people of color—remains.

In August 2016, the breakfast discussion group heard a presentation by Karen Branan, author of *The Family Tree: A Lynching in Georgia, a Legacy of Secrets, and My Search for the Truth*.[20] Branan had grown up in Columbus, spending her summers in Harris County (which is south of Troup), and wrote about a lynching that had taken place there in 1912. Her great-grandfather, the sheriff, and her grandfather, his deputy, looked the other way while a mob of about a hundred men hung and shot three Black men and a Black woman accused of killing one of Branan's cousins. After the presentation, Lou asked Branan if she'd ever heard of Austin Callaway. She had; she'd seen his name in a book.

Then Lou posed a question that few white Southern police chiefs, if any, had thought to ask before, especially not spare-me-the-bullshit conservatives like himself. Had Branan ever heard of a chief publicly addressing his department's role in a lynching?

"Well, you'll be the first to do that," she replied.

The workshops and breakfast meetings hadn't turned Lou into a different person. But many white people who took part in them, even those who were well educated and knowledgeable about current inequalities, felt themselves becoming more empathetic and humble as the conversation progressed; they realized how little they'd known about the everyday experience of being Black in the Deep South. Lou had started thinking. Perhaps memories of what had happened to Austin Callaway, and of the police department's culpability and indifference, were swirling around in the community's unconscious despite his name having been forgotten, the memories reactivated by police encounters today. Until efforts were made to bring that trauma to the surface, Lou and his officers might only be able to get so far in winning people's trust. Leave aside fears about LaGrange becoming the next Ferguson. Wouldn't it be a powerful gesture for the police chief to speak honestly about the events of decades earlier, to take some responsibility for them, and to affirm LaGrange PD's commitment to equal treatment and protection under the law?

Through the Hope in the Cities process, Lou had become friendly with Ernest Ward, a former LaGrange cop who now taught health and phys ed in an elementary school. He was also president of the Troup County NAACP and had a scraggly beard, as if to signal the distance between his law enforcement past and his activist present.

"Hey, I'm thinking about doing something in the way of an acknowledgment or an apology for Austin Callaway. Would you be willing to work with me?"

"Absolutely," Ward said.[21]

13

BLUE FOLDER

The Politics of Regret (2007) addresses a major change in the collective memories of nations around the world.[1] Written by Jeffrey Olick, the leading US scholar on the subject, the book notes how, in previous eras, countries often celebrated their historical "golden ages" with hero-worshipping speeches by politicians and ideology-laden history books for schoolchildren that told tales of the country's virtue and triumph. In the contemporary period, by contrast, nations have expended great energy telling stories of their "horrible, repulsive past"—and issuing formal apologies. Some examples "include Pope John II's remarks about both the Catholic Church's treatment of Galileo and Catholic individuals' behavior during World War II; British prime minister Tony Blair's acknowledgment of an English role in the Irish potato famine . . . and an official, though limited, Japanese recognition of wartime atrocities in Nanking."[2]

Olick became interested in collective memory and regret while trying to understand the political culture of West Germany in the postwar years, when the government sought to come to terms with and make amends for the evils of Nazism. In many other countries with terrible pasts—South Africa after apartheid, Rwanda after the genocide, Chile after the dictator Augusto Pinochet was deposed—apologies also featured prominently in public life.

Some argued that the world had been forced into soul-searching over collective responsibility because events of the twentieth century—the Holocaust in particular—were orders of magnitude worse than anything that had come before. Others believed that public apologies signaled a transition out of a premodern shame-based culture into a modern guilt-based one. The apologies were said, alternatively, to reflect the adoption of universal human rights ideals, with leaders denouncing their forebears for violating those rights, even if they hadn't been recognized at the time of the injustice.

Olick disagreed. The politics of regret, he thought, could be traced to a change in the way that contemporary societies understand history: as the product of people making choices for which they should be held responsible, rather than as God's will. And if those people belonged to institutions of which we remain a part, then isn't it our responsibility as stewards to acknowledge wrongdoing?

Public apologies could be beneficial, Olick argued, provided they were genuine, not opportunistic. Even if the victims of a historical injustice or their descendants couldn't forgive, the material reparations that might accompany an apology could go at least some way toward making up for their losses.

What's more, apologies could cause a "turn in the narrative basis of community." When done right—preceded by ample fact-finding, extensive consultation with affected groups, and serious consideration of how a nation or institution could have gone down such an immoral path—apologies create a watershed moment for communities to begin telling new stories of themselves. Olick quoted the political philosopher Hannah Arendt, who saw apologies and requests for forgiveness as promises for a better future. Those promises bind us to others. Without them, Arendt wrote, we would be "condemned to wander helplessly and without direction in the darkness of each man's lonely heart."[3]

• • •

ON A JANUARY EVENING IN 2017, standing in front of a packed crowd at Warren Temple United Methodist on East Depot Street, Lou Dekmar felt the gravity of the occasion. He didn't usually get nervous, but that night he was, his eyes darting from the audience, made up in no small part of Black men and women in suits and dresses, to his speech, which was cradled in a noticeably blue folder he'd set down on the podium. It didn't help that Lou's address—the main event—was to follow a moving introduction by Mayor Thornton, who confidently quoted scripture and appealed to the Methodist tradition he shared with many of those present (although he went to First United Methodist, a mostly white church in a wealthier neighborhood). Thornton was a practiced public speaker, Lou a curt uniformed cop who hadn't picked up a hint of a Southern accent despite living in the area for more than two decades. The stakes were high. It felt as if all of Black LaGrange was in that church. Plus, someone had alerted the press; reporters for the *New York Times*, NPR, and CNN were on hand.

After Lou finished his preliminaries, thanking everyone who'd made the evening possible, he hit his stride. "It's long been recognized," he said, "that attitudes and the traditions of life are passed down through each generation. African Americans alive decades ago can speak of incidents of terror and lynchings and share oral history about those times." That was what had happened in LaGrange with Austin Callaway's death. Lou told the story of the two elderly women who'd come into the police station, keepers of Austin's memory.

But Callaway's killing was not an isolated case. Thousands of African Americans had been murdered by white people in the decades around the turn of the twentieth century, Lou noted. The Black citizens who filled the pews would have known this history, but it could have been instructive for some of the white police officers standing along one wall. Police had sometimes been directly involved in these lynchings. Or they gave tacit consent, allowing them to occur. After, they failed to investigate the crimes or covered them up to protect the perpetrators. "As one that is proud to be a police professional," Lou said, "I believe this period was our darkest hour."

These killings were horrendous injustices. Beyond that, the lynchings had shaped the Black community's feelings about law enforcement, feelings that had been carried forward. "Weekly," Lou said, "I deal with African American citizens who are suspicious, untrusting, apprehensive about what the police do and say." It was imperative that Austin and his family receive some measure of justice, but it was equally important to heal historical wounds so that trust could be restored. (Lou believed that, on the whole, the police department in LaGrange treated Black and white citizens equitably today. In a city where that wasn't true, an apology for past wrongdoing wouldn't go very far toward establishing trust.)

"Undoubtedly, some in the white community will ask, why should we apologize for outrageous actions committed by a generation long gone or dead?" Lou anticipated the town's objections. "Others, in the Black community, may believe this is another hollow effort to gloss over centuries of injustice and cruelty. To each group, I say, the institution responsible for Austin's death is still here and its members bear the burden of that history."

"All citizens have a right to expect a police department to be honest, decent, unbiased, and ethical," Lou proclaimed. That was not the treatment Austin received. For that, and for Austin's death, Lou apologized. "As the LaGrange police chief," he said, "I sincerely regret and denounce the role our police department played in Austin's lynching, both through our action and our inaction . . . I'm profoundly sorry. It should never have happened."

• • •

CLARK JOHNSON, A RETIRED EDUCATOR, worked part-time at the Troup County Archives and was the official county historian. He was coauthor of several of the books sold in the gift shop and had written his master's thesis on the nineteenth-century history of LaGrange. He was the kind of proud Southerner who referred to the *New York Times*, without irony, as a Yankee paper. But he was dismayed by Austin Callaway's death. With the town talking about the case, he felt a responsibility, in the months following the apology, to find whatever additional information he could. After doing some digging, Clark was able to figure out why the search for Callaway's school records had turned up no results: Callaway wasn't from LaGrange.

Census rolls showed that in 1920, a four-and-a-half-year-old Austin Callaway was living in the unincorporated community of Bacon Level in

Randolph County, Alabama, right over the Georgia state line. He lived with his father, who was named either Sess or Gus—the census taker's handwriting is unclear—his mother, Ida, and an older sister, Minnie. Austin could have been a late-in-life baby; his father was fifty and his mother was forty-seven. Or he could have been adopted. Sess/Gus Callaway was a farmer, originally from Georgia. Ida's occupation wasn't listed, but she was from Alabama.

This led Clark to another discovery: a convict record, also from Alabama. In 1932, a sixteen-year-old, Pat Austin Callaway, was sentenced in Randolph County to fifteen to twenty years in prison for the crime of "assault to ravage"—attempted rape. The Austin living in Bacon Level would have been sixteen in 1932. While it's possible that Callaway committed the crime, Black men and boys were commonly accused of assaulting white women in response to perceived violations of Jim Crow social codes. Coupled with flimsy eyewitness testimony, such accusations were sometimes enough to get a white jury to convict (although historical research suggests that this depended, in part, on the social class of the accuser).[4] Whatever the circumstances, Callaway was looking at spending the next two decades behind bars.

Southern prisons were barbaric. But every year at Christmastime, eligible Alabama inmates would receive one grace: a furlough to spend the holiday and New Year's with their families. (Other states had similar practices.) In December 1937, having served five years of his sentence, Callaway, then twenty-one, left prison on a furlough and never came back. By January 2, he was considered an escapee.

Clark Johnson's theory was that to avoid capture, Callaway fled Alabama for LaGrange, where he'd also find decent employment prospects. Cotton production—Georgia's number one industry—had picked back up after the Depression, and the mills were buzzing, although "most of the workers . . . were poor," and "in the faces along the streets there was the desperate look of hunger and of loneliness," as Carson McCullers put it in *The Heart Is a Lonely Hunter*, her novel set around this time in a fictional Georgia town.[5] Austin Callaway couldn't have become a mill operative; the workforce remained segregated. But he might have been able to get a janitorial job. Outside the mill walls, Black people worked as day laborers, cooks, plasterers, cotton truckers, cleaners, gas station attendants, teachers, and nurses.

Clark theorized that on that night in September 1940, Callaway had been detained in LaGrange as a fugitive. LaGrange police notified the authorities in Randolph County, who came to get him, seizing him at gunpoint when the jailer failed to recognize their credentials. On the drive to Alabama, a scuffle might have broken out, and Callaway was killed. Liberty Hill, where he was shot, is on the route from LaGrange to Randolph County, so the killers could feasibly have committed the crime there. Callaway was found the next day by a white LaGrange family. In Clark's theory, the lynching was the work of outsiders.

Wes Edwards and Bobbie Hart gleaned other facts as they continued their own research—and drew a different conclusion. Several people in their nineties who'd lived in the Liberty Hill area remembered things from that night or had heard their parents discuss the lynching. The jailer in LaGrange had said that six masked men took Callaway from his cell, driving away in a single car. But the people who talked to Wes and Bobbie said it was more like one hundred cars gathered at the scene of the killing. They recalled that Callaway had been mutilated as well as shot. Talk around town was that Callaway had been doing odd jobs for a white woman and had asked to be paid in cash. She refused; words were spoken. Next thing anyone knew, he was under arrest. To Wes and Bobbie, it seemed likely that Callaway had been killed by LaGrange people. Also, one hundred cars plus kidnappers in masks sounded a lot like a lynching by the Ku Klux Klan. If that was true, the NAACP's interpretation of the case—that it represented a turn away from lynchings as spectacles—needed an update.

In the 1940s, the KKK was intensely active in Georgia, as much in Troup County as anywhere else in the state. Alexander Hughes, an archivist at the Troup County Archives and part of a younger generation intent on presenting a more inclusive version of local history, documented Klan activity dating back at least to the 1860s and continuing well into the twentieth century. The Klan found particular support in LaGrange. In 1922, Hughes reported, a "Klan circuit speaker" from Atlanta "addressed . . . a large crowd" in LaGrange on the topic of "the Ku Klux Klan and Law

Enforcement,'" declaring that "the Klan stood for 'law and order' and 'one-hundred percent Americanism.'" That speaker, Hughes wrote, "was introduced by a prominent LaGrange citizen, Judge F. M. Longley, who claimed membership in the Klan during his introduction. Longley served on the LaGrange City Council, as chairman of the county commissioners, a judge of the Troup County Superior Court, and as mayor of LaGrange."[6]

The elderly LaGrange residents who spoke to Wes and Bobbie said that decades later their families had continued to live in fear of the KKK. Gene Bowen, whose parents brought Callaway to the hospital after the shooting, told the *Atlanta Journal-Constitution* in 2017 that his family had kept quiet to avoid incurring the Klan's wrath.[7]

Klan violence at the time, seemingly sporadic, followed a pattern: attacks tended to occur around hotly contested statewide elections. Candidates for office sometimes had Klan connections and would rile their supporters into a racist frenzy as part of a get-out-the-vote effort.[8] The other reason was that Black Georgians had been making gains in their quest to secure voting rights. Racial violence was a reaction, aimed at dissuading Black people from exercising their right to vote, maintaining the Democrats' prohibition on Black participation in Southern primaries, and preserving white supremacy.[9]

September 8, 1940, the night when Callaway was lynched, was three days before the Georgia gubernatorial Democratic primary. Tensions were running high throughout the state. Perhaps Callaway had gotten into a dispute about wages at a moment when even the most minor transgression would be met with a furious response, the charge that he'd tried to assault a woman entirely fabricated. Perhaps he had the audacity to say that he planned to vote and was killed for it.[10] Or perhaps he had a closer tie to the white, mill-owning Callaway family or to other powerful figures in town than had been recognized.

Wes and Bobbie hadn't found all the answers, but they'd uncovered fragments of LaGrange history that some might prefer to keep buried.

• • •

WITH HIS APOLOGY, LOU HOPED to build greater trust between the police department and LaGrange's Black community. But trust is elusive, a difficult thing to measure—it's not as if there were rigorous before-and-after studies of police-community relations being conducted.

To Ernest Ward, the NAACP president in Troup County, Lou's apology was a profoundly meaningful gesture, a signal that a new day had dawned in race relations in LaGrange. Here was a white police chief vowing that LaGrange PD would never again fail a Black person—fail anyone—the way it had failed Austin Callaway.

Just as important as Lou's apology, Ward felt, was the collaboration and dialogue that preceded it. The Hope in the Cities workshops had been transformative, he believed. And the planning conversations for the apology were the first time Ward had felt that white men in positions of influence listened to and respected him. When he suggested language for the plaque to be placed outside Warren Temple, including the line that lynchers were "night-riding terrorists," others deferred to his judgment.[11] The nature of the group's endeavor—a collectively organized apology for a historical injustice—complicated the normal racial power dynamics. Maybe those conversations would allow LaGrange's white elite to glimpse the potential of shared governance. Ward gave credit to Lou and to Jim Thornton, who he considered the best mayor LaGrange had seen in a long while. He expected more progress on racial equity and inclusion to follow.

Trust building aside, the apology had an unanticipated benefit: it reinforced the respectful policing culture based on the rule of law that Lou had established in LaGrange.

Politicians and public officials, but also CEOs, university presidents, and leaders of other organizations—all are apologizing for past wrongs these days. Many of these apologies are pro forma, offering an inexpensive way to deflect criticism, made one week and forgotten the next.

But in the rare cases where such apologies are sincere and coupled with a commitment to not repeat the same mistake, they communicate a strong message. The message alone isn't likely to change an organization's culture, but it can solidify a shift already in process, enhancing people's knowledge of the organization's ethical stance and drawing a thick line between the abhorrent actions of the past and the behavior expected now. The misdeed can become a lesson in what the organization will no longer tolerate.

Some cops at the Warren Temple event didn't think Lou's apology made sense: no one who worked in the police department today was alive when Austin Callaway was killed in 1940. How can you apologize for something for which you're not personally responsible? Acknowledge the department's historical wrongdoing, fine, but don't apologize.

Robbie Hall was there, too. He understood their argument, but that's not how he felt. If Chief (as Lou's officers called him) thought that this would improve relations with the community, then it had Robbie's support.

He didn't have much personal interaction with Lou, who he viewed as a chain-of-command kind of leader, someone who frowned at chiefs and patrol officers getting too familiar. The only exception was when an officer erred royally—then Lou would haul him into his office for a talking-to. Robbie had never gotten in trouble like that. (From Lou's perspective, his commitment was to accountability, not chain of command. He avoided social relationships with his officers so that his ability to hold them accountable wouldn't be compromised.)

Nonetheless, Robbie knew that Lou's leadership had shaped him as an officer. He supposed his personality would be the same anywhere. But cops adapt to their work environment, and the distinguishing feature of LaGrange PD, as Robbie saw it, was its strictness, Chief Dekmar's strictness. There were rules, and you had to follow them: cops were to be respectful of all citizens, to treat them equally regardless of the color of their skin. They were supposed to use the absolute minimum level of force necessary to take suspects into custody. The culture of the department frowned on rule benders, unlike in other PDs, where cops who figure out how to circumvent rules might be treated as folk heroes.

Robbie believed that if he worked for a more loosey-goosey agency, he wouldn't be quite so careful never to slip up. Such an agency might not have provided him with the extra training he received at LaGrange, like CIT, which helped him be a better cop. In another department, a warrior mentality could easily have taken hold, instead of what prevailed in LaGrange, where cops prepared to defend themselves if attacked, but where the goal wasn't to vanquish foes so much as to restrain people who—perhaps in a moment of weakness and bad judgment—had decided to fight the law.

To Robbie, Lou's apology was a potent reminder of the high-minded agency he worked for. What that meant in practice wasn't always straightforward.

• • •

Cops in small communities know every inch of the towns they police. So when Robbie heard a call come in about a stolen car with a GPS tracking device pinging near an industrial area, he knew where to look.

The evening before, a woman and her boyfriend had stopped at a convenience store, leaving the woman's car, a silver Hyundai, running outside. Seconds later, the car was gone. A LaGrange officer took a report, entering the license plate into the system as stolen. The plate was viewed overnight by automated tag cameras on the interstate, and Robbie and his day-shift teammates had spent the morning cruising through the parking lots of motels off the highway to see if it had been left after a joyride.

Ashley, the car's owner, had meanwhile been blowing up the phone of the used lot where she'd bought it. The lot had installed the GPS tracker in case she failed to make payments. She was trying to get workers there to share the Hyundai's coordinates with the police so that she could get her car back, along with her driver's license, Social Security card, and two cash cards she'd left inside. But it was Sunday, and the lot was closed. Finally, the car lot owner received her messages and called the PD to report an approximate location for the vehicle.

Robbie was out by the LaGrange Mall when he was dispatched to Swift Street west of the cement plant. "That's gonna be near that closed-down nightclub," he radioed to Ryan Cadenhead, his assigned backup.

At 4:30 p.m., Robbie parked his car near a white wooden building with boarded-up doors, weeds, and encroaching rot. His boots crunched on leaves and twigs as he followed tire tracks in the grass. "We'll look back here and see what we can find," he said.

The Hyundai had been carefully hidden, tucked behind the nightclub so that it wouldn't be visible from the street. It glinted in the late afternoon light, a stark contrast to the ramshackle structure and its surroundings. "I guarantee you they left it here so they could come back and get it," Robbie said to Ryan. He kept his hand on his holstered gun as he advanced on the car, though he couldn't see anyone inside.

Satisfied that the car was empty, he donned a pair of black leather gloves and tried the driver's door with two fingers, to see if he could open it without disturbing any fingerprints. He could, and the smell of marijuana wafted out. "Who-ee!" said Robbie, wrinkling his nose.

"It's a shame we can't sit on the car and wait for them to come back tonight," he said. He began poking around inside the vehicle and emerged with a slender wallet that had been left on the driver's seat.

"What was the owner's name?" he asked Ryan.

"Think it was Ashley something."

Robbie flipped open the wallet. "Wait a second," he said.

He showed the contents to Ryan. They looked at each other and burst out laughing. It wasn't Ashley's wallet. "The suspect left his ID!" exclaimed Ryan.

A few minutes later, Ashley showed up, along with her boyfriend. The man from the car lot came as well, with an extra set of keys.

"Without the GPS, we'd have never found this car," the guy said, popping the hood to check on the battery. He was acting proprietary, considering that Ashley, his customer, was standing right there.

Ashley detailed the theft to Robbie. While she and her boyfriend were in the convenience store, a woman had come rushing in saying that two teenagers had stolen the car. The woman, who'd been out in the parking lot, said she'd confronted the thieves but backed off when one of the kids showed her a handgun. She recognized the armed kid from the neighborhood and began scrolling through Facebook on her phone. "That's him," she said, showing Ashley a photo. Ashley snapped her own photo of the image and was now showing it to Robbie.

The photo matched the Georgia State ID Robbie had found in the wallet: Jamal, an eighteen-year-old. "Same guy," Robbie said.

From his car, Robbie put in a call to one of the detectives. The case sounded open-and-shut, and Robbie wanted to go to the suspect's house and try to make an arrest.

The detective hemmed and hawed. Had the witness who'd seen the theft stuck around the convenience store to give a statement? On his car computer, Robbie scanned through the original officer's report, which was bare-bones. No mention of a witness. "That seems strange," the detective said. He asked Robbie to check the addresses of the suspect and victim. They lived a couple of blocks from each other in low-income housing near the convenience store. The detective found this suspicious, too. So did the victim know the suspect? Maybe she'd willingly loaned him her car? Maybe they were in on a fishy deal? Maybe, when the suspect failed to return the vehicle, the victim concocted the whole story? Was it possible that Ashley wasn't a victim at all? Without a statement from the witness, the case would fall apart in court, the detective said.

Detectives could sometimes rub Robbie the wrong way. Most were good at their job; a few were paper pushers who'd settled for a cushy gig behind a desk. Robbie thought this detective had it wrong. It could be that he was angling to mark the case unsolvable and get out of doing investigative legwork.

Another thought went unspoken: maybe Ashley's credibility was in question because she was Black and low income. People lie to cops all the time, including making false claims of being victims. It's one reason officers tend to become cynical. But Robbie was a savvy street cop with a solid bullshit detector, and he saw no reason to doubt Ashley, who seemed like a standard victim of car theft looking to recover her property. Would the detective have raised his questions if Ashley were white, if her car hadn't come from a used lot, if she'd lived in a more upscale neighborhood?

Lou Dekmar's commitment to equal justice under the law meant something to Robbie and the detective's attitude didn't sit right with him. But Robbie wasn't one to make a fuss, to bring every questionable decision by another cop to a supervisor. Maybe there *wasn't* enough evidence. These were hard calls to make.

14

SUPER HOOKS

On September 11, 2020—a day of national remembrance for the attacks of 9/11 and eighty years after the lynching of Austin Callaway—LaGrange officers Tyler Cox and Brandon Wright responded to a call on a street of modest 1960s-era single-family homes set among manicured lawns and towering pines. A young woman had called 911 to report that her uncle, Marcus Williams, had threatened to hit her and her mother—Williams's sister—with a stick. If the police didn't show up soon, she told dispatchers, she'd grab a kitchen knife and take matters into her own hands. Williams, fifty-one, was well known to the cops. He was mentally ill, addicted to cocaine and alcohol, and had a history of assaulting his family. When police would go to arrest him, he'd usually fight them, too.

After taking a quick statement from the woman, Cox and Wright spoke to Williams, who they found in shorts and a sweatshirt outside the house where the three lived. His responses to their questions were disjointed and delivered a mile a minute. When they asked if he'd threatened his niece with a stick, he picked up a pole lying on the ground and reenacted his threatening moves, holding it like a baseball bat before dropping it back down. At one point, he fell to his knees and screamed at the top of his lungs. Then he wandered over to a lawn chair in the driveway and took a seat.

Cox and Wright called Robbie for an assist. Robbie had dealt with Williams many times before and was known for dispensing good advice, which Cox and Wright needed. They'd have to take Williams into custody, and they knew that the minute they told him he was under arrest, the battle would be on.

When Robbie arrived, Cox and Wright walked over to meet the car.

"What's he done now?" Robbie asked.

"What hasn't he done?" Cox replied. "They got into it this morning. He picked up a stick and started coming toward her, talking about, 'I'm gonna kill you, you bitch,' this, that, and the other."

"So we got simple assault on her," Robbie said.

"That's right, and terroristic threats."

"Is he drinking again?"

"He was drinking last night. I really don't know what's in his Gatorade bottle."

"Well, he ain't gonna stop," Robbie said. "If y'all got a good case on simple assault, we might as well take him on that."

He pointed toward the driveway area where Williams was sitting; it was cluttered with debris. "We'll have to get him away from all that if he starts being foolish."

"There's sticks and stuff, poles, and a couple of pieces of metal," said Wright.

"Maybe you can bring him out in the yard, say, 'Hey, step over here and let me talk to you,'" Cox suggested to Robbie. "He's got some kind of trust in you."

"He can't have been out of jail a couple of days, and he's already been over here threatening?" Robbie sounded exasperated.

The officers knew where this was going. No amount of sweet talk would convince Williams to turn around for the handcuffs. It hadn't worked before, and today his lucidity seemed extra-compromised. The three cops weren't worried about being overpowered, but they didn't relish what would likely turn into a protracted struggle; Williams was decently strong. The cultural climate was also on their minds. The cops were white; Williams was Black. Only three months earlier, Derek Chauvin had murdered George Floyd. The country was a powder keg waiting to explode.

• • •

THE PROTESTS THAT CAME AFTER George Floyd's killing in every state across the country continued for weeks on end in the summer of 2020. The total crowd size, an estimated 15 to 26 million, surpassed all previous protest movements in American history. While a handful of protests turned violent, the great majority were peaceful and heartfelt.

In LaGrange, forty or so people gathered on June 1 at Lafayette Square. Most were in T-shirts; it was a hot Georgia day. The crowd was mixed, Black and white. Kids held signs that said, "My Life Matters" and "Stop Police Brutality."

For a little over an hour, the protesters listened to speeches delivered over a portable PA system. A young Black man started things off with a prayer: "The police officer, we don't hate you; we love you. God, we ask you to forgive the ones that don't know what they're doing. We ask you to forgive the ones who think they're doing the right thing but are doing the wrong thing."

He was followed by an event organizer, a white woman, wearing a tank top on which she'd scrawled, "I Stand with Black Lives Matter." She lamented systemic racism and police violence, insisting that white people had a duty to stand in solidarity with their Black brothers and sisters. Another woman, Black, took the microphone and told the crowd about her three boys, how she worried about them every day. One of them went to college in Carrollton. Everyone knows how racist Carrollton is, she said. Her son was constantly profiled by police there for driving a nice car. When he and his friends were pulled over, the first question from the cops was when had they last smoked weed? When her kids had parties, the cops showed up, looking for gang activity. "They just want to live free," she stated.

Several speakers were running for local office. Yvonne Lopez, a candidate for the Troup County Commission, was a respected Black leader in LaGrange, the head of Ark Refuge Ministries, which ran a transitional housing facility. George Floyd's death was part of the centuries-long mistreatment of Black Americans, she said. And the only way to bring racial inequality to an end was for Black people to begin voting more of their own into office.

Lopez had been born in Baltimore, where "when we come out of the womb, we are taught to hate the police." In LaGrange, she'd wanted to know more about the PD. So she did some ride-alongs. From that experience and from interacting with the cops through her job, she'd had a change of perspective. "For the first time in my adult life," she said, "I felt compassion for the police department. Now, all police officers are not good. But I'm going to tell you, for the most part, the police department in LaGrange, Georgia, is a very good place. I feel absolutely safe here. I feel like they genuinely care. And I believe in my heart what happened in Minnesota would never happen here in LaGrange. . . . And that's because of the leadership of Chief Dekmar."

• • •

IN FACT, LOU HAD JUST published a short opinion piece in the *LaGrange Daily News*.[1] He'd received an email from a resident seeking reassurance that LaGrange cops had been trained never to do what Derek Chauvin had done. To Lou, the query missed the mark. "The death of George Floyd is not a police training issue but is a result of a troubled culture," he wrote, castigating the Minneapolis department. "The bystanders that called out for the police to stop were not trained in use of force but recognized what the police ignored, a fellow human being in pain, unsympathetically and unnecessarily being fatally injured." Most of all, Lou stated, "the action of the officer kneeling on Mr. Floyd's neck" and "the failure to intervene by the three other officers present on the scene" indicated "a lack of core values" in the police organization. By contrast, "the culture of LPD is one of community partnerships, collaboration and respect for human life. That can only occur if our incidents of use of force are rare and consistent with best practice, department policy, and training."

Lou concluded, "Like anyone viewing the George Floyd video, I was sickened by what I saw. It was outrageous and, in my opinion, criminal.

I also know it's not reflective of the police officers I know and work with on a daily basis."

• • •

At the Williams house, Robbie went in to speak with Marcus's sister and niece. They told him that along with that day's incident with the stick, Williams had punched a friend, a young woman, in the lip the night before. He'd been out with the woman, and she was dropping him off when he'd become enraged. His niece had been asleep at the time, but the woman texted her a photo that showed her mouth swollen and bleeding. It looked as if she'd been hit so hard that she'd bitten through her lip.

"That's battery all day long," Robbie said.

The niece told Robbie she was done with her uncle and was filing to evict him. Brandon Wright began making calls to the woman who'd been punched to see if she'd give a statement, while Robbie and Tyler Cox returned to the question of how to take Williams into custody. He was still sitting in the driveway.

"Is he near the sticks now?" Robbie asked Cox. Williams's access to items that could be used as weapons remained a concern.

"Yeah, they're all propped up, right there. There's plenty of stuff for him to grab hold of," said Cox.

"If we get him when he's sitting, one of us go left, one of us go right, he won't be able to get his hands on them sticks," Robbie said.

The cops walked over to Williams.

"Why'd you hit that girl last night, Marcus?" Robbie asked.

"Man, she hit *me*. I busted my lip."

"Your lip don't look busted to me!" Robbie replied.

Williams, who was barefoot, announced: "I'm walking to my cousin's house."

"Well, put your socks and shoes on; maybe we can help with that," said Robbie, careful not to hint that Williams was about to be arrested.

"Yes, sir," said Williams.

While Williams finished with his shoes, Robbie stepped away to speak to his sergeant over the radio. "We've got two counts of simple assault and a possible battery if we can get the other victim to cooperate." Robbie went on: "You just may want to ease this way because it will turn out probably like it did last time," when Williams made an effort to kick the officers who'd arrested him.

Robbie was formulating a plan. LaGrange PD had recently purchased a BolaWrap, a nonlethal device that looks a little like a Taser but is a restraint and not designed to achieve compliance through pain. If you need to arrest someone who won't agree to be handcuffed—someone who's mentally ill, for example, and who can't process instructions—you aim the BolaWrap's laser pointer at them. When you pull the trigger, the device shoots out a long cord that wraps around the person, immobilizing them long enough so you can get them handcuffed.

Robbie had trained on the BolaWrap and thought it could work to contain Williams's legs. But you weren't supposed to deploy the device on bare skin because there were hooks at the end of the cord that could cause an injury.

Robbie saw that Williams had some clothes near his chair.

"Why don't you put them blue jeans on, man?" Robbie called to him.

"What blue jeans?"

"The ones behind you!"

"They ain't no blue jeans; they're shorts!" said Williams.

"Well, they long! Why don't you put them on!" said Robbie.

"Why, it ain't gonna rain!"

"It *is* gonna rain!"

Williams looked up at the blue sky. "When's it gonna rain?" he asked.

"Today," said Robbie. "It's forty, sixty percent chance." That was a lie, but Robbie hoped it might work.

"I'll bet you it rains about five, about ten, eleven o'clock at night; what you think?" said Williams.

"Let me ask you a question," said Robbie, changing tactics. "Why'd you threaten them with a stick?"

"I wasn't gonna hit them," said Williams. "I love them. I'm crazy about my niece."

The niece came outside, and Williams stood up, immediately beginning to shout. She had his money, and he needed some of it.

"Don't yell, Marcus," said Robbie.

"Can I get ten dollars of my money?" Williams asked.

"Not right now," Robbie replied.

"Why?"

"Hang on, Marcus," said Robbie.

"Nah, I ain't gonna hang on." Williams took a few steps away from the house. He seemed to realize all of a sudden that he was in trouble.

"Marcus, stop," said Robbie.

"Don't start that shit with me," said Williams. "Don't start that shit with me. Don't start that shit with me." With that he took off running down the street.

"Mr. Williams is now running full sprint," Robbie said into his radio.

"I ain't running after him," he told the younger officers, who were about to. "I'll go get my car."

Cox and Wright caught up to Williams after about a block. He'd lost steam. Robbie got there moments later. "Leave him standing like that," he told Cox and Wright over the car's loudspeaker.

Robbie got out of his cruiser, BolaWrap in hand. "Back up, y'all."

"Put your hands down by your sides," Robbie said to Williams, aiming the laser pointer at his torso, which was covered by his sweatshirt. The leg option was out.

"You don't got to tase me!" yelled Williams.

"Put your hands behind your back," Robbie said.

Williams didn't. His hands were down, but his body had tensed in anticipation of a fight ahead.

"Put your hands behind your back," Robbie said again. There was a "pow" sound as the BolaWrap cord shot out of its canister and wrapped around Williams's arms and torso. "Ow," he said. The cord hadn't landed tight enough to immobilize his arms, but it did give Cox and Wright enough time to grab Williams's hands and get them behind his back.

They couldn't cuff him, though; Williams was trying furiously to pull away.

Robbie threw the BolaWrap aside so that he could join the fray.

"Go to the ground; go to the ground," Robbie told his colleagues. Williams resisted, but after a few seconds, they were able to get him off-balance and tip him over in the middle of the street.

Ground grappling is at the heart of the jiujitsu method that Robbie had taken to practicing five days a week at Invictus Combatives, the exercise the only thing keeping him afloat during a period of social upheaval. COVID had forced Robert Moore to close the dojo to the public, but a core group of friends had continued to train there. One of the grappling techniques is "super hooks," and Robbie was confident in his skill with it. Super hooks involves mounting an opponent, using the pressure of your hips to keep his hips on the ground and controlling his limbs with yours.

When Williams came down on his back, Robbie got right on top of him. Williams tried to kick and wrestle, but Robbie super-hooked his legs and pinned him with his hips, being sure to keep the pressure off his chest. After three minutes of intense grappling, with Robbie repeating, "Stop, Marcus. Marcus, stop," and everyone sweating and grunting, the three cops were able to reposition Williams so that he was on his stomach. He was still resisting too much to get cuffs on, but when a detective arrived, and then a Troup County sheriff's deputy, the five officers together were able to secure the handcuffs. They rolled Williams onto his side to allow him to breathe more easily.

No punches were thrown. No Taser was used, nor a chemical irritant or a baton or a kick. Guns stayed holstered. No one swore or threatened Williams or even raised their voices. When it was over, he was taken to the hospital and then to jail.

In an ideal world, Williams would have had access to treatment for his mental illness and addiction and would never have threatened his family. But the world we live in isn't ideal. When a violent man needs to be arrested, this—or some version of it—is how it should happen.

If James H. Cone, the theologian read by the Alterna group, were alive today, he might argue that the police stop has taken the place of the lynching tree as among the most powerful symbols of Black oppression.[2] Changing law enforcement so that it can stand for something different is the moral responsibility of Lou Dekmar and Robbie Hall and every chief and police officer in America.

CONCLUSION

When I joined the Berkeley police in 1992, I thought I was signing on to a progressive police agency with a rich, admirable history. In the early twentieth century, Berkeley had one of the most advanced police departments in the nation. Its influential chief, August Vollmer, believed that police and social workers should act together to address the root causes of crime; that officers should be college educated; and that the department would be well-served by adopting new technologies for patrolmen (like radios) and new investigative techniques for detectives (like mapping crime patterns). Professional policing, Vollmer insisted, was essential to good governance.

Parts of Vollmer's vision and influence remained intact during my time there. Most officers in Berkeley had bachelor's degrees. The chief, Dash Butler, favored strong police-community relations and tried to hire cops with ties to the city, people who'd thrive in its diverse, eclectic environment. Berkeley officers attended neighborhood watch meetings, swung by after-school programs, and walked or rode bicycles in the commercial districts to connect with those passing through.

But this approach to policing sat uneasily with another, more menacing perspective. In a period when crime and violence dominated the local news, a contingent of Berkeley cops came to think of themselves as the only thing standing between civilization and chaos. It was their job, they maintained, to strike fear in the hearts of anyone contemplating criminal activity. They saw stop and frisk as crucial. Find a crack rock? Great. A weapon? Even better. Someone with a minor warrant? Take him in. The community would thank them for these efforts, and if they didn't, screw 'em. Do what you have to do and watch your back.

Enough Berkeley officers swore by this creed that on the street a macho, aggressive policing culture was the name of the game.[1] The officers I was closest to weren't a macho bunch, but certain elements did rub off on us.

Christine, my best friend then and a doctoral student in clinical psychology, watched with concern as I got put through the mill of cop culture. She saw me become more aggressive, more depressed, less inquisitive. One night, while I was getting coffee at a 7–Eleven, a jerk of a cop, an older guy who'd joined Berkeley PD after serving in another state, looked at me and said, "Gross, in twenty years, you'll be just like me." That's when I knew I had to get out, and when I first started thinking about the sway that culture has over people's lives.

As I CAME TO KNOW the officers in Stockton, Longmont, and LaGrange, I realized that were I a rookie today in those agencies, soaking up their healthier cultures, I'd have stood a better chance of becoming the cop I wanted to be: one who knows that you can't have social justice without criminal justice because no one prospers without public safety, but who also understands that unequal law enforcement is no justice at all. The kind of cop who adjusts their policing to serve the changing needs of the community because anything less is undemocratic; one who's always prepared for a fight, but who knows in their bones that only a tiny percentage of people pose an actual threat and acting otherwise means *you're* the one who presents a danger; a cop who recognizes the distinction between criminal behavior and mental illness or addiction; one whose mantra is "de-escalate, de-escalate, de-escalate"; one who sees protecting people's constitutional and human rights to be as important as arresting suspects. One morally and emotionally mature enough to prevent a minor traffic stop from exploding into a pointless altercation.

In Longmont and LaGrange, particularly, the path to becoming that cop—to becoming an ethical, responsible police officer—would have been laid out from the get-go. That's what a positive policing culture can do. It can't solve all the problems of the police. It's not a substitute for structural change in the justice system or in American society generally. But it can guide officers, young and old, toward worthy behavior.

* * *

IN STOCKTON, ERIC JONES ANNOUNCED that he'd be retiring at the end of 2021, which would mark a decade of serving as chief and three decades with the department. He imagined moving on to a position at the federal, state, or county level, where he could continue working on police reform or advise other police agencies on procedural justice. The summer before, Black Lives Matter protests in Stockton had been comparatively small, nothing like the huge crowds that turned out in San Francisco or Oakland. While Stockton activists took credit for making sure the protests remained nonviolent (there were only a few minor scattered incidents), police commanders thought the peace reflected the trust that had grown between the department and the community.

Still, improving the department's performance on racial equity was near the top of Eric's priorities in the year and a half that followed. Harry Black, the city manager, convened an equity review board that met quarterly to discuss the PD. Eric, confident that procedural justice was now sufficiently established that his cops and the union wouldn't balk, talked with the board about policy changes that could make a real difference: the routine spot checks of bodycam footage he'd previously thought premature, restrictions on vehicle stops to reduce racial disparities, recruiting and retaining a more diverse workforce, further tightening the use of force policy, new ways to make the department's performance data visible to the public. If implemented by Eric's successor, these changes would represent the fruition of his incremental approach: slowly alter the department's culture, and then layer on new policy. Stay one step ahead of your officers, not three. Make sure that reforms are more than window dressing.

But a spike in violent crime—terrible in itself—threatened to reverse this progress. Consistent with national trends, Stockton saw an alarming 40 percent rise in its homicide rate in 2020. That rate remained elevated in the first half of 2021, though by summer it had begun to moderate. Nonfatal shootings were up, too. Criminologists pointed to a range of factors to explain the tumultuous surge: stress from the pandemic; disruptions to drug markets; a sudden increase in gun ownership in response to social uncertainty, with people drawing weapons over trivial disputes; an anti-police climate leading officers to second-guess routine enforcement and creating a groundswell of resignations and early retirements. In this context, calls mounted for a return to harsh policing strategies.

As Eric saw it, the department's task was to try to keep public safety from devolving further while holding the line on improvements he'd made to the force. Slippage could happen easily. In December 2020, two newer CRT officers allegedly assaulted a seventeen-year-old Black boy following a vehicle pursuit. After an investigation, Eric fired them both.

DRAKE WIEST LEFT STOCKTON PD for Fairfield in April 2020. He loved working gangs, but the team was in transition. Rob Barrington had taken the sergeant's exam and would soon be promoted, heading back to patrol. Other officers were transferring to investigations. The main reason Drake took the new job, though, was to shave off two hours from his commute and be closer to his wife and daughter, getting that pay raise to boot. He'd have to do field training all over again, but he didn't mind.

Eric's accelerated reforms came too late for Jesse Smith, who by early 2020 had had it with how slowly things were changing in Stockton. He got an idea. The Stockton Unified School District maintains its own police force, with thirty-seven officers patrolling the district's sixty schools. The SUSD Department of Public Safety doesn't have the greatest track record, either. In 2019, the district entered into a legal settlement with the California Attorney General's Office, which had found that Black, Latino, and disabled students were being systematically over-policed. The settlement committed the district and department to an overhaul managed by an independent monitor.

Jesse was hopeful that these reforms would stick; they were state mandated, and the SUSD force was more diverse at all levels than Stockton PD. The man who would become its new chief, Richard Barries, was Black and had a strong personal stake in racial equity and empowerment. Jesse was offered a sergeant's position; here was his chance to help rebuild a police agency from the ground up. SUSD Public Safety had signed on not only to procedural justice but to dismantling the school-to-prison pipeline, prioritizing restorative justice and social service referrals rather than arrests for students who commit offenses while on school property. For Jesse, it was a perfect fit, an opportunity to do policing right. He traded in one uniform for another.

Eric and his team were devastated by Jesse's departure. That he left because he'd lost faith in Stockton PD's commitment to reform made it that much harder to swallow. But incremental police reform always reflects a utilitarian calculus: you believe that the benefits of cautious change—avoiding a disruption in operations that could compromise public safety, avoiding blowback from your officers—will outweigh the costs. Those costs include the people who might be hurt by bad policing in the meantime and allies you lose who are tired of being asked for patience.

* * *

In Longmont, Mike Butler retired in July 2020. He felt some ambivalence, as policing in this country had a long way to go.

A month earlier, he joined a tense, virtual city council meeting. The council was considering a resolution condemning the killing of Black people by law enforcement. Mike had been asked to field questions. Struggling to find the right words, and not entirely succeeding, he said of George Floyd's murder, "It's a black mark for us. I've said for years that the actions of one police officer can upset the equilibrium of an entire community. Well, these actions upset the equilibrium of an entire country."

After emphasizing that what happened to Floyd could never happen in Longmont—because of the officers hired, the training they were given, and the policies that were in place—Mike concluded: "The police profession in the eyes of many seems broken. And I'm not going to say it's not broken. There is a brokenness about it, and these latest incidents have highlighted that brokenness. There's a part of me that says, you know what, I don't want to leave because I think I can help. But there's also a part of me, the bigger part of me, that says good luck to the next person. That's where I'm landing." After a lifetime of public service, Mike was ready for a change.

Retirement suited him. He continued to speak at community events. He did consulting for other police departments that had heard about Longmont's innovations and wanted to emulate them. He and Carol began leading the Urantia study group, alternating weeks with Mo Siegel. Mike saw friends, including Dan Benavidez, the activist.

In the summer of 2021, Mike and Carol made it out to Maine, a state they'd always wanted to visit. One night in Acadia National Park, at Eagle Lake, he took a breathtaking photograph of the stars plastered everywhere above a mountainous horizon.

MIKE WAS A UNICORN AMONG police chiefs, the ethos he established at Longmont PD as unique as his character. But that singularity also posed a problem. Herman Goldstein wrote in *Policing a Free Society*: "It is rare to find an enlightened police leader whose immediate subordinates approach him in competence."[2] If that's true, how does a unicorn chief who has built a positive department culture safeguard it for the future?

The answer is that the chief needs to make sure that those who report to him and are apt to succeed him are committed to the same values and principles. That means reform-minded leaders must be extremely picky when it comes to promotions into the top ranks, and they should be effective mentors to the captains, lieutenants, and deputy chiefs in their agencies.

In this one area, Mike had arguably fared less well. Many lower-ranking officers were committed to his Longmont way of policing and would continue doing the job as Mike had inspired, enabled, and encouraged them to do it, no matter who became chief. But at the top of the command structure, Jeff Satur's commitment was harder to gauge. By all appearances, he was a SWAT guy before he was anything else.

The leadership vacuum created by Mike's departure proved real and consequential. In his absence, a small number of patrol officers and sergeants who'd disliked his approach became more vocal. Vijay Kailasam, for one, butted heads with them. It made for an uncomfortable workplace.

It took a year for Harold Dominguez, Longmont's city manager, to announce Mike's replacement. It wasn't Jeff Satur, who'd remain as deputy chief. Dominguez gave the job to a longtime cop and police administrator from Georgia, Zach Ardis. Ardis told the *Longmont Leader* that he was drawn to Longmont because he "saw things happening" there "that were light years ahead of what other cities are doing."[3]

Around the same time that Mike retired, Sandie Campanella left to take a new job as an investigator at the Boulder County District Attorney's Office. The DA, Michael Dougherty, elected in 2018 as part of a national wave of progressive prosecutors, set up a dedicated domestic violence unit, and Sandie's reputation preceded her. In addition to investigating cases, she'd be able to establish countywide systems to track DV, identify potentially lethal offenders, and advocate for wraparound services for victims—social, mental health support, medical. Sandie couldn't have done more to prepare for her departure, leaving Longmont domestic violence investigations in Edna Munoz's capable hands.

* * *

After the arrest of Marcus Williams in LaGrange, Robbie Hall's commitment to jiujitsu deepened. Like many other cops who practice the martial art, Robbie was apoplectic when he heard that the New York City Council passed a law weeks after George Floyd's murder outlawing not just choke holds for NYPD officers but the application of any pressure to the back or chest that would compress a person's diaphragm. Choke holds have no place in policing, but pinning someone by the hips is integral to moves like super hooks, and Robbie felt strongly that these moves were safe and necessary. As he saw it, if cops didn't have access to them, they'd end up resorting to far more dangerous techniques (and weapons) when people resisted arrest. LaGrange didn't have the same use of force restrictions as New York, so Robbie kept going back to Invictus Combatives to practice, and began teaching jiujitsu-inspired defensive tactics to other officers in the department.

Robbie had never aspired to promotion beyond corporal, but now it was on his mind. He knew he'd make a good sergeant; he was already doing informal mentoring and supervising. To get the extra stripe on his shoulder, Robbie would have to pass a sergeant's exam—and earn his associate's degree. His wife encouraged him, and in 2021, at age forty-nine, he enrolled in an online college.

LOU DEKMAR HAD NO IMMEDIATE plans to retire, not least because he'd been working on important changes to the department's firearms training. For decades, police officers were taught that, faced with a lethal threat and the need to shoot, they should aim for the chest or the head and keep shooting until the threat is neutralized. Shooting someone in a limb to temporarily disable them might seem like a better option, but when your adrenaline's going, getting that much precision with a handgun is hard. If you miss, you might pay the ultimate price.

Lou had spent time thinking about this. Sometimes multiple shots to the chest made sense, no matter how horrifying that might seem—in a gun battle, for example. And regular cops weren't able to strike flailing arms, sharpshooter style. But you didn't have to be a particularly good shot to strike in the pelvic region, stomach, or upper thigh, where the wound would less likely be lethal. What if that was enough to end the threat? Wasn't it worth trying, if it meant the difference between taking a life and not?

Lou's firearms instructors investigated the feasibility of the idea and developed a training plan. They called it "Shoot to Incapacitate." With practice in simulated scenarios, LaGrange PD officers believed that it was doable.

Lou's other big project stemmed from a partnership he'd formed with the Georgia Innocence Project, which works to free people wrongly convicted of crimes. In 1981, LaGrange PD arrested a Black man named Terry Talley, charging him with a string of sexual assaults. Talley was convicted and sentenced to life. But Innocence Project lawyers became convinced that the police and the Troup County District Attorney's Office had gotten the wrong man. Lou tasked one of his detectives with reopening the case. In February 2021, Talley's conviction was overturned, and he was released from prison.

When Lou was told that this was the first time a police department had fully cooperated with the Georgia Innocence Project on an investigation, he was taken aback. How could other agencies *not* cooperate if their officers had put an innocent man behind bars?

He'd remained involved with CALEA and wondered whether the commission might require that agencies investigate when presented with credible exculpatory evidence after a conviction. Perhaps that could begin to right some of the wrongs of the past. Lou wrote up a proposed accreditation standard and submitted it for review.

* * *

THE CHALLENGES THIS COUNTRY FACES in getting the professional, equitable, and humane policing it needs are formidable. The aggressive culture of policing I encountered twenty-five years ago prevails in too many departments, and racial inequities are entrenched.

Amid national outrage about police abuse, the temptation has arisen to either write off policing or impose a plethora of legal and policy restraints to bring police into line. But we can't write off the police, not in the foreseeable future. The January 6, 2021, insurrection at the US Capitol made clear even to skeptics that democracy is not sustainable without law enforcement, whatever the shortcomings of the police response that day. No less vividly, the recent nationwide rise in violent crime, coming on the heels of deficiencies in police staffing, shows that we remain reliant on the police for community safety. And while restraints on police behavior are needed, public institutions like the police need more than rules to function effectively. They also require an animating spirit, a culture, one that offers employees a sense of mission, purpose, and identity, and that steers them toward doing the right thing. Changing cop culture must become a new national priority.

If a turnabout is possible in a place like LaGrange, with its history of slavery, racism, and police malevolence, then in principle it's possible anywhere. The most important lesson to be drawn from the three cities I studied is that when it comes to remaking a police department, chiefs play an indispensable role. Herman Goldstein was right: their leadership matters. Yet chiefs won't make progress with superficial, off-the-shelf solutions: a little procedural justice here, some racial reconciliation there, and you're done. In Stockton, Longmont, and LaGrange, cultural change occurred only because the chiefs displayed inventiveness and ingenuity, creatively combining elements from their personal experience, the world of criminal justice reform, and local circumstance to come up with new models of policing—and implementation strategies—custom-built for their agencies. The chiefs also exhibited organizational savvy, skill at communicating with cops and citizens, historical awareness, humility, and perseverance.

The problem is that these attributes are in short supply among police leaders. Frequently, risk-averse mayors or city managers install competent but anodyne chiefs, their goal to placate constituents without disturbing the status quo. Or they'll put in place top cops who are all talk when it comes to reform but have no follow-through. If we're serious about change, appointments should be given to respected high-ranking officers who have a clear and compelling vision for how the culture of a police department could be improved (which might include building on the success of predecessors), who pledge to engage in continuous dialogue with the public and be open to ideas that emerge from that exchange, and who have a workable plan for achieving their goals in the face of resistance from officers and unions. They also need time: in many cities, revolving-door appointments of two to three years are now the norm for police chiefs, making it almost impossible for them to build the support for change that Eric Jones, Mike Butler, and Lou Dekmar were able to muster.

We could take steps to increase the creative potential of chiefs so that they're better equipped for the work before them. Universities should bolster certificate or graduate programs that put police leaders in touch with the widest possible spectrum of researchers, thinkers, law enforcement professionals, activists, and citizens from around the country and around the world. Philanthropies and nonprofits should sponsor conferences and events that similarly bring chiefs and their staff into conversation with voices they don't normally encounter. Some of this is being done already, but not enough. States and the federal government could spur further innovation by awarding grants to cities willing to experiment with new approaches, funding research, and disseminating information about changes in culture that prove successful.

We would benefit, too, from far more inclusive recruiting practices to encourage our best and brightest to consider careers in law enforcement, especially those who don't fit the traditional policing mold. That's how we'll find the next generation of unicorns and change-makers.

But changing cop culture requires one more thing: the community.

As citizens, we will not get the policing we need by treating all cops as either villains or heroes and retreating to the comforts of a fixed set of positions and ideologies. Recognizing that some police departments perform to higher standards than others and that improvement is possible, our job is to press our local agencies to rethink their culture and operations; to support chiefs and officers who are trying to do precisely that; to make sure that departments have the resources they need to change; to volunteer our time for programs like the Longmont Community Justice Partnership or the racial trust-building initiative in LaGrange; and to sit down with the police at every opportunity, listen to what they have to say, and communicate our hopes and fears, our experiences and expectations, and the firmness of our resolve for justice. Institutions change as people change them, together.

Better policing lies over that mountainous horizon.

NOTES

INTRODUCTION

1. Frank Edwards, Hedwig Lee, and Michael Esposito, "Risk of Being Killed by Police Use of Force in the United States by Age, Race–Ethnicity, and Sex," *Proceedings of the National Academy of Sciences* 116, no. 34 (2019): 16793–98.
2. Emma Pierson, Camelia Simoiu, Jan Overgoor, et al., "A Large-Scale Analysis of Racial Disparities in Police Stops across the United States," *Nature Human Behaviour* 4 (2020): 1–10.
3. Li Zhou, "Where Americans Stand on Policing Today," *Vox*, April 9, 2021, https://www.vox.com/22372342/police-reform-derek-chauvin.
4. Jennifer Agiesta, "CNN Poll: Most Satisfied with Chauvin Verdict, but Partisans Divide," CNN, April 27, 2021, https://www.cnn.com/2021/04/27/politics/cnn-poll-chauvin-trial/index.html.
5. Joshua M. Chanin, "Examining the Sustainability of Pattern or Practice Police Misconduct Reform," *Police Quarterly* 18, no. 2 (2014): 163–92.
6. Joel Miller, Paul Quinton, Banos Alexandrou, and Daniel Packham, "Can Police Training Reduce Ethnic/Racial Disparities in Stop and Search? Evidence from a Multisite UK Trial," *Criminology & Public Policy* 19, no. 4 (2020): 1259–87; Robert E. Worden, Sarah J. McLean, Robin S. Engel, Hannah Cochran, Nicholas Corsaro, Danielle Reynolds, Cynthia J. Najdowski, and Gabrielle T. Isaza, "The Impacts of Implicit Bias Awareness Training in the NYPD," 2020, https://www.theiacp.org/sites/default/files/Research%20Center/NYPD%20Implicit%20Bias%20Report.pdf.
7. President's Task Force on 21st Century Policing, *Final Report of the President's Task Force on 21st Century Policing* (Washington, DC: Office of Community Oriented Policing Services), 11–12.

8. Mallory Newall, Chris Jackson, and Johnny Sawyer, "Americans' Trust in Law Enforcement, Desire to Protect Law and Order on the Rise," *Ipsos*, March 5, 2021, https://www.ipsos.com/en-us/americans-trust-law-enforcement-desire-protect-law-and-order-rise.
9. The book might be read by my fellow sociologists as a series of case studies of organizational problem-solving, creativity, and adaptation, with a focus on cultural change.
10. "US News Special Report: Stockton, Calif., Is the Most Diverse City in America," *US News & World Report*, January 22, 2020, https://www.usnews.com/info/blogs/press-room/articles/2020–01–22/us-news-special-report-stockton-calif-is-the-most-diverse-city-in-america.

1: MUDVILLE

1. Leonard Gardner, *Fat City* (1969; repr., New York: New York Review Books, 2015), 7.
2. Ronald Eugene Isetti, *Competing Voices: A Critical History of Stockton, California* (Denver: Outskirts Press, 2019).
3. Quoted in Isetti, *Competing Voices*, 44.
4. See Michael Fitzgerald, "Going to Bat for Casey's Mudville," *Record*, April 9, 2004, https://www.recordnet.com/story/news/2004/04/09/going-to-bat-for-casey/50703416007/.
5. Although Stockton's Black population increased by more than 200 percent between 1940 and 1950, there'd long been a Black community in the area. Lawrence B. De Graff and Quintard Taylor report that beyond San Francisco and Sacramento, "Marysville, Grass Valley, and Placerville in the Mother Lode country and Stockton in the Central Valley were the only other cities in antebellum Northern California that had a sizable black presence." See their "Introduction: African Americans in California History, California in African American History," in *Seeking El Dorado: African Americans in California*, ed. Lawrence De Graff, Kevin Mulroy, and Quintard Taylor (Seattle: University of Washington Press, 2001), 12.
6. Jack Harlow, "Whats Poppin," https://genius.com/Jack-harlow-whats-poppin-lyrics.
7. One of the best studies of this hollowing-out process remains William Julius Wilson, *When Work Disappears: The World of the New Urban Poor* (New York: Knopf, 1996).
8. Gerald W. Haslam, *The Other California: The Great Central Valley in Life and Letters* (Reno: University of Nevada Press, 1993).
9. Jason Zengerle, "Can the Black Rifle Coffee Company Become the Starbucks of the Right?" *New York Times*, July 14, 2021, https://www.nytimes.com/2021/07/14/magazine/black-rifle-coffee-company.html.
10. See Richard Rosenfeld, "Crime and the Great Recession: Introduction to the

Special Issue," *Journal of Contemporary Criminal Justice* 30, no. 1 (2013): 4–6, and the other papers in the issue. Also relevant is Richard Rosenfeld, "Studying Crime Trends: Normal Science and Exogenous Shocks," *Criminology* 56, no. 1 (2018): 5–26.

11. Aaron Chalfin, Benjamin Hansen, Emily K. Weisburst, and Morgan C. Williams, Jr., "Police Force Size and Civilian Race" (National Bureau of Economic Research Working Paper 28202, 2020). Yet the study also found that "investments in police manpower lead to larger numbers of low-level 'quality of life' arrests, with effects that imply a disproportionate burden for Black civilians who are arrested" (p. 4).

2: I DON'T GANGBANG NO MORE

1. On the connection between poverty and violent crime, with particular reference to the experience of people living in impoverished Black neighborhoods, see Elliott Currie, *A Peculiar Indifference: The Neglected Toll of Violence on Black America* (New York: Metropolitan, 2020). On social bonds, Robert J. Sampson, Stephen W. Raudenbush, and Felton Earls, "Neighborhoods and Violent Crime: A Multilevel Study of Collective Efficacy," *Science* 277, no. 5328 (1997): 918–24. On lead toxicity, Christopher Muller, Robert J. Sampson, and Alix S. Winter, "Environmental Inequality: The Social Causes and Consequences of Lead Exposure," *Annual Review of Sociology* 44 (2018): 263–82.
2. See David M. Kennedy, *Don't Shoot: One Man, a Street Fellowship, and the End of Violence in Inner-City America* (New York: Bloomsbury, 2011).
3. Anthony A. Braga, David L. Weisburd, and Brandon Turchan, "Focused Deterrence Strategies and Crime Control: An Updated Systematic Review and Meta-Analysis of the Empirical Evidence," *Criminology & Public Policy* 17, no. 1 (2018): 205–50.
4. Thomas Abt, *Bleeding Out: The Devastating Consequences of Urban Violence—and a Bold New Plan for Peace in the Streets* (New York: Basic Books, 2019), 88.
5. The police department wouldn't be the only city agency trying to prevent shootings. Stockton maintains an Office of Violence Prevention staffed by "peacekeepers," civilians with street knowledge who receive training in mediation and gang conflict and attempt to intervene in disputes before they turn deadly. So that gang members will trust them, the peacekeepers preserve a firewall between themselves and the cops. Research on the effectiveness of these kinds of "violence interrupter" programs has yielded mixed results, but some studies suggest that such programs, along with efforts by nonprofit organizations to improve the quality of life in urban neighborhoods, can play a significant role in curbing violence. For discussion, see Patrick Sharkey, *Uneasy Peace: The Great Crime Decline, the Renewal of City Life, and the Next War on Violence* (New York: W. W. Norton, 2018). Also, John Jay College Research Advisory Group on Preventing and Reducing Community Violence, "Reducing

Violence without Police: A Review of Research Evidence" (New York: Research and Evaluation Center, John Jay College of Criminal Justice, City University of New York, 2020), esp. 8–11.

6. Two useful overviews are Eric H. Monkkonen, *Police in Urban America, 1860–1920* (Cambridge: Cambridge University Press, 1981); and Samuel Walker, *Popular Justice: A History of American Criminal Justice*, 2nd ed. (New York: Oxford University Press, 1998). On the South, see Dennis C. Rousey, *Policing the Southern City: New Orleans, 1805–1889* (Baton Rouge: Louisiana State University Press, 1996).
7. If crime was high, fear of crime was even higher as part of a broader reaction against urbanization. Loïc Wacquant notes that "by the 1870s, the idiom of wilderness was transferred from the Western frontier to the urban frontier, and the inner ring of cities portrayed as an abyss of anonymity, depravity, and artificiality, whose 'semi-barbarous' residents threatened to capsize the societal edifice." See his *The Invention of the "Underclass": A Study in the Politics of Knowledge* (Cambridge, MA: Polity, 2022), 17. On riots as a key stimulus to the growth of American police forces, see Roger Lane, "Urban Police and Crime," in *Modern Policing*, ed. Michael Tonry and Norval Morris (Chicago: University of Chicago Press, 1992).
8. Sidney L. Harring, *Policing a Class Society: The Experience of American Cities, 1865–1915* (New Brunswick, NJ: Rutgers University Press, 1983). For a review of the rapidly growing historical literature on policing, class inequality, and race, see Elizabeth Hinton and DeAnza Cook, "The Mass Criminalization of Black Americans: A Historical Overview," *Annual Review of Criminology* 4 (2021): 261–86.
9. Ernest Jerome Hopkins, *Our Lawless Police: A Study of the Unlawful Enforcement of the Law* (New York: Viking Press, 1931), 195–96.
10. Brandon T. Jett, *Race, Crime, and Policing in the Jim Crow South: African-Americans and Law Enforcement in Birmingham, Memphis, and New Orleans, 1920–1945* (Baton Rouge: Louisiana State University Press, 2021). Gunnar Myrdal wrote of the Southern policeman during this period that "he stands not only for civic order as defined in formal laws and regulations, but also for 'white supremacy' and the whole set of social customs associated with this concept." See his *An American Dilemma: The Negro Problem and Modern Democracy*, 20th anniversary ed. (New York: Harper & Row, 1962), 535.
11. William A. Westley, "Violence and the Police," *American Journal of Sociology* 59, no. 1 (1953): 34–41.
12. In 1954, Lohman would be elected sheriff of Cook County.
13. Westley, "Violence and the Police," 38–39.
14. Westley, 35. These tendencies may have been shaped by the unique history of American policing. Reflecting on police brutality in the nineteenth century, Samuel Walker observes that "the problem was deeply rooted in political conflicts surrounding the police. Patrol officers were unqualified

and untrained, while their supervisors were more concerned about their political patrons than about good policing. Correctly perceived as political agents, police officers never won the respect of the public." See his *Popular Justice*, p. 62.

15. These are studies in progress. One paper published from their collaboration, concerned less with resistance than other dynamics of police-citizen interaction, is Geoffrey Raymond, Lillian Taylor Jungleib, Don Zimmerman, and Nikki Jones, "Rules and Policeable Matters: Enforcing the Civil Sidewalk Ordinance for 'Another First Time,'" in *The Ethnomethodology Program: Legacies and Prospects*, ed. Douglas W. Maynard and John Heritage (New York: Oxford University Press, 2022).
16. Jerome H. Skolnick, *Justice without Trial: Law Enforcement in a Democratic Society* (New York: Wiley, 1966).
17. Skolnick, 42.
18. Two other early studies that spoke to police culture are Egon Bittner, "The Police on Skid-Row: A Study of Peace Keeping," *American Sociological Review* 32, no 5. (1967): 699–715; and Albert J. Reiss Jr., *The Police and the Public* (New Haven: Yale University Press, 1971).
19. Joe Goldeen, "Widow Spirals into Homelessness," *Record*, February 7, 2015, https://www.recordnet.com/story/news/2015/02/08/widow-spirals-into-homelessness/35201031007/.
20. The San Joaquin County District Attorney's Office investigated this incident and published a report clearing the officers involved of wrongdoing.
21. For an analysis of such practices nationally that links them to an increasingly precarious labor market, declining levels of public assistance for the poor, and backlash against civil rights gains, see Loïc Wacquant, *Punishing the Poor: The Neoliberal Government of Social Insecurity* (Durham, NC: Duke University Press, 2009). These themes are also explored in Michelle Alexander, *The New Jim Crow: Mass Incarceration in the Age of Colorblindness* (New York: New Press, 2010).
22. Stockton was included in the study because Eric agreed to have the police department take part in the National Initiative for Building Community Trust and Justice, a US DOJ–funded collaboration between academics and practitioners intended to "improve relationships and increase trust between communities and the criminal justice system and advance the public and scholarly understandings of the issues contributing to those relationships." The project helped coordinate some of the training and trust-building work in Stockton that I describe in the following chapter. On the initiative, see their website: https://trustandjustice.org/. For an overview of the study, see Jocelyn Fontaine et al., "Evidence of Change in Six Cities Participating in the National Initiative for Building Community Trust and Justice," Urban Institute, 2019, https://www.urban.org/sites/default/files/publication/100706/2019.11.11_ni_community_survey_brief_final_0.pdf. Calculations are my own.

3: PJ

1. Skolnick, *Justice without Trial*, 60. This quotation is from a section of the book comparing American and British police culture.
2. James Q. Wilson, *Varieties of Police Behavior: The Management of Law and Order in Eight Communities* (Cambridge, MA: Harvard University Press, 1968).
3. Elizabeth Reuss-Ianni, *Two Cultures of Policing: Street Cops and Management Cops* (New Brunswick, NJ: Transaction Books, 1983), 14–15.
4. As criminologist Robert Reiner has pointed out in correspondence, it is curious that Wilson and Skolnick, studying the Oakland police department at approximately the same time, could reach such different conclusions. Skolnick reflected on the discrepancy years later, suggesting that Oakland PD was legalistic in some respects with a traditional police culture under the surface. Jerome H. Skolnick, "Enduring Issues of Police Culture and Demographics," *Policing and Society* 18, no. 1 (2008): 35–45.
5. Wilson, *Varieties of Police Behavior*, 200.
6. Wilson, 236.
7. Wilson, 258.
8. Elizabeth Hinton, *America on Fire: The Untold Story of Police Violence and Black Rebellion Since the 1960s* (New York: Liveright, 2021), 313, 320. In response to these disturbances, and as an extension of his previously announced war on crime, President Lyndon Johnson disbursed millions of dollars in grant money and transferred a substantial amount of military hardware to local police departments, in what Hinton argues should be seen as a domestic counterinsurgency effort, one that set the stage for intensive policing of urban communities in the 1980s and beyond.
9. Robert Sheehan, "The Changing Role of Boston's Finest," *Boston Globe*, March 16, 1969, 20A.
10. Wilson, *Varieties of Police Behavior*, 283.
11. The idea of police culture as flexible and variegated is in line with a new generation of research that draws on more sophisticated sociological theories of culture. See, for example, Janet B. L. Chan, *Changing Police Culture: Policing in a Multiracial Society* (Cambridge: Cambridge University Press, 1997). For a review of contemporary research emphasizing variability, see Tom Cockcroft, *Police Culture: Themes and Concepts* (New York: Routledge, 2013), esp. 79–103. An important study that finds more universality than variation is Bethan Loftus, *Police Culture in a Changing World* (Oxford: Oxford University Press, 2009). For general introductions to research on police culture see John P. Crank, *Understanding Police Culture*, 2nd ed. (New York: Routledge, 2015); and Eugene A. Paoline and William Terrill, *Police Culture: Adapting to the Strains of the Job* (Durham: Carolina Academic Press, 2013). Crank identifies a large number of themes found by scholars to be part of the culture of the police,

from domination and the "righteousness" of force to suspicion, danger, unpredictability, the seductions of crime, solidarity, and morality. He argues: "Until advocates of police change recognize the importance of culture, they will continue to be as surprised as they have been for the past 100 years at the profound limitations of reform efforts to yield real and enduring changes" (p. 13).

12. Max Weber, "The Three Types of Legitimate Rule," *Berkeley Journal of Sociology* 4, no. 1 ([1922] 1958): 1–11.
13. Tom R. Tyler, *Why People Obey the Law* (New Haven: Yale University Press, 1990).
14. Tracey L. Meares and Tom R. Tyler, "Policing: A Model for the Twenty-First Century," in *Policing the Black Man*, ed. Angela Davis (New York: Knopf, 2017), 164.
15. E.g., Alex S. Vitale, *The End of Policing* (London: Verso, 2017), 14–15.

4: TAKE SOME GIRLS

1. At the request of the task force, I've changed the name of the officer depicted in this sketch.
2. R. Andrew Chesnut, *Devoted to Death: Santa Muerte, the Skeleton Saint* (New York: Oxford University Press, 2012).
3. I've drawn on multiple sources to reconstruct the events that follow. Particularly helpful is Rick Braziel, Devon Bell, and George Watson, "A Heist Gone Bad: A Police Foundation Critical Incident Review of the Stockton Police Response to the Bank of the West Robbery and Hostage-Taking," Police Foundation, 2015, https://www.policefoundation.org/wp-content/uploads/2015/08/A-Heist-Gone-Bad-Critical-Incident-Review.pdf.

5: ENEMY NUMBER ONE

1. Robert E. Worden and Sarah J. McLean, *Mirage of Police Reform: Procedural Justice and Police Legitimacy* (Berkeley: University of California Press, 2017).
2. John P. Crank and Robert Langworthy, "An Institutional Perspective of Policing," *Journal of Criminal Law and Criminology* 83, no. 2 (1992): 338–63. Crank and Langworthy's paper was informed by a broader literature in organizational theory. See especially Karl Weick, "Educational Organizations as Loosely Coupled Systems," *Administrative Science Quarterly* 21, no. 1 (1976): 1–19; and John Meyer and Brian Rowan, "Institutionalized Organizations: Formal Structure as Myth and Ceremony," *American Journal of Sociology* 83, no. 2 (1977): 340–63.
3. Worden and McLean, *Mirage of Police Reform*, 183.
4. Worden and McLean, 187.
5. E.g., Jordi Blanes i Vidal and Tom Kirchmaier, "The Effect of Police Response Time on Crime Clearance Rates," *Review of Economic Studies* 85, no. 2 (2017): 855–91.
6. E.g., "How Target, Google, Bank of America and Microsoft Quietly Fund

Police through Private Donations," *Guardian*, June 18, 2020, https://www.theguardian.com/us-news/2020/jun/18/police-foundations-nonprofits-amazon-target-microsoft.

7. Robert J. Sampson and Dawn Jeglum Bartusch, "Legal Cynicism and (Subcultural?) Tolerance of Deviance: The Neighborhood Context of Racial Differences," *Law and Society Review* 32, no. 4 (1998): 777–804.
8. For an alternative, more political conceptualization of legal cynicism, see Monica C. Bell, "Police Reform and the Dismantling of Legal Estrangement," *Yale Law Journal* 126, no. 7 (2017): 2054–2150.
9. Arthur Niederhoffer, *Behind the Shield: The Police in Urban Society* (New York: Doubleday, 1967).
10. Peter Moskos, *Cop in the Hood: My Year Policing Baltimore's Eastern District* (Princeton: Princeton University Press, 2008).
11. Moskos, 46.
12. Ryan Grim and Aída Chávez, "Minneapolis Police Union President: 'I've Been Involved in Three Shootings Myself, and Not a One of Them Has Bothered Me.'" *Intercept*, June 2, 2020, https://theintercept.com/2020/06/02/minneapolis-police-union-bob-kroll-shootings/.
13. Research shows that many Black Minneapolis residents continued to experience disrespectful and disproportionate policing during and after the implementation of PJ reforms. See Michelle S. Phelps, Christopher E. Robertson, and Amber Joy Powell, "'We're Still Dying Quicker Than We Can Effect Change': #BlackLivesMatter and the Limits of 21st-Century Policing Reform," *American Journal of Sociology* 127, no. 3 (2021): 867–903.
14. For discussion of such technology, see Rob Voigt, Nicholas P. Camp, Vinodkumar Prabhakaran, and Jennifer L. Eberhardt, "Language from Police Body Camera Footage Shows Racial Disparities in Officer Respect," *Proceedings of the National Academy of Sciences* 114, no. 25 (2017): 6521–26. More generally, see Victoria A. Sytsma, Eric L. Piza, Vijay F. Chillar, and Leigh S. Grossman, "Measuring Procedural Justice Policy Adherence during Use of Force Events: The Body-Worn Camera as a Performance Monitoring Tool," *Criminal Justice Policy Review* 32, no. 9 (2021): 938–59.
15. Sarah Brayne, *Predict and Surveil: Data, Discretion, and the Future of Policing* (New York: Oxford University Press, 2021).
16. Tina Rosenberg, "A Strategy to Build Police-Citizen Trust," *New York Times*, July 26, 2016, https://www.nytimes.com/2016/07/26/opinion/a-strategy-to-build-police-citizen-trust.html.
17. My calculations.

6: EBK

1. Robert Reinhold, "Stockton Journal; Gangs Selling Crack Give Rise to New Wild West," *New York Times*, June 21, 1988, https://www.nytimes.com/1988

/06/21/us/stockton-journal-gangs-selling-crack-give-rise-to-new-wild-west.html.

2. Jill Leovy, *Ghettoside: A True Story of Murder in America* (New York: Spiegel & Grau, 2015).
3. Wesley Lowery, Kimbriell Kelly, Ted Mellnik, and Steven Rich, "Murder with Impunity: Where Killings Go Unsolved," *Washington Post*, June 6, 2018, https://www.washingtonpost.com/graphics/2018/investigations/where-murders-go-unsolved/.
4. Currie, *A Peculiar Indifference*, 145.
5. Forrest Stuart, *Ballad of the Bullet: Gangs, Drill Music, and the Power of Online Infamy* (Princeton: Princeton University Press, 2020).
6. One of the enduring challenges for gangs as organizations is that they bring together people who have what Martín Sánchez-Jankowski calls "defiant individualist" character traits, arising in the context of resource deprivation. See his *Islands in the Street: Gangs in Urban American Society* (Berkeley: University of California Press, 1991). For a discussion of some of the strategies that gangs (in prisons) use to overcome this challenge, see David Skarbek, *The Social Order of the Underworld: How Prison Gangs Govern the American Penal System* (New York: Oxford University Press, 2014).
7. Tyrese Johnson, "Rep Your City: The Hottest in Stockton," Thizzler.com, May 17, 2019, https://www.thizzler.com/blog/2019/05/17/rep-your-city-the-hottest-in-stockton.html.
8. This was a telephone survey carried out on my behalf by SurveyUSA. Although response rates were undoubtedly low among the small number of Stocktonians heavily involved in crime, who'd have the most information to share, tipsters outside such circles can be critical for solving crimes as well, as the Celestine case shows. Among the other findings from the survey: about 60 percent of Stockton residents said they were either very satisfied or satisfied with the performance of Stockton PD; 22 percent said they or one of their immediate family members had been harassed by Stockton officers, as compared to 69 percent who said this had never happened, with no major differences between white, Black, and Latino residents; 47 percent of Stockton residents overall said they thought Stockton PD was doing either an excellent or good job treating racial and ethnic groups equally, as compared to 22 percent of Black residents; and just under half of the Stocktonians surveyed said they'd heard "not very much" about the department's reform efforts.
9. Kyle Peyton, Michael Sierra-Arévalo, and David G. Rand, "A Field Experiment on Community Policing and Police Legitimacy," *Proceedings of the National Academy of Sciences* 116, no. 40 (2019): 19894–98.
10. Steve Large, "Stockton Leads State in Drop in Police Shootings," August 13, 2019, https://sacramento.cbslocal.com/2019/08/13/stockton-leads-state-in-drop-in-police-shootings/.
11. My calculations from the crowdsourced database mappingpoliceviolence.org.

Included in these numbers: Jesse Smith and his CRT partner shot and killed a man in 2015 as he attempted to run them over.

12. My calculation from data on use of force incidents provided by the department. This number is an approximation, as multiple officers may use force on the same arrest.
13. Also my calculations from department-provided data. Most large cities like Stockton generate a relatively small percentage of their municipal revenue from fines, including fines that stem from traffic tickets. In Stockton, that number is around 2.5 percent—on the high side compared to other cities with more than three hundred thousand residents. See "Fines and Forfeitures," Urban Institute, https://www.urban.org/policy-centers/cross-center-initiatives/state-and-local-finance-initiative/state-and-local-backgrounders/fines-and-forfeitures#revenue.
14. Bocar A. Ba, Dean Knox, Jonathan Mummolo, and Roman Rivera, "The Role of Officer Race and Gender in Police-Civilian Interactions in Chicago," *Science* 371, no. 6530 (2021): 696–702.
15. David Weisburd, Cody W. Telep, Taryn Zastrow, Heather Vovak, Anthony A. Braga, and Brandon Turchan, "Reforming the Police through Procedural Justice Training: A Multicity Randomized Trial at Crime Hot Spots," *Proceedings of the National Academy of Sciences* 119, no. 4 (2022): 4. The fact that officers in the study were being closely observed by researchers may have minimized loose coupling, although such observation wouldn't bear on the causal effect of procedural justice training per se, as officers in both the treatment and control conditions were observed. For a review of other experimental and observational research on procedural justice in policing, see Paige E. Vaughn, Benjamin Feigenberg, and Leah Luben, "Procedural Justice Training for Police," University of Chicago Crime Lab, March 10, 2021, https://urbanlabs.uchicago.edu/attachments/6e9553d31bdca8b974dc15851afd780b58db44fc/store/18a2d1610a8bb8547d6de7d4c835393910fbbb510c028480a3b54daec650/Procedural+Justice+Training.pdf.

7: BELONGING REVOLUTION

1. Brook Wilensky-Lanford, *Paradise Lust: Searching for the Garden of Eden* (New York: Grove, 2011), 141.
2. For a careful review of what's known about the scope, roots, and effects of mass incarceration, see Jeremy Travis, Bruce Western, and Steve Redburn, eds., *The Growth of Incarceration in the United States: Exploring Causes and Consequences* (Washington, DC: National Academies Press, 2014). There is considerable debate about how large a role rising crime rates played in the expansion of the prison system. Some scholars emphasize fear more than actual crime; others note that the system continued to expand even after crime fell off; and still others argue that even if crime was the proximate cause of

growing public investment in prisons, underlying factors—like the perceived need to contain and discipline young men of color from poor families who couldn't find their way in the postindustrial economy—drove the increase. Three particularly engaging studies of these topics are Elizabeth Hinton, *From the War on Poverty to the War on Crime: The Making of Mass Incarceration in America* (Cambridge, MA: Harvard University Press, 2016); Michael Javen Fortner, *Black Silent Majority: The Rockefeller Drug Laws and the Politics of Punishment* (Cambridge, MA: Harvard University Press, 2013); and James Forman, *Locking Up Our Own: Crime and Punishment in Black America* (New York: Farrar, Straus and Giroux, 2017).

3. In *Prison Break: Why Conservatives Turned against Mass Incarceration* (New York: Oxford University Press, 2016), David Dagan and Steven Teles explain how and why conservatives in the pre-Trump era helped to bring about this decline, after earlier having led the charge for mass incarceration. On the liberal contribution to mass incarceration, see Naomi Murakawa, *The First Civil Right: How Liberals Built Prison America* (New York: Oxford University Press, 2014).
4. Ample social scientific evidence could be cited in support of both claims. On the effects of mass incarceration for inequality, for example, see Sara Wakefield and Christopher Uggen, "Incarceration and Stratification," *Annual Review of Sociology* 36 (2010): 387–406. On community effects, see Jeffrey D. Morenoff and David J. Harding, "Incarceration, Prisoner Reentry, and Communities," *Annual Review of Sociology* 40 (2014): 411–29. On the moral side of the equation, see Reuben Jonathan Miller, *Halfway Home: Race, Punishment, and the Afterlife of Mass Incarceration* (New York: Little, Brown, 2021). Franklin Zimring's *The Great American Crime Decline* (New York: Oxford University Press, 2008) and Patrick Sharkey's *Uneasy Peace* demonstrate that mass incarceration wasn't the main driver of historic crime rate declines from the mid-1990s on.
5. Daniel W. Van Ness and Karen Heetderks Strong, *Restoring Justice: An Introduction to Restorative Justice*, 5th ed. (New York: Routledge, 2014), 27.
6. Howard Zehr, *Changing Lenses: A New Focus for Crime and Justice* (Scottdale, PA: Herald Press, 1990), 179.
7. Lawrence W. Sherman et al., "Twelve Experiments in Restorative Justice: The Jerry Lee Program of Randomized Trials of Restorative Justice Conferences," *Journal of Experimental Criminology* 11, no. 4 (2015): 501–40.
8. US Department of Justice, *National Survey of Victim-Offender Mediation Programs in the United States* (Washington, DC: Office of Justice Programs, 2000).
9. On funding, see David R. Karp and Olivia Frank, "Anxiously Awaiting the Future of Restorative Justice in the United States," *Victims & Offenders* 11, no. 1 (2016): 50–70. The quotation is from Thalia González, "The State of Restorative Justice in American Criminal Law," *University of Wisconsin Law Review* (2020): 1147–97, 1156–57. On school discipline, see Thalia González, "Restorative Justice from the Margins to the Center: The Emergence of a New Norm

in School Discipline," *Howard Law Journal* 16 (2016): 101–44. On progressive prosecutors, see Bruce A. Green and Lara Abigail Bazelon, "Restorative Justice from Prosecutors' Perspective," *Fordham Law Review* 88 (2020): 2287–2318.

10. See, for example, Robert B. Putnam, *Bowling Alone: The Collapse and Revival of American Community* (New York: Simon & Schuster, 2000).
11. A useful history of Longmont is Erik Mason, *Longmont: The First 150 Years* (Brookfield, MO: Donning Company, 2020).
12. Brooklyn Dance, "'It Woke Longmont Up': Community Remembers 40 Year Anniversary of Police Shooting of Two Latino Men," *Longmont Times-Call*, August 15, 2020, https://www.timescall.com/2020/08/15/it-woke-longmont-up-community-remembers-40-year-anniversary-of-police-shooting-of-two-latino-men/.
13. It's bad policy that in the US we allow people in their early twenties to serve as police officers, despite our knowledge that the human brain doesn't fully mature until age twenty-five or so.
14. Clifford Geertz, "Ethos, World-View and the Analysis of Sacred Symbols," *Antioch Review* 17, no. 4 (1957): 421–37, 421.

8: I WILL BE HURTIN'

1. Frank Edwards, "Family Surveillance: Police and the Reporting of Child Abuse and Neglect," *RSF: The Russell Sage Foundation Journal of the Social Sciences* 5, no. 1 (2019): 50–70, 52.
2. Dorothy Roberts, *Shattered Bonds: The Color of Child Welfare* (New York: Basic Books, 2002), vi.
3. For example, Olga Khazan, "American Police Are Inadequately Trained," *Atlantic*, April 22, 2021, https://www.theatlantic.com/politics/archive/2021/04/daunte-wright-and-crisis-american-police-training/618649/.

9: TOY HANDCUFFS

1. Michael K. Brown, *Working the Street: Police Discretion and the Dilemmas of Reform* (New York: Russell Sage Foundation, 1981).
2. Brown, 135.
3. Brown, 223.
4. Brown, 226.
5. Brown, 229.
6. Brown, 232–33.
7. Brown, 236.
8. Herman Goldstein, *Policing a Free Society* (Cambridge, MA: Ballinger, 1977).
9. Goldstein, 1.
10. Goldstein, 13.

11. Goldstein, 257.
12. Goldstein, 261.
13. Goldstein, 168.

10: VICTIM WHISPERER

1. Lawrence W. Sherman and Richard A. Berk, "The Specific Deterrent Effects of Arrest for Domestic Assault," *American Sociological Review* 49, no. 2 (1984): 261–72. Later research called this finding into question, showing differential effects depending on the city, the race or ethnicity of the victim, whether the offender was employed, and other factors. See, for example, Richard A. Berk, Alec Campbell, Ruth Klap, and Bruce Western, "The Deterrent Effect of Arrest in Incidents of Domestic Violence: A Bayesian Analysis of Four Field Experiments," *American Sociological Review* 57, no. 5 (1992): 698–708; and Janell D. Schmidt and Lawrence W. Sherman, "Does Arrest Deter Domestic Violence?" *American Behavioral Scientist* 36, no. 4 (1993): 601–9. A recent research review finds no consistent effect of mandatory arrest on reoffending. See Susan J. Hoppe, Yan Zhang, Brittany E. Hayes, and Matthew A. Bills, "Mandatory Arrest for Domestic Violence and Repeat Offending: A Meta-Analysis," *Aggression and Violent Behavior* 53 (2020), 101430.
2. A provocative argument about the contribution feminists thus made to mass incarceration is Aya Gruber, *The Feminist War on Crime: The Unexpected Role of Women's Liberation in Mass Incarceration* (Berkeley: University of California Press, 2020).
3. Rachel Louise Snyder, *No Visible Bruises: What We Don't Know about Domestic Violence Can Kill Us* (New York: Bloomsbury, 2019), 45.
4. Rosa Brooks, "One Reason for Police Violence? Too Many Men with Badges," *Washington Post,* June 18, 2020, https://www.washingtonpost.com/outlook/2020/06/18/women-police-officers-violence/.
5. Wilson, *Varieties of Police Behavior*, 251.
6. Goldstein, *Policing a Free Society*, 225.
7. Goldstein, 228. Contemporary scholars are divided on how much power police chiefs have to change police culture. For a discussion of this with respect to the possibility for "transformational leadership," see Tom Cockcroft, "Police Culture and Transformational Leadership: Outlining the Contours of a Troubled Relationship," *Policing* 8, no. 1 (2014): 5–13. Cockcroft argues, based on the work of Bethan Loftus, that it will be easier for chiefs to change superficial aspects of culture, such as whether cops feel comfortable openly espousing racist opinions, than deeper elements like worldviews. Longmont is interesting sociologically because it represents a case of deeper, leadership-driven change.
8. Jal Mehta and Christopher Winship, "Moral Power," in *Handbook of the Sociology of Morality,* ed. Steven Hitlin and Stephen Vaisey (New York: Springer, 2010).

9. Mehta and Winship, 426.
10. Mehta and Winship, 428.

11: RAISING THE CAIN

1. Although the conviction was reversed on appeal, the doctor, Robert Schmunk, was retried and convicted of involuntary manslaughter.
2. Alvin W. Gouldner, "Cosmopolitans and Locals: Toward an Analysis of Latent Social Roles—I," *Administrative Science Quarterly* 2, no. 3 (1957): 281–306.
3. One retired Black officer told me that when he joined the department in the late 1970s, he wasn't allowed to write tickets for white people he'd pulled over.
4. For a social-scientific account of how such referral practices, along with help-seeking behavior by job applicants in segregated social networks, reproduces racial inequalities in hiring, see Nancy DiTomaso, *The American Non-Dilemma: Racial Inequality without Racism* (New York: Russell Sage Foundation, 2013).

12: AUSTIN CALLAWAY

1. Michael Sierra-Arévalo, "The Commemoration of Death, Organizational Memory, and Police Culture," *Criminology* 57, no. 4 (2019): 632–58.
2. Seth Stoughton, "Law Enforcement's 'Warrior Problem,'" *Harvard Law Review Forum* 128 (2015): 225–34
3. Stoughton, 227–28.
4. Radley Balko, *Rise of the Warrior Cop: The Militarization of America's Police Forces* (New York: PublicAffairs, 2013).
5. For an introduction, see Jeffrey K. Olick, Vered Vinitsky-Seroussi, and Daniel Levy, eds., *The Collective Memory Reader* (New York: Oxford University Press, 2011). Also useful is Joachim J. Savelsberg and Ryan D. King, "Law and Collective Memory," *Annual Review of Law and Social Science* 3 (2007): 189–211; and Geneviève Zubrzycki and Anna Woźny, "The Comparative Politics of Collective Memory," *Annual Review of Sociology* 46 (2020): 175–94.
6. "A Day to Celebrate the American Promise," *National Review*, July 4, 2021, https://www.nationalreview.com/2021/07/a-day-to-celebrate-the-american-promise/.
7. Nikole Hannah-Jones, "America Wasn't a Democracy, until Black Americans Made It One," *New York Times*, August 14, 2019, https://www.nytimes.com/interactive/2019/08/14/magazine/black-history-american-democracy.html.
8. Sierra-Arévalo, "The Commemoration of Death," 641.
9. For discussion of some of these functions, see Peter K. Manning, *Police Work: The Social Organization of Policing* (Cambridge, MA: MIT Press, 1977), 4–10.
10. Glenda Major and Clark Johnson, *Treasures of Troup County: A Pictorial History of Troup County* (LaGrange, GA: Troup County Historical Society, 1993);

John Lawrence et al., *Travels through Troup County: A Guide to Its Architecture and History* (LaGrange, GA: Troup County Historical Society, 1996); Glenda Ralston Major, Forrest Clark Johnson III, and Kaye Lanning Minchew, *Troup County* (Charleston, SC: Arcadia Publishing, 2007); Glenda Ralston Major, Forrest Clark Johnson III, and Kaye Lanning Minchew, *LaGrange* (Charleston, SC: Arcadia Publishing, 2011).

11. Major and Johnson, *Treasures of Troup County*, 19.
12. Michael D. Schulman and Jeffrey Leiter, "Introduction," in *Hanging by a Thread: Social Change in Southern Textiles*, ed. Jeffrey Leiter, Michael Schulman, and Rhonda Zingraff (Ithaca, NY: ILR Press, 1991), 8.
13. Donna Jean Whitley, "Fuller E. Callaway and Textile Mill Development in LaGrange, 1895–1920" (PhD diss., Emory University, 1984), 185.
14. Edward E. Baptist, *The Half Has Never Been Told: Slavery and the Making of American Capitalism* (New York: Basic Books, 2014).
15. Chris Boner, the former director of the Callaway Educational Association, made this comment in an interview with Scott Smith in April 2011. Smith discusses it in his book *Legacy: The Secret History of Proto-Fascism in America's Greatest Little City* (self-pub., 2011).
16. James H. Cone, *The Cross and the Lynching Tree* (Maryknoll, NY: Orbis Books, 2011), 3.
17. Jason M. McGraw, "Defining Lynching in Order to End It: The Lynching of Austin Callaway and How It Shaped the Debate on How to End Lynching," Civil Rights and Restorative Justice Project, Northeastern University, 2014, https://repository.library.northeastern.edu/downloads/neu:m04286351?datastream_id=content.
18. Rob Corcoran, *Trustbuilding: An Honest Conversation on Race, Reconciliation, and Responsibility* (Charlottesville: University of Virginia Press, 2010), 9.
19. For a different approach, emphasizing shared experience more than common ground, see Adam B. Seligman, Rahel R. Wasserfall, and David W. Montgomery, *Living with Difference: How to Build Community in a Divided World* (Berkeley: University of California Press, 2015).
20. Karen Branan, *The Family Tree: A Lynching in Georgia, a Legacy of Secrets, and My Search for the Truth* (New York: Atria, 2016).
21. There is some disagreement in town as to whether Lou came up with the idea for the apology. Bobbie Hart maintains that it originated with the Alterna group. Ernest Ward disputes this, while also noting that there were multiple streams of inquiry into the Austin Callaway case happening at once, all important in their own way.

13: BLUE FOLDER

1. Jeffrey K. Olick, *The Politics of Regret: On Collective Memory and Historical Responsibility* (New York: Routledge, 2007).

2. Olick, 121.
3. Olick, 147; Hannah Arendt, *The Human Condition* (Chicago: University of Chicago Press, 1958), 237.
4. For discussion of this for an earlier period, see Diane Miller Sommerville, *Rape & Race in the Nineteenth Century South* (Chapel Hill: University of North Carolina Press, 2004).
5. Carson McCullers, *The Heart Is a Lonely Hunter* (1940; repr., Boston: Mariner, 2000), 6.
6. Alexander O. Hughes, "Hidden History: The Ku Klux Klan in Troup County," *Georgia Historical Quarterly* 106, no. 2 (2022): 200–25, 212.
7. Brad Schrade, "Family Reveals 76-Year-Old Secret in Georgia Lynching." *Atlanta Journal-Constitution*, March 16, 2017, https://www.ajc.com/news/family-reveals-year-old-secret-georgia-lynching/vH0uCAwkC4dKqEAnATj2II/.
8. See, for example, William Anderson, *The Wild Man from Sugar Creek: The Political Career of Eugene Talmadge* (Baton Rouge: Louisiana State University Press, 1975).
9. The legality of this prohibition was undercut by a 1944 US Supreme Court decision, *Smith v. Allwright*, where the court ruled that it was unconstitutional for the Texas Democratic Party to make discriminatory rules concerning primary voting. But other Southern states, like Georgia, refused to recognize the ruling. Black Georgians sued the Georgia Democratic Party and won, while a voter registration drive added more than one hundred thousand previously disenfranchised people to the voting rolls, with the promise of more Black voter registration to come. For discussion of this period, see Stephen G. N. Tuck, *Beyond Atlanta: The Struggle for Racial Equality in Georgia, 1940–1980* (Athens: University of Georgia Press, 2001).
10. Tuck also tells the story of Maceo Snipes, a Black man living in Taylor County, to the east of Troup and Harris. Before the 1946 primary, the Georgia KKK threatened to attack any Black person who went to the polls. Snipes, a veteran, would not be deterred. He cast his ballot and was murdered on his porch three days later. Tuck, *Beyond Atlanta*, 71.
11. Not everyone was deferential. Some people thought that trust hadn't yet developed to the point where it could withstand such direct language.

14: SUPER HOOKS

1. Louis Dekmar, "George Floyd Is Not a Police Training Issue," *LaGrange Daily News*, May 29, 2020, https://www.lagrangenews.com/2020/05/29/george-floyd-is-not-a-police-training-issue/.
2. Indeed, Cone often wrote critically of the police, describing them as agents of racial oppression.

CONCLUSION

1. On the origins of such a culture, particularly among cops in California, see Joe Domanick, *Blue: The LAPD and the Battle to Redeem American Policing* (New York: Simon & Schuster, 2015), 60–62. To be clear, aggression is sometimes required in law enforcement—but as a tactic to be used when the situation calls for it, not as an overall demeanor.
2. Goldstein, *Policing a Free Society*, 229.
3. Monte Whaley, "New Public Safety Chief Ardis Wants to Build on Longmont's Successes," *Longmont Leader*, April 9, 2021, https://www.longmontleader.com/local-news/new-public-safety-chief-ardis-wants-to-build-on-longmonts-successes-4201183.

ACKNOWLEDGMENTS

This book wouldn't have been possible without the cooperation and support of a host of people, scattered across the country. My biggest debt is to the nine main officers I've profiled, who graciously endured more questions than I'm sure any of them bargained for. Thank you for sharing your experiences.

Beyond these officers, I've talked with countless other cops, along with citizens, attorneys, activists, politicians, reporters, nonprofit workers, and academics in Stockton, Longmont, LaGrange, and elsewhere. Some are named in the book; the rest provided invaluable background information. My gratitude extends to all.

Jen Marshall at Aevitas Creative Management saw the need for a reported book on police culture and reform, and was incredibly supportive throughout the writing process. At Metropolitan, Riva Hocherman proved that ink-all-over-the-page editing isn't a thing of the past. She sent me back to the drawing board again and again, each time with astute observations that completely changed how I understood the manuscript. Hannah Campbell, the book's production editor at Holt, was terrific. Domenica Alioto helped with plotting and pace.

Parker Henry was every bit the obsessive fact-checker I'd hoped she would be. I take full responsibility, of course, for any errors that may remain and will post corrections as necessary to my Colby College web page. Thanks as well to Christopher Brehm, for corroborating my analysis of survey data; and to Michael Fitzgerald in Stockton, Erik Mason in Longmont, and John Tures in LaGrange for local gut checks on chapters. Thanks also to the many scholars and writers I've discussed in the book, whose fair-minded comments on what I'd written about them (solicited during fact-checking) clarified my thinking.

For insightful suggestions on drafts of the manuscript, I thank Julian Go, Eric Klinenberg, Eyal Press, Richard Rosenthal, Patrick Sharkey, and Christopher Winship.

Projects such as this require significant institutional support. I am lucky to work at Colby, whose commitment to truth-seeking on issues vital to our democracy is second to none. President David Greene and Provost Margaret McFadden, thank you. I also want to acknowledge financial support from Colby's Goldfarb Center for Public Affairs and Civic Engagement. Katie Queally, Amber Churchwell, and Tara Strelevitz (former students) and Ivan Knoepflmacher (a current student) provided excellent research assistance. Leslie Lima gave outstanding administrative support.

Words will never be able to fully express the depth of my gratitude—and love—for my family. To my wife, Jessica Berger Gross, thank you not only for your literary brilliance, which I've had the fortune to surround myself with for the past two decades, but also for being the wonderful, kind, and enchanting person you are. You inspire me. Every page of this book is better because of your notes, encouragement, and humanity.

My son, Lucien Gross, gave ridiculously good editorial feedback. Your talent and intelligence are beyond anything I've ever encountered, and you're a lot of fun to hang out with, too. You're going places, kid. Just remember the thing Ben Parker said.

INDEX

ABOUT THE AUTHOR

A former patrol officer in the police department in Berkeley, California, **Neil Gross** is a professor of sociology at Colby College. A frequent contributor to the *New York Times*, he is the author of two previous books and has also taught at Harvard and Princeton. He lives in Maine.